THE
UNITED
STATES
AND
AFRICA

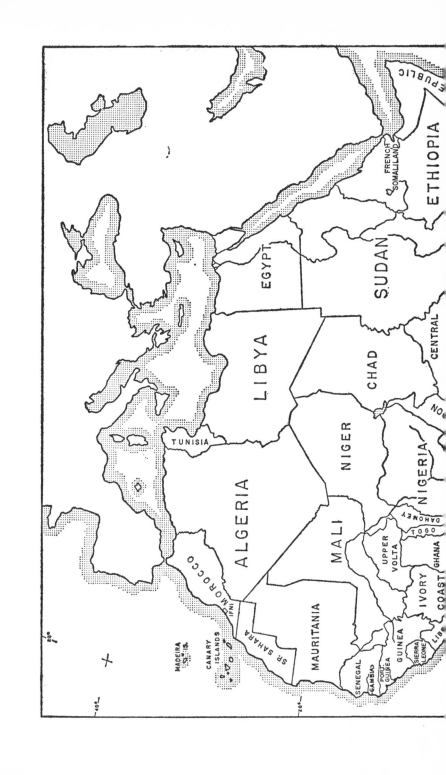

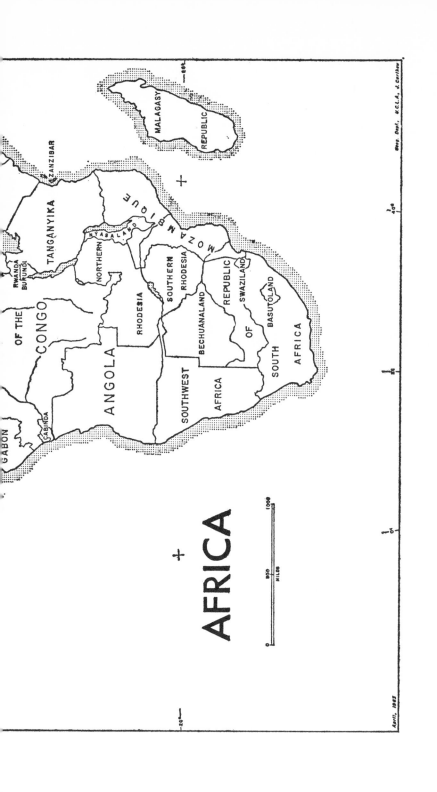

AFRICA

MILES

April, 1963

Geog. Dept., U.C.L.A., J. Carithew

THE
UNITED
STATES
AND
AFRICA

Edited by

WALTER GOLDSCHMIDT

REVISED EDITION

THE AMERICAN ASSEMBLY

Columbia University

Essay Index Reprint Series

BOOKS FOR LIBRARIES PRESS

FREEPORT, NEW YORK

INTERNATIONAL STANDARD BOOK NUMBER:
0-8369-1781-2

LIBRARY OF CONGRESS CATALOG CARD NUMBER:
75-117751

PRINTED IN THE UNITED STATES OF AMERICA

Preface

The many changes in the African scene since 1958 and the continual high demand for a study using the approach of THE UNITED STATES AND AFRICA have led us to undertake this completely revised edition—again under the editorial supervision of Dr. Walter Goldschmidt of the University of California at Los Angeles. Originally, this volume was prepared as background reading for participants in the Thirteenth American Assembly, at Arden House, the Harriman Campus of Columbia University, May, 1958. Subsequently, it was used for a series of regional Assemblies and as a book of basic readings on Africa by colleges and universities throughout the country.

As in the first edition, the opinions expressed herein are those of the authors and do not necessarily represent the official views of The American Assembly or the Carnegie Corporation of New York, whose generosity made the original Assembly study possible.

Henry M. Wriston
Chairman
The American Assembly

Contents

ECONOMY

SOCIETY

APPENDIX

Introduction:
Africa Enters a New Era

WALTER GOLDSCHMIDT

The political shape of Africa is becoming clear. The colonial era is rapidly drawing to a close and the continent is now largely made up of independent states. These states have inherited the boundaries established by the European governments who partitioned the land in the nineteenth century, and these are likely to remain for some time, with but minor modifications. The basic institutions of government have been patterned after Europe, although the spirit in which these governmental institutions operate varies from one country to another. Economic expansion and incipient industrialization are everywhere. The independent states are establishing their own social and political institutions, and discovering and making friends in the international community, according to the perceptions and predilections of their respective leadership.

When The American Assembly met at Arden House, in the spring of 1958, to discuss the relationship between the United States and the people of Africa, it had before it a draft of the first edition of this book. At that time, aside from three European oligarchies and two old political states (Liberia and Ethiopia), there were six new independent countries (Egypt, Libya, Tunisia, Morocco, Sudan, and Ghana); in the intervening five years some twenty-four new nations have been created. There is little doubt that the whole continent will sever its colonial ties. When, in its final report, the Assembly stated that its "fundamental premise is that the peoples of Africa will ultimately determine their own relationships with each other, with Europe, and with the rest of the world," it could not know how rapidly this assumption would become reality. This new edition brings out the changing circumstances with respect to Africa as these have modified basic problems and policies.

In accordance with the tradition of The American Assembly, several subsequent regional and local meetings were held, and each of these in turn prepared an independent report and recommendations. In every case, the participants agreed not only that Africa was moving rapidly to independent status, and that in fact it should so move, but also that the United States should do all in its power to aid such movement. They further agreed that the United States should in no way endeavor to make its aid conditional upon political commitments to the West.

As matters turned out, events in Africa were so far along that, save in the former Belgian Congo, the United States had little to do other than watch. As we have observed the family of nations grow through political development in Africa, we have seen that each of the nations has taken its own stance; some remain closely tied to their former metropolitan countries, others have taken a generically pro-Western position, while many have shown varying degrees of sympathy to Communism and to the Soviet Union. The essential fact, however, is that these nations are self-determining and that they have thus enlarged the third force in the international community.

A second recurrent theme in these Assemblies concerned the importance of economic development in Africa. Most of them echoed the Arden House conclusion that "a rapid tempo of economic development is essential, requiring a continued flow of capital to Africa." The Southern Assembly felt that "the most pressing needs . . . are in the infrastructure of the economy —communication, transportation, power, public services, and education." Technical assistance was stressed by the Western Regional Assembly, among others.

A third theme was the need for greater mutual understanding.

One specific recommendation was that the United States Government expand its official relations with Africa, including the formation of an independent African desk in the Department of State. The latter has long since been created, and a comparison of our African programs today (described by Vernon McKay in the Appendix to this edition) with those detailed in the first edition of this book reveals great progress in our official relations with Africa. Educational exchanges have shown satisfactory growth—the Peace Corps being the most obvious but by no means the only example. The flood of popular and technical books, of articles in magazines and scholarly journals, of radio and television reportage, all attest to the awakening American interest in and understanding of African affairs.

Africa is on the threshold of a new era. The exciting events of the past few years will be followed by a period of social adjustment and hard work. In this volume, we endeavor to set before you the character of these problems and the nature of the task ahead—both for Africans themselves and for Americans who have a natural interest in Africa.

The nature of this interest is set forth by Rupert Emerson in the first essay. The following six papers divide themselves into the fields of politics, economics, and social affairs. On each of these broad topics there are two essays. James Coleman treats the political scene in Africa, describing the different kinds of political organization in relation to their origins and circumstances, and the problems involved in developing institutions of government; Vernon McKay deals with the African states in the world community of nations. In the field of economics, Elliot Berg classifies the types of economic organization characteristic of the nations of Africa, and the problems inherent in maintaining a viable economy; Andrew Kamarck discusses the international trade and economic relationships of the African nations. In social matters, Walter Goldschmidt discusses the cultural backgrounds and social values of the African people and the problems of adjustment to the modern world; St. Clair Drake is concerned with the organization of society and the development of new social institutions.

Africa is a large area. The second largest continent, it contains 11½ million square miles—nearly 4 times that of continental United States. Its variant terrain is the home of 220 million people of many races and a wide variety of cultures. In the north are the ruins and remnants of classic civilization; in the south, there have been more than 300 years of European occupation and of struggle between the African and the European who made his home in Africa. Between lies that part of Africa which gave it the sobriquet of the Dark Continent—a phrase that does not appear subsequently in these essays, so out of joint with the times is it—and within this are elaborate kingdoms as well as simple tribes living, so far as we can tell, much as they did in the time of the Ptolemies. This vast and variant area is the subject of the essays in this volume.

*THE
UNITED
STATES
AND
AFRICA*

1. The Character of American Interests in Africa

RUPERT EMERSON

On October 7, 1957, in accordance with the custom of the community, a Negro was refused a glass of orange juice in a restaurant in Dover, Delaware. This turned out to be not a trivial repetition of a familiar injustice, but a globe-circling incident that symbolized America's interest in the new Africa. The Negro was Komla Agbeli Gbedemah, Finance Minister of Ghana, who was in this country, among other purposes, to represent at meetings of the International Bank and Monetary Fund the first tropical African state to win its independence. Within two days of his encounter with Jim Crow, he received an urgent invitation from the White House to breakfast with President Eisenhower and with Vice-President Nixon, whom he had entertained at dinner in Accra earlier in the year. It was reported that the White House tactfully omitted orange juice from the breakfast menu.

Only a century ago, much of the interior of this Africa which has now become so close a neighbor remained a still unexplored mystery. It was not until 1871 that Henry Morton Stanley, an American by adoption, addressed his famous "I presume" to David Livingston. As Africa was the last continent to be opened to the world at large, so was it the last to be discovered by the United States—although discovery is perhaps a less apt word for what has happened than rediscovery. The American fashion in continents is a fluctuating one. Europe is always with us; Asia and South America swim in and out of the center of our consciousness as the prevailing tides of the time dictate. Africa, rising and falling in American awareness, has never rivaled the other continents in its ability to capture our interest, and it barely does so now. In the last years, however, it has shot ahead spectacularly.

AMERICAN CONTACT WITH AFRICA

The Earlier Period

Present American awareness of Africa, more widespread than it has ever been in the past, dates back no further than to World War II when strategy, politics, and economics all combined to force the United States to pay attention to a part of the world it had hitherto largely ignored. Of the earlier links with Africa little need be said, since for the most part they do not give much of a clue to the nature of the contemporary American interest. By far the greatest of them in its consequences was the slave trade, which provided the United States with the ancestors of a tenth of its present population. There were a long series of tangles with the Barbary States at the end of the eighteenth and beginning of the nineteenth centuries. The founding of Liberia in the 1820's, itself deriving from the slavery issue, established one spot on the African coast to which the United States had a special attachment from that time forward. American delegates participated in the Berlin Conference of 1884–85, which laid down some of the ground rules for the already active scramble for Africa.

These and similar contacts, including continuous trade relations of a somewhat desultory kind, indicate how slight and episodic American contact with Africa has usually been. The role of the United States as a great power, the pressures of global war, and the shrinking of the world's horizons put an end to the possibility that either continent can hereafter be disinterested in the affairs of the other. Developments since 1945 have hammered home the lesson taught us by World War II. Three major lines, closely interrelated, come immediately to mind.

Expanding American Interests after World War II

The first of these, but by no means necessarily the most lastingly significant, is the Cold War, which has compelled us to take stock of the advantages a friendly Africa gives and the penalties we would suffer if African countries were to be taken into the Soviet orbit. The shock that Egyptian, Syrian, and Iraqi fraternization with the U.S.S.R. gave us was a foretaste of the effect which similar African dealings would have. As leader of the free world coalition, the United States must be profoundly concerned with what happens in a continent that occupies a fifth of the earth's surface.

The second is the immense change which is under way in Africa. Colonialism has been challenged in all its aspects. The old assumption that Africa is a subordinate attachment to Europe has been swept away. The radical nature of the change is reflected in the fact that whereas only four African states were members of the United Nations at its start in 1945, the 17th session of the General Assembly, in 1962, counted thirty-two African members, with a substantial number still to come as the remaining colonies achieve independence. Within the U.N. and outside it, the drive for social and economic development is gathering momentum as a means of securing equality with the formerly dominant West and of making independence a working reality. In this era of anticolonialism, it is an inevitably relevant matter that the imperial powers from whom the Africans have so recently won freedom are among our major allies in the free world and NATO.

The third is the pained American discovery that our own resources in raw materials are far from inexhaustible and that we must rely on other parts of the world. Measured against American trade, investment, and aid programs elsewhere, the economic involvement of the United States in Africa continues to be slight, but it has been growing constantly of late and there is every reason to assume that it will be of increasing importance. Furthermore, the United States cannot help being concerned with the economic significance of Africa for its

European allies, and, in particular, with the effects on the trade patterns of Africa and the world at large of the Common Market with its eighteen associated African states.

Whether it takes one side or the other on particular controversies or situations in Africa—or even if it seeks merely to abstain—the United States cannot evade the fact that what it does, and often what it does not do, will have a great influence on the fate of Africa.

Similarly, whether they like it or not, Americans must reconcile themselves to the realization that what goes on in Africa may have a decisive influence on the future direction of their lives.

The troubled affairs of the Congo have given the most vivid demonstration of these facts.

WHAT IS AFRICA?

What is this Africa with which the United States has come to be increasingly entangled? We have grown accustomed in recent times to nationalist drives in many parts of the world: Can we expect that African peoples in the years immediately ahead will generally follow the same revolutionary patterns as those we have seen in Asia and elsewhere, or are African conditions so different as to indicate that precedents derived from elsewhere are more dangerous and misleading than helpful?

African Diversity

As befits a great continent, Africa is marked by great diversity. This diversity can be looked at in a number of ways, the most familiar of which is the separation into North Africa and Africa south of the Sahara. It is the latter that is normally thought of as the real Africa—the Negro Africa of the tropics, or *l'Afrique noire* —in contrast to the Mediterranean Africa of the North. Islamic in religion and peopled largely by Arabs, North Africa in many respects attaches to the East rather than to the continent lying to the south, although both Arabs and Islam have penetrated deeply south of the desert. A further subdivision which might usefully be added severs the Republic of South Africa from its neighbors to the north, on the ground that, despite its strong African majority, it is for present purposes a predominantly European country.

Colonial Influences

A third feature that distinguishes the African territories from each other is derived from the colonial regimes which have been imposed upon them. How far into the future the differences will perpetuate themselves there is no current way of estimating, but it is evident that the decades of rule by the British or the French, the Belgians or the Portuguese, have a very significant influence in shaping the African peoples.

On the whole continent, Liberia is the only country that can boast an unbroken record of independence during its lifetime, and even it has in the past occasionally been regarded as an American protectorate. The component parts of South Africa had shorter or longer periods of British rule, Egypt was under British control for several decades after 1882, and Ethiopia fell briefly to the Italian Fascists in 1935–36. For all the rest of Africa, independence is a very recent matter. In some measure because of failure of the great powers to agree to any other solution, Libya came to independence in 1951; the Sudan, Morocco, and Tunisia followed in 1956. In Africa south of the Sahara, the freeing of Ghana in 1957 loosed the flood that reached its height in 1960 when, in addition to Nigeria, almost all the French territories and the Belgian Congo emerged from colonialism.

The widespread use of the language of the colonial power, including English in Liberia, is the most obvious outward symbol of what has taken place under Western rule. But the cultural penetration goes much deeper. The impact of the culture and institutions of the colonial overlord has been very great on the Western-educated elites who are the heirs of imperial power in Africa, or who protest that they should be its heirs. Even the relatively short period of German rule in Togoland and the Cameroons left an imprint that has not yet vanished. Each of these colonially-created territories has a distinctive identity of its own, despite the division of each between the British and the French after World War I. In the case of Togoland, British Togo opted, not without reluctance, to join Ghana; the northern Cameroons, under British administration, voted to merge with the northern region of Nigeria, but the southern Cameroons decided to link its destiny with the adjoining French Cameroon.

It will be long before the differences which have been imposed on the peoples of Africa by the colonial powers lose their sharp edges. Economically and politically, as well as culturally, bonds have been established that may well continue to be regarded as advantageous by both the former colony and the metropolitan power. The Commonwealth has so far demonstrated that it has a great attraction for countries emerging from British rule. Moreover, with the exception of Guinea, the ex-French territories have remained intimately linked to France, although the more formal bonds of the French Union or Community have largely vanished. Even Guinea has indicated its interest in resuming closer relations with France if appropriate terms can be negotiated.

The Problem of White Settlers

One last and troublesome line of distinction should be added. In most of Africa, the Africans themselves have a clear title to their countries once the colonial tie is broken. There are a few areas, however, in which white settlement, occasionally combined with substantial Asian settlement, has raised immensely difficult issues for the future. These difficulties are most inescapably apparent at the two ends of the continent. In South Africa the Europeans—themselves unhappily divided between Afrikaners and those of British descent—have been able to maintain a still almost unchallenged supremacy, although they account for only some 3 million of a total population of 14 million. In the north, Algeria presented the gravest problem, with its European population of 1.2 million out of a total of 10 million, but the winning of independence in 1962 was the signal for the departure of the great bulk of the Europeans.

In the rest of Africa, the British territories that have caused the most serious complications, because of the diversity of the races inhabiting them, are Kenya and the Rhodesias. In both areas, the recently fashionable slogan of "partnership" has broken down badly. The Europeans who had taken up residence in the Belgian Congo and in French West and Equatorial Africa were mostly transients rather than settlers, and though numerous did not present as serious a challenge as did the settlers in other parts of the continent. The troubles following independence in the Congo led to the flight of the majority of the Europeans, although some returned as conditions grew quieter. In most of the other ex-French dependencies, friendly relations with France made it possible for the Europeans to stay on. The relatively large European population in Angola was presumably one of the causes of the uprising in that country that began early in 1961, but Salazar continues to promote emigration to Angola in order to make the Portuguese "presence" there unmistakable, and to establish the validity of his claim that Portugal has no dependencies but only provinces of a single and indivisible state.

So long as colonialism was accepted as one of the facts of life, white settlement could also be accepted as a natural accompaniment. Indeed, colonization in this older sense was defended as an essential instrument in the great task of bringing civilization to the Africans—although the record suggests that actually the presence of white settlers has often imposed a ceiling on the advancement of colonial peoples rather than encouraged it. (Incidentally, this was not the case in South Africa, and it is one of the tragedies of apartheid that South Africa's role as a training ground for African advancement has been so gravely impaired.) Bringing with them the techniques and scientific knowledge of highly developed societies, the settlers have demonstrated their ability to produce much more efficiently than the Africans and to speed economic development, but they have been little inclined to share either their talents or their economic well-being with the people of the country. In self-protection, they have avoided pushing the African ahead to the point where his competition might endanger their supremacy. Like other segments of mankind, the settlers have been prone to concentrate on their own interest, and a significant part of that interest has been defined as a need to secure title to much of the best land and to maintain an ample supply of cheap and tractable African labor.

The situation changed drastically when anticolonialism took over and the Africans began to speak for themselves. The west coast dependencies and other comparably all-African countries could move to independence with no profound stirring up of racial issues. However, in territories where locally established Europeans—in violation of all democratic precepts, though not perhaps of the existing balance of social and economic power— laid claim to political as well as economic predominance, revolutionary consequences are likely to flow from the abandonment of the colonial ties.

In Kenya, where some 65,000 Europeans, less than half of whom can properly be regarded as settlers, confront an African population one hundred times as large, the assumption that this is an African country has come to almost universal acceptance, and the former white monopoly of the desirable highlands has been abrogated. The delay in Kenya's advance to independence in the last years has been due far less to racial conflict than to tribal and other disagreements within the African community.

In the Federation of Rhodesia and Nyasaland, which has virtually come to the end of its days, the two extremes are Nyasaland, where fewer than 10,000 Europeans live among nearly 3 million Africans, and Southern Rhodesia, where 223,000 Europeans have for decades monopolized all political power and economic advantage in a territory inhabited by over 3 million Africans. In both Nyasaland and Northern Rhodesia, the transition to African government, and presumably to independence, is well under way; it is difficult to believe that Southern Rhodesia will not soon follow on the same path, but the dominant European minority is still unprepared to yield or even to share its prerogatives. Good will, patience, and forbearance, in quantities which can be hoped for but not realistically expected, will be required to make possible a peaceful transition from white minority supremacy to the supremacy of Africans still unendowed with economic command of their own country. For the local

Europeans, the descent from being in effect masters of all they survey to the position of a tolerated minority in a country that may have been their home for several generations must be at best a painful one, and in Kenya as well as in the Rhodesias the economic consequences may be grave.

By now, the United States has had ample occasion to sample the difficulties that such situations as these present, and even more serious ones are likely to be under way. South Africa's problems have made an annual appearance in the United Nations; the affairs of former French North Africa, and particularly Algeria, have often occupied the Assembly, and the Rhodesias have come to more recent prominence. The embarrassment that Britain feels when it must act or take public stands in relation to South Africa or the Rhodesias is inevitably shared in some measure by the United States, which also has large investments and raw material interests in these countries. Membership in the United Nations forces all countries to stand up and be counted on many issues on which they would no doubt frequently prefer to operate behind the scenes or even play no role at all, and the multiplication in numbers of the anticolonial bloc also multiplies the number of issues brought into the United Nations arena.

African Poverty

Although there are many "poor whites" among them, the European settler communities are oases of prosperity in a desert of African poverty. Africa is poor, its economy is stunted, its social patterns are by and large primitive, and its people are still largely illiterate. These are basic conditions of its past and present. The tragic cycle of poverty repeats itself endlessly: malnutrition, ill health, lack of sanitary and medical facilities, inadequate skills and techniques, lack of capital, and an economy based either on low-standard subsistence production or on export industries from which Africans derive a meager living wage. A *Review of Economic Conditions in Africa,* published by the United Nations in 1951, came to the summary conclusion that "Africa as a whole is economically among the least developed areas of the world, with very low levels of production and consumption." Three-quarters of its population are engaged in agriculture—the highest proportion of any of the continents, although Asia, with 70 per cent, comes in a close second. Its agricultural productivity, however, is the lowest of all the continents, whether measured as production per person or per hectare. Its soil is often infertile and, with a few exceptions such as the cocoa of Ghana, the flourishing sectors of its economy have been introduced and controlled by aliens. Mining, processing, and manufacturing are for practical purposes wholly in European hands, with the great bulk of their products headed directly for export to supply the needs of richer and more diversified economies. Although Africans are steadily rising in the economic hierarchy, the essential African contribution, aside from the resources of the earth itself, has been bare labor power.

To historical "if's" there can never be wholly conclusive answers, but there is on the face of it no reason to assume that, if there had been no European intervention, Africa would have overcome its own age-old poverty. Similarly, if the Europeans were wholly to withdraw, there is no reason to assume that the living standard of Africans, freed from exploitation, would begin a prompt and sustained upward spurt. What we know as the modern world originated in Europe, and it is the Europeans who must take the praise or blame for introducing Africa to that modern world. Up to now the Africans have had only a meager share of the material wealth their continent can produce, and it still remains true that they are likely to be able to move ahead only if they receive substantial admixtures of outside aid, wisely administered and geared to their needs. However great the basic resources of the continent and the existing or potential abilities of its inhabitants, for present purposes African capital, entrepreneurial talent, and skilled manpower remain inadequate to the task of pushing through effective development programs.

The White Man Rules, the Black Man Obeys

The great gap between the developed societies of the West and the backward societies of Africa shows clearly enough the failure of the imperial powers to bring their African wards up to any approximation of those standards that are taken for granted in the imperial centers. European governments and settlers can be credited with laying some of the essential foundation for Africa's economic and social advance under colonial rule, but the bulk of the people are still just in the opening stages of the transition into the modern age. The government revenues from which much of that transition must be financed stay almost everywhere at a discouragingly low level. On the educational score, as late as 1950, in most of the African territories, from 85 to 90 per cent of the adult population was estimated to be illiterate, and the figure fell to 55 to 60 per cent in the Union of South Africa and to 60 to 65 per cent in the Belgian Congo. In 1958, a UNESCO estimate concluded that illiteracy in Africa for those over fifteen years old, was still 80 to 85 per cent. The moral drawn by Chester Bowles from this unhappy tale of poverty and backwardness is that, for the African, "'the political equation becomes a simple one; the white man rules, the black man obeys. Therefore, the white man is rich while the black man is poor. A more ominous revolutionary situation is difficult to imagine."

African Political Movements

Anticolonialism and Nationalism

In terms of this equation, African political movements and actions have so far generally been surprisingly mild and restrained —in good part, to be sure, because of the readiness of the colonial powers to yield gracefully. Of course, exceptions come immediately to mind, of which recent samples would be the Mau Mau rising in Kenya, the open warfare and terrorism in Algeria, and disturbances and repressions in South Africa and the Rhodesian Federation. The over-all trend has been toward well-organized and popularly based demands for an end to colonialism.

Once the early phases of colonial pacification were left behind, an extended time of quiet usually followed, broken only by local and inconsequential disorders, which frequently drew their inspiration from religious leaders and themes. The most significant and ultimately unanswerable challenge to the colonial powers came at the next stage with the emergence of modern, forward-looking nationalist movements, led by the new Western-educated elite. These men spoke the idiom of the West and presented their case in the familiar terms of the West's own experience and philosophy.

Asia did not succeed in giving effective expression to the demand for a speedy end to its own colonial subjugation until after World War I, and it was not until after World War II that Africa followed the same path. Once the movement toward decolonization got under way, it swept ahead at an almost incredibly rapid pace. Given the strength of the world anticolonial movement, and the hold that it already has on Africa, it is difficult to believe that the colonial system can perpetuate itself for long anywhere on the continent, including the variations now being enforced in South Africa.

The Colonial Setting

Although northern Angola has seen some anticolonial violence recently, the territories which up to now have experienced the least political activism are those attached to Spain and Portugal —certainly not those territories which have made the largest advances toward liberty, progress, and well-being. There is good reason to suggest that although some of this is due to the readiness of the colonial authorities to engage in ruthless suppression of rebels, the more significant factor is their failure to stimulate the social and economic development that has everywhere paved the way for nationalism. The ability, particularly of Portugal, to isolate its dependent peoples from world currents is markedly reduced as the anticolonial forces sweep Africa, and the existence of free African countries such as the Congo and Tanganyika as neighbors of Angola and Mozambique makes possible a mobilization of revolutionary forces which was previously excluded.

Until almost the eve of independence, the Belgian Congo, despite the disruption of traditional society brought about by Western rule and unusually extensive economic penetration, was dominated by an unabashed paternalism and was singularly barren of political agitation. It was not until late in 1957 that the first elections ever to be held in the Congo cautiously and tentatively produced a slate of municipal councillors. Belgian policy deliberately denied political expression to all elements of the Congo population, including the Belgians, on the ground that some reasonable facsimile of an indigenous middle class, as well as an educated mass, must be created in order to furnish a safeguard against rule by a tiny minority of whites or of Western-educated Congolese. Looking ahead to perhaps another half-century of colonial rule, the Belgians were quite unprepared for the risings which took place in Leopoldville in January, 1959, and a year and a half later the Congolese were hastily endowed with independence, despite their almost total lack of experience in the management of a modern society.

It was the British and the French who, in their different fashions, gave the largest measure of political liberty to their dependencies, made higher education possible for the largest number of Africans, and have, in consequence, been confronted with the most urgent demands for equality and freedom. After World War II, these powers brought into being a new style of colonialism that may be honestly characterized as one intended to secure the advancement of colonial peoples. Only in areas of white settlement, as has been seen, has this policy run into serious difficulties. For Britain, the new course meant the translation to Africa of the policy of granting independence which had long since been applied to the older Dominions and which, after 1945, was extended to India and other Asian dependencies. It is Britain's hope that independence will not exclude membership in the Commonwealth, but the possibility of bidding both colonialism and Commonwealth farewell remains open—an option that has so far been exercised only by Burma.

France found it more difficult to break away from her traditional policies of assimilation and centralization, but in 1956 she conceded independence with surprising suddenness and completeness to Tunisia and Morocco, and under De Gaulle's leadership not only freed all the sub-Saharan territories, but made peace with Algeria as well. This was a far cry from the Brazzaville colonial conference of 1944, which had stated that France's

colonial mission made any evolution outside the French imperial
bloc impossible, and had dismissed any notion of self-government
for the colonies, even in the distant future. For a time, it seemed
as if there might be a realization of the dream that the peoples of
the French African territories, including Madagascar, should
be content with equality with other Frenchmen in a unitary
French system revolving about Paris, but the demand became increasingly insistent for the recognition of the distinctiveness of
the African peoples and their political independence. A vigorous
effort is being made by France to maintain close ties of all kinds
with her former colonies. This effort appears to have had a large
degree of success; but it must also be recognized that in the years
ahead the emergence of a more radical nationalism, protesting
the present continued dependence on France, is to be expected,
and this may imply impairment of relations with the United
States as well.

The Re-evaluation of Colonialism

Somewhat paradoxically, the repudiation of colonialism came
at a time not only when the colonial powers had begun to change
their spots, but also when their good name had begun to be re-
habilitated. In recent years, the widespread assumption that the
boasted *mission civilisatrice* was a sheer fraud, and that exploitation and repression were the real core of imperialism, has been
challenged by a counterview which asserts—hesitantly, except for
the few outright apologists for imperialism—that perhaps there
has been some good in the evil old system after all. Among the
sources of this re-evaluation, two in particular may be mentioned.

Some of the peoples who have recently come to independence
have discovered, perhaps to their own surprise, that they owe
significant debts to the imperial power from which they have
parted. The establishment of a democratic constitution, the creation of a modern administrative system, including the training
of a body of civil servants, and the installation of an impartial
and practiced judiciary would rank high in the list of political
benefits. Beyond such things as these, which could be multiplied
by examples in other spheres, there is the discovery that over the

years cultural ties have been woven which make mere condemnation of the relationship difficult and unreal. For African leaders who have been educated in French or British universities and who have shared in greater or lesser degree the life of the metropolitan center, it is impossible wholly to cast off the cultural imprint and the human ties that have resulted. When peoples part in anger and with bloodshed, such ties can be broken, though not without pain; when the separation is on an agreed and friendly basis, as in the case of most of the African colonies, friendships and shared culture remain to bridge the gap.

A second factor serving to lessen the ill repute of colonialism is the comparison frequently drawn between countries that have had an intensive experience of Western colonial rule, and other underdeveloped areas that have had none or only a brief touch of it. The basic assumptions of the earlier liberal and leftward theory of imperialism make inescapable the conclusion that the free countries should be well ahead of the colonies, which have by definition been ground under the imperial heel. Much testimony bears witness to the contrary, and it is not only the testimony of the colonial powers that have an obvious axe to grind. In the course of his explorations *Inside Africa,* John Gunther found Liberia backward because the country had not had the advantages of enlightened colonialism, and he added:

> It is a striking phenomenon that three of the independent states of Africa—Ethiopia, Libya, and Liberia—should be the poorest and most backward on the continent, much poorer than most of those dominated by white powers.

In March, 1957, corroboration of this thesis came from an unexpected quarter. Charles T. O. King, Liberian Ambassador to the United States, was moved to speak in defense of his country by the dispatches of newspapermen who had accompanied Vice-President Nixon to Ghana's independence ceremony and who had portrayed Liberia as largely primitive and lagging materially behind the newly freed British colony. This verdict the ambassador did not contest. On the contrary, trampling under foot the convictions of all good liberals, he explained that this state of affairs arose from the fact that his country had always been independent and had therefore never reaped the advantages of colonialism. The difference, he continued, was between the home of a man who has had to accomplish everything by his own sweat and toil and that of a man who has enjoyed a large inheritance. In a number of recent cases where independence has been achieved on the basis of amicable agreement, the nationalist leaders have given warm praise and thanks to the colonial authorities who have brought them this far along the road.

Dependent Peoples Repudiate Colonialism

Colonialism, it has become increasingly apparent as it comes to an end, is not to be written off as all evil; but it is even more apparent that it has been rejected with growing passion by all those upon whom it has been thrust. It has, for good or ill, provided one of the essential channels through which the lore and skills of the West could be made available to—or forced upon—the peoples of Africa; but the price the Africans had to pay was subordination to alien rule. Even where oppression and exploitation cease to play any serious role, save as slogans with which to beat the imperialists, the basic fact of superiority and inferiority continues. If their leaders represent them correctly, Africans reject neither friendship with the West nor what the West can provide to help them climb into the modern age, but they do reject the assumption of white overlordship. What is sought is equality in status and recognition of the right of all people to set their own course in the world, including neutralism or alignment with the Communist powers if they so choose.

Leaders and Masses

Anticolonialism is a major ingredient in the political movements which have been mushrooming in Africa since the end of World War II. It is more difficult to determine to what extent these movements also embody the more positive aspects of nationalism. Are the rising leaders who lay claim to the title of nationalists able to speak on behalf of peoples who have in fact achieved a substantial measure of national solidarity? On two major counts, there must be serious doubt.

In Africa as in Asia, the leadership that has been coming up is widely separated in background and outlook from the mass of the people and particularly from the peasantry. Although the ferment of change is at work throughout in greater or lesser degree, the peasants remain only distantly aware of the great world beyond their horizons and still cling strongly to the old established ways of life. The rising new elements, on the other hand, have made a drastic breach with the old, have come to a high degree of familiarity with the West, and literally as well as figuratively are likely to speak an alien language. Their goals and patterns of thought have been in good part shaped for them by their exposure to Europe or the United States, while the masses have grown up within the framework of the old society, which follows them even to the great urban centers of Africa.

To the pained surprise of the colonial administrator, the people increasingly gave their effective allegiance to the new elite, which no longer protested particular grievances but challenged the legitimacy of the entire colonial system and ridiculed the claim of the expatriate official to be the real representative of the people's interests. But the joining of forces between mass and leadership that has been accomplished in the struggle to win freedom from alien domination cannot conceal the fact that there is an immense gap between the people at large and the Western-educated and in many respects Western-orientated elite. In Africa, this has characteristically taken the form of an opposition between the chiefs as the traditional rulers and the young men who appear as advocates of a new order. That the forces which represent the new will win out seems highly plausible, but there may be bitter conflicts within African societies as they feel their way toward a new and independent course. There is no present means of estimating what combination of the traditional and the Western-inspired will ultimately emerge in different parts of the continent.

Africa's Political Future

The second major problem directly concerns the shape of Africa's political future. What will be the geographic and demo-

graphic dimensions of the new Africa breaking out from the confines of colonialism? In an age that pays tribute to the right of
self-determination of peoples, the easy answer is that the African
nations will determine their own configuration, but this assumes
that the nations are already in existence and capable of taking
decisions. Almost without exception, however, the new states are
the direct heirs of the colonial regimes, taking over intact the
frontiers imposed on Africa by the European empire-builders,
which more often than not arbitrarily lumped diverse peoples
together, divided close-knit ethnic groups into two or more parts,
and in some instances created political entities with little prospect
of being politically or economically viable. Nationalists are rising
in many African quarters: What remains open to question is
whether the corresponding nations have as yet come into existence. It is tempting to suggest that in most other parts of the
world the nations have preceded the nationalists who have arisen
to plead their cause, whereas in Africa the nationalists have made
their vigorous appearance before the nations are more than a
phrase in oratorical imagination.

In Asia, the problems were real enough. India saw Pakistan
split away, and both successor states are troubled by inner ethnic
cleavages; Burma and Indonesia have so far failed to establish
their full internal unity; and Malaya is an unstable mixture of
races. But even when this has been said, it still remains highly
dubious in most of Africa that nations can now be found comparable to those which have been able to take over elsewhere as
empires toppled and peoples seized their own destinies. In North
Africa, there is no occasion to doubt the reality of the Egyptian,
Moroccan, and Tunisian nations that have won their separate
statehood, even though there are minority problems which may
still prove serious. Algeria perhaps presents a more doubtful case,
but a nation seems at least to be in the making. Libya has the
weakest claim to embody a people which has come to a sense of
common identity.

It is in Africa south of the Sahara that there is found the most
widespread discrepancy between the pretensions of those who
assert their prerogatives as champions of their nations and the
social reality that lies behind them. For the most part, the peoples

of Africa have had a very limited consciousness of social cohesion. Even though there have been impressive native empires, such as the one from which Ghana derived its name, strong kingdoms like that of the Baganda and some large tribal groupings such as the Kikuyu and Wachaga, the effective sense of the "we" who together form a community has normally not reached far afield. Everywhere in Africa, European rule has been too short-lived to make possible the kind of colonial creation of nations that took place in the Philippines, Indonesia, and even in India.

Tribalism, Nationalism, and Africanism

The social reality of Africa has been and largely continues to be tribal in nature, dividing the continent into a multiplicity of distinct and often warring communities marked off from each other by language, custom, and structure. As both caste and language affiliations are still of great political importance in India, so in Africa the tribal attachments that many had thought anachronistic have shown their vitality by their resurgence within the orbit of the new political parties and institutions. What to the outsider and the early nationalist had the look of a single Nigerian nation-in-the-making soon separated into its component regional parts of the Hausa and Fulani in the north, the Yoruba in the west, and the Ibo in the east—with a number of lesser peoples rising to assert their right to equally distinctive treatment. To glance only at nearby territories in West Africa, the people of the Northern Territories and the Ashanti in Ghana have protested "imperialist" domination by the coastal peoples with whom they were often at war in the past; and the Ewe of the two Togolands and Ghana have sought a tribal unity which cut across all existing political lines. Uganda independence was undoubtedly delayed by conflicts of interest among pre-colonial kingdoms, and their differences remain a dominant and potentially disruptive problem today. Undoubtedly the British system of indirect rule has maintained tribal divisions that the more centralized French system has worked to minimize—as witness the local protest against breaking the two French African federations down into their twelve constituent parts—but tribalism is so deep-rooted in the African tradition as to be a negligible matter virtually nowhere.

It is on the basis of considerations such as these that Lord Hailey, in the 1957 edition of his monumental *African Survey,* suggests that it is advisable to use the term "Africanism" rather than "nationalism" to describe contemporary political movements. African peoples, united only by the accidents of history, as he sees it, lack the tradition of common origin and a common outlook on their political future: "The majority have in the past missed the dynamic influence of the concept of territorial nationalism." Lord Hailey's "Africanism" does not assume a drive toward a single Pan-Africa, but is portrayed as having two phases, of which one is the positive reconstruction of African countries in "'the characteristic spirit of Africa as interpreted by modern Africans," and the other is the negative rejection of European dominance, perhaps inspired by a traditionalist revolt against modern influences.

Questions for the Political Future

Since Africa's history has differed profoundly in many respects from the history of other parts of the world, it is conceivable that the continent will evolve some other foundation for its political systems than the nationalism which has taken over elsewhere. It is more probable, however, that its nations are merely retarded in their development and, reversing the customary course, will follow in the wake of the urban Westernized leaders who have prematurely declared their existence. The political facts of the situation have dictated that the anticolonial struggle should in the first instance be directed against the existing colonial government and that the successor states should be the old colonies under new African management. The political map of the continent still has significant elements of uncertainty, however, even though it appears to have been widely recognized that any effort to tinker with existing boundaries might open the door to chaos. This consideration has entered into the widespread African hostility to the secession of Tshombe's Katanga from the Congo, for fear that it might lead to a further Balkanization of Africa on tribal lines.

As soon as one begins to challenge the solidity of the present African states, any number of questions immediately arise. Does the political future lie with Nigeria as a whole, in the limits arbitrarily established by the British, or with its tribally-determined regions, or with an expansion to take in such neighboring territories as Dahomey or Niger? Will the twelve successors to the two French African federations maintain their separate identity, or will a series of mergers and unions take place, and if so, on what lines? Will the disintegrating Federation of Rhodesia and Nyasaland be replaced by some new federal structure agreed upon by future African governments, and what will be its relation to neighboring countries? What success is likely to attend the several existing unions or groupings of African states, and what are the prospects for one or another version of a broader Pan-Africanism?

These, and many others like them, are questions to which no crystal ball presently available can give more than a highly speculative answer, but we may be sure that in the unfolding of the answers, the United States will find itself confronted with a series of baffling decisions. What precise form African states should take may be a matter of little moment to American statesmen, but if serious instability and perhaps revolutionary upheaval are to mark Africa's coming to maturity, the United States can have no real hope of standing aloof from Africa's troubles in these days of global involvement. Nor will any easy formula of support for national aspirations be of much help, since it may be precisely the identity of the nation that is in dispute, the battle perhaps being joined by those who see the basic national interest as pointing in the traditionalist rather than in the modernist direction, or toward a Pan-African rather than a more parochial version of Africa's destiny.

ECONOMIC AND SOCIAL DEVELOPMENT

Whatever the turn of events in Africa, and whatever its political shape, one immense task that lies ahead is that of social and economic development. In the colonial areas this was the almost exclusive responsibility of the imperial powers, which can with some legitimacy contend that technical assistance and aid programs are nothing new under the sun but have been a regular feature of colonialism. However, a fundamental shortcoming lies in the fact that a great part of the development undertaken under colonial auspices concentrated on the building up of export industries to meet the demands of outside markets, with only incidental attention, at best, paid to the well-being of the Africans or to securing rounded African economies. After World War II, there was a significant reappraisal of the responsibility of the imperial powers to their colonial wards. The changed temper of the times was clearly reflected in the planned development launched under the British Colonial Development and Welfare Acts, the *Fonds d'Investissement pour le Développement Economique et Social de la France d'Outre-Mer,* and the Ten Year Development Plan for the Belgian Congo. In all of these it was recognized that Africa still required a very large amount of not directly profitable investment in order to lay the foundations—including those in education, health, and other social welfare measures—on which a viable and coherent economic structure might be built. However short they fell of African requirements, they represented a beginning of great importance. In more recent years, the efforts of the colonial or ex-colonial powers have been supplemented by aid both from several other countries and from international organizations.

The American Role in Development

The American role in African development has been a limited one, whether measured in absolute terms or, even more strikingly, in relation to the vast sums which have been devoted to Europe and Asia. As calculated in the report of Representative Frances P. Bolton's 1955 African mission, from July 1, 1945, to December 31, 1955, the United States gave away without requirement of repayment a total of $46,142,413,000, of which Africa received only $71,595,000, or 0.15 per cent. In the same period, the United States lent a total of $16,140,524,000, of which Africa received $342,713,000, or 2.12 per cent. It should be noted that of this latter sum, $151,714,000 went to the Union of South Africa and $60,686,000 to the Rhodesias, both areas of white settlement already substantially developed. The International Cooperation Administration reported that the cumulative total of American foreign assistance, military and economic, from fiscal year 1946 through fiscal year 1960, came to $84,090,800,000, of which $822,-100,000, or less than one per cent, went to Africa. Of this latter sum, $483.9 million was earmarked for Morocco, Tunisia, and Libya, while $115 million went to Ethopia and $44.1 million to the Sudan, leaving a very meager residue for the countries south of the Sahara.

The reason for such relatively slight attention to Africa was obviously not that the continent's needs were small, but rather that the United States could not operate freely in the colonies of other Western nations. As the colonial status of the African territories came to an end, active American participation increased substantially, but in general the United States was hesitant to assume a leading role in furnishing aid to countries that for the most part retained a special relationship to, and were being aided by, the former mother country. According to the official *Statistical Abstract of the United States (1962)*, the major American assistance to Africa rose from $122 million, net, in 1959, to $282 million in 1961. The share of Morocco, Tunisia, and Libya remained high, amounting to $189 million in 1961.

Other considerations have also entered into United States underplaying of Africa. It could be said that in a world where the warning sirens are constantly shrieking in one corner or another, Africa has still not become enough of a danger point to command full American attention. Since the defeat of the German and Italian forces, there has been no direct military threat to the continent, although the Congo crisis raised the possibility that the Soviet Union or the United States, or both, might intervene. Africa does not contain countries of sufficient military consequence to merit the kind of armaments support which the United

States has lavished elsewhere, and the American desire to sign up as many countries as possible in military pacts of the SEATO and CENTO variety has happily receded. As far as economic aid is concerned, it seems clear that most of the African states have not yet reached a point of development where they could make effective use of massive injections of capital. Far more must be done, however, than has hitherto been seriously contemplated if the African peoples are to come to the kind of equal place in the world which is alone likely to keep them reasonably stable and at peace. How large a responsibility for the huge load of African development the United States should assume, and whether or not it should channel a more sizable fraction of its aid through the United Nations, remain issues for future settlement.

COMMUNISM IN AFRICA

Under present conditions, the one sure stimulant for greater American attention to Africa would be an increase in Communist activity. Up to now there is no reliable evidence that the Communists have established a really firm foothold in any part of the continent, although they have begun to penetrate a number of countries. It is foolish to look for a Communist under every nationalist bed—to turn against colonialism requires no journey to Moscow—but it is equally foolish not to recognize that both under and in the nationalist beds there is ample and attractive room for Communists to congregate. A disinherited proletariat, often crowded into disreputable and segregated shantytowns; a growing middle class of traders, small business men, teachers, clerks, and professional men; disoriented societies moving from primitive isolation to participation in a worldwide money economy and an anarchy of world political rivalry; the remnants of colonialism, and independent states resting on shaky foundations —these are elements ready-made for the Communist. Under conditions such as these, the inevitable Communist appeal to Africa can be countered only if, with Western aid, African peoples come to a sense that their rising expectations are being met without resort to the drastic methods of Communism and that colonialism no longer threatens their mastery of their own societies.

Increased Soviet and Chinese Interest in Africa

There is ample evidence of increasing interest in Africa on the part of the Soviet Union and Communist China, leaving no doubt of an intensive Communist drive to win over the African peoples as they emerge from colonialism, or at least to break such continuing attachments as they may have to the West. Diplomatic relations have been established by the Communist states by no means only with the leftward inclined Ghana-Guinea-Mali trio but also with a number of other countries. Economic connections between the Communist and the African states have multiplied, although there are still relatively few of them, and several signs—for instance, in Guinea—indicate that the first enthusiasm of some Africans for intimate intercourse with the Communist world has cooled perceptibly as the result of experience.

Within the U.S.S.R., the study of African culture and languages is being actively pursued, and African students have been encouraged to come to the Soviet Union and other countries of the Soviet bloc. Through Youth Festivals and at international gatherings the charms of Communism are displayed to eager watchers. The effort of Communist propaganda to pin the label of imperialism on the West, while the Soviet Union remains the champion of freedom, often meets with success among people whose ears are attuned to just this kind of message. Hungary is far away and European; the Portuguese territories, Southern Rhodesia, and South Africa are close at hand and of immediate African concern. To African students in Western countries, the Communists offer sympathetic help and a doctrine that links imperialism and capitalism and has the persuasive look of explaining their ills and answering their needs. Particularly for those who are themselves victims of discrimination abroad (and fail to win the solace of a White House breakfast), both the Marxist creed and the party organization of the Communists are often distinctive features of their Western experience, as President Nkrumah of Ghana has testified in his autobiography.

Strategic and Economic Space for Europe

A Communist take-over in any African country would be a dangerous opening wedge for entry into a continent that has hitherto been held as an inviolate preserve of the free world—although many Africans are skeptical of applying the term "free world" to powers that so recently ruled colonial Africa and still hold large parts of it. The stake of the West and of the United States in Africa is great. Negatively, the primary concern is to ensure that the Communist bloc secures neither the prestige nor the material gains that would flow from enlisting Africa, or any substantial part thereof, in its camp. Strategically, the vital importance of North Africa to Europe was demonstrated in World War II, and Dakar, offering potential command over South Atlantic shipping lanes, juts out as the nearest point for an invasion of the Western hemisphere. At a time when defense in depth has become essential, the continent of Europe must watch Africa's turbulent developments with intense interest.

As Western Europe looks, perhaps somewhat wistfully, at the strategic area it once commanded in Africa, so it looks with a greater measure of hope at the economic opportunities the continent offers. The concept of a Eurafrica which would permanently wed the two highly diverse continents is perhaps an idle dream, if only because many influential Africans are very wary of any venture that might have the effect of binding their countries in perpetual economic servitude to highly developed Europe. This view found expression in the repudiation by Ghana and Nigeria of association with the European Common Market, but a dozen former French territories have welcomed their ties with the Common Market and want them strengthened. For these territories, the present benefits, including direct financial aid and links with Europe's flourishing economic community, outweigh the fears of a neocolonialism that would substitute more subtle economic bonds for the overt political controls of colonialism.

To a crowded Europe, Africa holds the promise of a frontier land still susceptible of great expansion, both as a market and as a source of raw materials, plus an almost unexplored industrial potential. Its riches in strategic and other minerals are impressive. In industrial diamonds, columbium, cobalt, chromium, and beryllium, Africa either heads the list of world producers or stands close to the top; it is a significant producer of tin, manganese, copper, and antimony; and its large reserves of iron ore and bauxite are just beginning to be tapped. The uranium of the Congo and South Africa has contributed to the unfolding of the atomic age. The French discovery of oil in the Sahara has enhanced the importance of Algeria, and Libya has also come into new riches. To this mineral wealth, Africa adds through its agriculture a variety of foodstuffs and industrial materials, such as cocoa, coffee, tea, vegetable oils, cotton, and pyrethrum.

The United States has a direct interest in many of these products, but it is probably of less importance to the United States to assure its own access to Africa's resources and markets than to make sure that its European allies are not cut off from them.

THE INTERESTS OF THE UNITED STATES

Economic Stake

The United States cannot help but be profoundly concerned with denying the Communist bloc entry to Africa and keeping the lines between Africa, Europe, and America open. From an economic standpoint, however, direct American involvement in Africa has been relatively slight, although moving upward. In 1961, American imports from Africa came to $582,588,000, or 4.03 per cent of American imports from all countries, while exports to Africa amounted to $826,826,000, or 3.96 per cent of all American exports. South Africa was well ahead as the best of America's African customers and suppliers, taking goods valued at $228,082,-000 from the United States and sending goods valued at $122,-390,000 in return.

Private American investment in Africa has lingered at a comparatively low level, although it has also been growing. In 1961, of an estimated total direct American investment abroad of $34,684 billion, investment in Africa came to only $1.07 billion, but this latter figure had risen from $664 million in 1957 and

$925 million in 1960. In 1961, American investment was distributed among the regions of Africa in the following amounts: North Africa, $260 million; East Africa, $56 million; West Africa, $341 million; and Central and South Africa, $413 million. Again the Republic of South Africa led the list of individual countries, with an American investment estimated at $304 million. The West African figure is swollen by a large sum representing ships owned by United States–controlled companies and registered under the Liberian flag. In the mid-1950's, it was estimated that, excluding the special case of Liberia, about 30 per cent of American investment had gone into mining, 30 per cent into distribution of petroleum, 20 per cent into manufacturing, and 20 per cent for all other activities. G. Mennen Williams, Assistant Secretary of State for African Affairs, has recently called for a greater boldness on the part of American investors in both the magnitude and the diversity of their activities in Africa.

Missions, Students, and American Negroes

The ending of colonialism and the emergence of African states as independent actors on the world stage has led to a great increase in contact between Africans and Americans. One traditional area of contact has been the missionary work so long undertaken by American churches, with notable results not only in direct religious impact, but also in education and medical services. American missionary activity in Africa expanded immensely in the decades following World War I, and has continued at a high level. A few years ago it was calculated that since Catholic missions in Africa were staffed primarily by Europeans, less than 10 per cent of American Catholic missionaries overseas were operating in that continent, whereas American Protestant churches were concentrating 30 per cent of their overseas missionary work in Africa.

The exchange of officials between the United States and African countries has expanded immensely. African countries that could previously have only a scant and vicarious representation in the United States, through the embassies of the colonial powers, have now opened embassies of their own in Washington and are further represented at the United Nations. On its side, the United States has hastened to make up for lost time by establishing embassies and consulates in the newly independent countries, equipped with information, cultural, and economic aid services.

The sudden leap in general American interest in Africa, as well as the need to train Africanists who could fill the great gaps in American knowledge about Africa and furnish experts to deal with African issues, has led large numbers of American students to concern themselves with African affairs, and many to visit Africa. American foundations have devoted a substantial share of their resources to African projects, and the Peace Corps has operated in several African countries. On the other side, the Institute of International Education reports that during the academic year 1961–62, 3,930 African students, coming from no fewer than 41 different African lands, attended American educational institutions, an increase of 39 per cent over 1960–61. These are men and women who are likely to be numbered among the leaders of the new Africa when they return, and the effect which their American experience has upon them may be of decisive consequence in shaping the attitudes they adopt toward the development of their own countries and toward the world at large. To name only two who have risen to the highest place in the political life of their countries, both President Nkrumah of Ghana and Governor-General Azikiwe of Nigeria are products of American universities.

A distinctive element in the relations between the United States and Africa is contributed by the 20 million Negro Americans. Even though they have for the most part long since decided that their goal is equality with all other Americans and not any form of separatism, the American Negroes inevitably watch Africa's development with a vivid interest that is strongly reflected in the Negro press. The desirability and effectiveness of drawing upon Negroes to represent the United States in Africa is a matter which has led to wide debate. The way in which Negroes are treated here has a great bearing on the esteem, or lack of it, in which Asians and Africans hold the United States. Vice-President Nixon was well justified in pointing out in his report to the President, when he returned from Ghana's independence ceremonies, in 1957, that every instance of prejudice in this country is blown up abroad and results in irreparable damage to the cause of freedom: "We cannot talk equality to the peoples of Africa and Asia and practice inequality in the United States." Little Rock and the University of Mississippi are well-enough known in Africa without its being necessary for Senator Ellender of Louisiana to export domestic controversies by commenting in Southern Rhodesia, late in 1962, that Africans are incapable of leadership and that nowhere has he seen Africans who are ready for self-government.

Africa's Desires and America's Hesitations

In the world of today it is inevitable that the threat of Communist expansion should capture much of American attention. It should not be forgotten, however, that for most Africans, like most Asians, Communism is far from constituting their greatest problem, and that the bulk of the issues with which Africa confronts the United States would be substantially the same if the Soviet Union had never come into existence. Approaching the matter from another angle, there can be no real doubt that if we are to win Africans to our view of the world it will be because we have dealt with them as human beings in their own right and not as instruments in what they are inclined to regard as our private and somewhat incomprehensible feud with Moscow and Peking. A decent and rising standard of living, education, self-respect, equality, and freedom—it is of such things as these that African aspirations are compounded, and we are most unlikely to persuade the Africans that such aspirations are to be achieved by enlistment in an anti-Communist crusade. Neutralism—at best a neutralism shaded in our direction—seems certain to be the dominant African mood for a long time to come.

The United States and Colonialism

Aside from the domestic problems of segregation and discrimination, the most difficult and urgent issue with which the United States must deal in its African relations continues to be colonialism and its immediate aftermath. All over the world, intense interest is displayed in the position which the United States adopts when it is faced, within the United Nations or outside it, by questions involving either particular colonial or racial situations, as in Angola, Southern Rhodesia, or South Africa, or more general propositions, such as the 1960 declaration on colonial independence, which the General Assembly adopted unanimously, but with the United States abstaining. In the years ahead, as in the past decade or two, the United States will repeatedly come up against the demand that it take a stand on issues such as these, and the answers are by no means always simple and easy to come by.

Traditional American anticolonialism has undoubtedly lost much of its earlier sharp cutting edge as the American position in the world has changed. From enthusiastic support for self-determination, there has been a drift toward regret that there should be so much turmoil. The United States still finds it impossible to turn its back on rising peoples, but from time to time it gives plain enough indications that it wishes they would sit tight and not start trouble. The effect on Africans was portrayed by Tom Mboya, then General Secretary of the Kenya Federation of Labour, who wrote in 1956 that for Africans America was identified as the symbol of anticolonial struggle, but that as a result of the American alliance with the colonial powers, and its neutrality on colonial issues, "this feeling is gradually changing to puzzled disappointment."

The dilemma confronting the United States is a very real one. The closest friends and most significant allies of the United States are the West European powers that have in the past been the most successful in gathering colonial possessions under their imperial wings. Even though these allies have in great part divested themselves of their overseas dependencies, it is inevitable that they should in some important respects and on some important issues base their policies on interests and assumptions that are at variance with those of the United States. A particularly unfortunate problem is presented by Portugal, a NATO ally which denies that its extensive overseas holdings are non-self-governing dependencies, which is sure to be confronted by mounting disaffection in its African territories, and which appears incapable of meeting the kind of demands which the present anticolonialist era insistently puts forward. In the United Nations, and presumably even more vigorously behind the scenes, the United States, although it has tried to soften the tone and content of the more hostile resolutions, has usually lined up with Portugal's critics, but this has not eliminated the charge that NATO's support and arms are what enable Portugal to carry on expensive colonial warfare in Angola (a charge that was also made concerning the French in Algeria). Relationships are further complicated by Washington's desire to extend its tenure of a strategically important base in the Azores, held by agreement with Portugal.

Pressed on one side by its Western allies, the United States must on the other side do what it can to work on friendly terms with the anticolonial bloc, often divided within itself, whose claims and aspirations tend to increase proportionately to the expansion of its numbers in the United Nations. The Kennedy Administration has been generally more sympathetic to the African position than was its predecessor, although this is in part attributable to the fact that the passage of time has somewhat clarified the nature of the revolutionary changes that have so abruptly swept the continent. It has made an evident effort to keep in close touch with what might be labelled moderate African opinion, but it is equally evident that issues arise from time to time where the United States feels itself compelled to part company with some of its African friends, as, for example, on radical proposals for dealing with South Africa or Southern Rhodesia.

One point which is clear is that the United States cannot hope, and should not try, to compete with the Communist states in hastening to embrace every anticolonial move, no matter what its nature. The most urgent and immediate Communist aim is to pry Africa loose from any intimate ties to the West, and this can be no part of the American purpose. Quite apart from its concern with the interests of its European allies, the United States is committed to a responsible policy that excludes the possibility of merely jumping aboard the anticolonial bandwagon.

It is evident that a policy of responsibility and moderation in relation to Africa is bound to run into trouble. The difficulties that such a policy encounters have been well illustrated in the Congo—a testing ground of the first importance for America's ability to deal with the new Africa—where American activities have been alternately praised and damned by almost all the different African and European leaders. It is more likely that these difficulties will grow rather than that they will diminish. The first revolution of anticolonialism, bringing independence, is in all probability only a forerunner of other revolutions to come. What guise will they take, and what will be the American response? The movement toward Pan-Africanism should in principle be welcomed by the United States, and "African socialism" should create no impassable barriers, but a swing toward condemnation of the United States as the evil genius of the neo-colonialists would offer scant ground for cooperation.

Caution there must be, and awareness that American actions and inactions may have drastic consequences. Responsibility and moderation are appropriate guide posts for American policy, but they offer wider latitude for collaboration with Africans in the achievement of African goals than has so far been accepted. We must seek to overcome the impression that we have an eagle eye for Communist abuses, but look with tolerant indifference on the equal or worse abuses in colonial domains. If the United States pleads neutrality and looks the other way when South Africa elbows its African majority aside, can it expect better than a suspicious neutrality when it seeks to rally Africa's people to the free world's standards? Africa remains to be convinced that the American concern for freedom and equality embraces the black man as well as the white.

POLITY

2. The Character and Viability of African Political Systems

JAMES S. COLEMAN

America's principal interest in Africa's political systems is that they be democratic and stable. No other goals would be compatible either with the declared aims and the known aspirations of the African peoples, or with the expressed ideals and the national interest of America. Immediate strategic interests or the imperatives of rapid economic and social development may require greater stress on order and stability, and the present prospects for achieving either goal in most of Africa appears quite remote. Nevertheless, the development of democracy and the maintenance of stability remain as long-range objectives. We will therefore focus upon those forces and situations in contemporary Africa having a bearing on their realization.

Once these objectives are declared, we must emphasize at once that stability does not mean the rigid maintenance of a static society. Nor does democracy mean the presence of any particular set of formal institutions. For us, stability can mean only that governments are sufficiently responsive to popular pressures to insure that change is orderly and that political authority itself is maintained. For us also, the minimum elements in democracy are freedom from alien rule, the existence of effective and regularized restraints on the exercise of political power, and a political climate in which dissent and opposition are not only tolerated but are provided a legitimate functional

39

role in the political process. Stable African democracies could emerge from quite different social and historical circumstances than those characteristic of Western societies. Indeed, we should not be insensitive to the possibility that special conditions found in developing African societies, or that a unique, possibly accidental, sequence and convergence of historical events, could serve as functional equivalents to those circumstances with the development of contemporary Western democracies.

VARIETY OF THE AFRICAN POLITICAL SCENE

The popular image of colonial Africa has tended to be one of a vast, undifferentiated continent. Now that the African peoples have lifted the steel grid of colonialism from more than three-fourths of the face of their continent and have thrust themselves onto the world stage, the complexity and diversity of both the old and new Africa become strikingly evident. True, Africa is a single continent; but the voices, the situations and problems, and the forms of political organization are many and varied.

Africa's diversity is nowhere more strikingly revealed than in the prevailing and emergent forms of government under which the African people live and are seeking to work out their destinies. All of the classical types of polities are represented, ranging from a medieval monarchy, through black and white oligarchies and static colonial regimes, to new tutelary democracies and single-party mobilization systems. An awareness and understanding of this political multiformity is important to enable the outsider to comprehend and interpret current political events and to sensitize policy-makers and their critics to the limitations and opportunities presented by the different political systems. Policies welcomed and successful in one country may be rejected and totally inappropriate for another. Such political diversity obviously must be fully appreciated for any realistic assessment of the prospects for democracy and stability.

Despite the extraordinary diversity of African political systems, certain general types may be seen which share sufficient similarities to permit some form of classification. The criteria of classification have varied during the past two decades. Prior to and immediately following World War II, African territories were classified according to the imperial power exercising control. By the mid-1950s, the character of the emergent political forms introduced a new and crucial variable. Today, however, the basic distinction is between (1) independent African states (including the two historic African states of Ethiopia and Liberia, and the new and emergent African states that have won or consolidated their independence during the past decade, or now stand on the threshold of receiving it), and (2) colonial and European settler oligarchies (Portuguese Angola and Mozambique, Southern Rhodesia, and the Republic of South Africa), which constitute the final bastion of entrenched European colonialism and minority racial domination in the modern world.

Independent African states constitute a comparatively novel type of polity among contemporary political systems. What sets them off as a type—and there are exceptions—is not that they are *sui generis*, but that they represent in the most extreme form those generic attributes of most new states in the developing areas, namely, economic underdevelopment, cultural pluralism, and shortage of high-level manpower. African states tend to cluster at the bottom of any ranking of countries by the conventional indices of economic development. Few countries reflect such a high degree of cultural fragmentation, or are so heavily dependent upon the external world for expatriate technical and administrative personnel. Among other things, this means that the burdens of modernization and the problems of political integration that their political systems confront are more awesome, and the likelihood of success less predictable, than elsewhere.

Historic African States

The Republic of Liberia and the Kingdom of Ethiopia share most of the foregoing attributes, yet they stand apart from other African states. They are not only the two oldest independent states in Africa, but, except for the brief Italian occupation of Ethiopia, they escaped the colonialism that engulfed the rest of the continent. This unique experience has meant that, alone among African peoples, they have enjoyed the dignity and national pride which go with a long history of national independence. But they have missed the economic and educational development and the widespread popular demand for rapid modernization that colonialism brought to most of Africa. Their economies, social structures, and political systems have remained relatively static for the past century, although recently there have been substantial changes. The two systems are both oligarchies dominated by a culturally distinct minority: In Liberia, it is the Americo-Liberian aristocracy; in Ethiopia, the Amhara ruling class.

The power structures and political processes within these ruling oligarchies are quite different. In Ethiopia, the Emperor is, in theory and in fact, the supreme source of all power. There are no regularized restraints upon his power, for the constitution and all modern political institutions are his own creation, and all the political actors are his appointees. There are no parties or pressure groups, and no independent or opposition newspapers. A cult has been built around the present Emperor, who has consolidated and maintained his power through the shrewd appointment and manipulation of subordinates and foreign advisers. In Liberia, political institutions and the political climate are democratic in theory. In fact, however, the political process is controlled by the Americo-Liberian oligarchy in Monrovia through the True Whig Party, which has dominated the political scene since 1870. Opposition parties have appeared, but as Thomas Hodgkin observes, "opposition remains an affair of cliques . . . [and], as in any one-party State, there is a tendency for opposition to be confused with heresy." Under the presidency of Mr. Tubman—in office since 1943—the system is relatively stable, but only qualifiedly democratic within the oligarchy.

Several factors should be kept in mind in considering the continued stability and progressive democratization in Liberia and Ethiopia. The first of these is that, in contrast to South Africa, the Liberian and Ethiopian oligarchies are not closed systems. The original Americo-Liberian founding families have assimilated to a considerable degree with the tribal peoples in the Liberian hinterland. In Ethiopia, no rigid social or official bar has been set against the advancement of members of the conquered tribes and their acceptance in the Amhara ruling group. In both governments, some of the high officials come from tribal groups traditionally dominated by the oligarchies.

Second, the present leaders, President William Tubman of Liberia and Emperor Haile Selassie of Ethiopia, are themselves among the principal driving forces toward the modernization and integration of their societies, and both have made cautious gestures in the direction of eventual democratization. As several of the more stable democracies in the world today came about through the progressive democratization of former oligarchies, it might be that it is easier to democratize a stable but adaptable oligarchy than to stabilize an excessively egalitarian society. In any event, whether the present trends in Liberia and Ethiopia continue depends largely on the successors to Tubman and Selassie.

A third point concerns the social and political consequences of the current programs of economic expansion and development in these hitherto stagnant societies. Such development may serve only to strengthen and enrich the present dominant class, as happened in the early stages of the commercialization of the economies of certain oligarchic societies in Latin America. In the long run, however, economic change and growth are bound to unleash a process of social change and movement, which in turn will have its own internal dynamic and should lead to fundamental changes in social structures. For example, neither country now has an indigenous middle class, or a wage-earning class of any significance. Indeed, one of the explanations for the self-perpetuative quality of these oligarchic systems is that heretofore there have been no opportunities outside government employment for the acquisition of status, wealth, or power. Economic development should operate to change this.

A final consideration is the future political role and pretensions of the new university-educated elites emerging in both countries. Until recently, very few Liberians had received a university education. The majority of the first generation of university-trained Ethiopians, who were just beginning to assert themselves in the social life of the country, were murdered by the Italians in the massacres of 1937. During the last decade, however, several hundred Liberians and Ethiopians have been sent abroad by their governments to study in universities, and more are being sent each year. Others are pursuing higher studies in the new universities of Liberia and Addis Ababa. Most of these university graduates are employed by their respective governments in comparatively high status positions, and this is likely to continue. These men constitute a distinctly new class, whose importance is out of proportion to its size and whose future political orientation will be decisive in the political development of the two countries.

This new class may acquire a vested interest in the existing oligarchies and become their strongest defenders and perpetuators, but it is more likely that in due course elements within this elite will be the primary sources of political ferment and change. Not all belong to the oligarchy by origin, and the attractions of becoming national leaders of their "oppressed" groups may be overwhelming. While they assume a posture of defensive pride in their systems in their relations with outsiders, most of them are thoroughgoing modernists who are known to be dissatisfied with the pace and direction of change and the limited role they are allowed to play. This was dramatically revealed in the abortive coup led by Ethiopian intellectuals against the present regime, during the Emperor's absence from the country in December, 1960. The coup failed because key leaders in the Army decided at the last moment to remain loyal to the regime. They supported the objectives, but disagreed with the timing of the revolt.

New and Emergent African States

Since the end of World War II, twenty-nine former African dependencies have become sovereign states, and three more (Kenya, Nyasaland, and Northern Rhodesia) are clearly destined for early self-government under indigenous political leadership. The implications—both external and internal—of this sudden and massive increase in the number of sovereign entities in Africa are profoundly significant. The impact of this array of new states upon international organization and politics is discussed in Chapter 3; here we are concerned with the common characteristics and patterns of internal political development of these states. Before turning to these, however, a few observations on the character of the colonial legacy are in order.

The Colonial Legacy

The most striking characteristic shared by the new states is their recent emergence from the colonial experience. However history might judge modern Western colonialism in Africa, there is little question that it created the present political entities; it has given them distinct legal personalities, and except for Portuguese and Spanish-dominated areas it has operated to produce— albeit in varying degrees and in some respects unwittingly— a set of conditions conducive to the modernization and the democratization of their societies. The new and emergent states of Africa have had comparatively greater exposure to modernity than have Liberia and Ethiopia, which missed the colonial experience. This is shown by higher levels of economic development, more widespread education, the emergence of new classes (such as an educated salaried group, a nascent middle class and proletariat, cadres of political and opinion leaders, and a small core of trained civil servants), and a whole array of aspirations of a distinctly modern character. Another characteristic is the wider popular involvement in modern social and political processes, as a result of the development of mass nationalist movements as the vehicles for the attainment of independence. Moreover, in the terminal stages of colonial status, most colonial governments earnestly sought to introduce massive social change and to endow the emergent political systems with democratic institutions. As a result of this social and political mobilization under colonialism and the drive for independence, a number of elements—the declared national goals, the dominant political symbols, the social expectations, and the standards for judging political action in the postindependence period—became ultra-populist and ultrademocratic in character. In these and other respects, it could be argued that the colonial experience has greatly enhanced the democratic potential of the new states.

On the other hand, these positive elements are largely negated by other aspects of the imperial legacy. One is the comparative recency and brevity of the very developments noted above. At most, they have occurred on any meaningful scale only during the last decade. Indeed, in the former Belgian Congo, no serious efforts to develop an indigenous administrative and political capacity were made until the disastrous headlong rush to independence in the six months preceding the transfer of power in July, 1960. The simple fact is, of course, that none of the colonial powers intended to create modern self-governing democratic states in Africa. Western racialism and ethnocentricity perpetuated a widespread belief that the European "presence" in Africa was permanently necessary and desirable. When postwar African nationalism forced a change and imposed a timetable aimed at early independence, procedural and institutional innovations of a "democratic" character were launched on a "crash program" basis. Thus, although most new African states have possessed all of the paraphernalia and pretensions of democratic government at the time of independence, their leaders and peoples have had extremely limited experience with modern democratic institutions. Since survival of such institutions depends heavily upon acceptance and commitment by a people accustomed to their use and confident in their ultimate effectiveness in satisfying wants and attaining goals, the significance of the democratic component of the colonial legacy can be vastly exaggerated.

The critical factor is not that the African peoples have had only a limited experience with the institutions and procedures of democracy; rather, it is that a colonial milieu is not one in which the idea and spirit of democracy—that cluster of attitudes and feelings supportive of the democratic process—can be acquired. On the contrary, a colonial regime is essentially one of bureaucratic authoritarianism, in which government is viewed as the initiator of all public policy, as well as the source of all amenities and of most good jobs. A colonial government rules through petition and administration, and not through political competition and compromise. The public does not participate in the political process; it is "administered" by a bureaucratic elite, which by the system's definition knows what is best. The present generation of African leaders and citizenry was socialized into this type of political system. It is most likely that their orientation, attitudes and feelings towards the present system, and their perception of their role within it, have been determined far more by the type of governmental process they observed during the period of "pure" colonialism than by the last-minute "democratic" innovations made immediately prior to independence.

There are other facets of the colonial legacy that are relevant for our analysis, but these can be examined more appropriately within the context of the following discussion of some of the general characteristics and dominant trends among the political systems of the new and emergent states.

Some General Characteristics of New African States

Three characteristics common to most of the new states are particularly significant for an understanding of contemporary political structures and trends: (1) their lack of integration, (2) their internal organizational weakness, and (3) their comparative smallness.

Lack of integration. Africa's new states are examples par excellence, of the "unintegrated" political systems that have precipitatedly emerged from modern colonialism. Internal discontinuities and divisions are many and varied, but three have particular political significance: tribal and sectional tensions, the traditionalist-modernist dichotomy, and the yawning gap between the affluent new political elite and the class of clerks, teachers, skilled artisans and students who have been, or manifestly will be, less successful in obtaining the fruits of independence.

Political integration is made difficult by the cultural heterogeneity and artificial boundaries that are common characteristics of most national societies in their early formative stages. They are particularly marked in African states, largely because during

Cultural and Regional Obstacles to Integration in some African States

SUDAN

DOMINANT ARAB-MOSLEM NORTH

UNDERDEVELOPED CHRISTIAN—PAGAN SOUTH

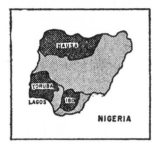

HAUSA

YORUBA

LAGOS

IBO

NIGERIA

REGIONALLY DOMINANT GROUPS

REGIONAL MINORITY GROUPS

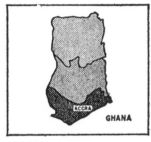

ACCRA

GHANA

DEVELOPED SOUTHERN REGION

ASHANTI AND ADJACENT TOGOLAND

UNDERDEVELOPED NORTHERN TERRITORIES

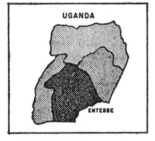

UGANDA

ENTEBBE

DOMINANT BUGANDA KINGDOM

LESS DEVELOPED BANTU SOCIETIES

UNDERDEVELOPED NILOTIC NORTH

MONROVIA

LIBERIA

DOMINANT AFRO—AMERICAN AREAS OF SETTLEMENT

UNDERDEVELOPED TRIBAL HINTERLAND

FREETOWN

SIERRA LEONE

ADVANCED AND FORMERLY DOMINANT CREOLE AREA OF SETTLEMENT

UNDERDEVELOPED PROTECTORATE

the scramble for Africa, the metropolitan countries arbitrarily bunched together diverse pre-colonial African societies into colonial administrative units. Moreover, not only are the peoples within states divided by tribe, religion, and differences in level of development, but several of the international boundaries cut across ethnic groups and thus divide formerly homogeneous cultural communities. Some of these obstacles to integration are illustrated by the accompanying maps of six African states.

Colonialism exerted a unifying influence by "holding the ring" within which objective forces of integration, such as more intensive social intercourse and economic interchange, could operate; by imposition of a common administrative, legal, and educational system; by creating a nationally minded educated class; and by simply being the common enemy against which nationalist movements were able to organize a "national" opposition. But, as African colonialism has been comparatively short-lived, these integrative influences have been uneven and limited. Moreover, certain colonial policies—particularly the British policy of "indirect rule"—tended to preserve and exacerbate tribal or regional separatism.

The latter has been further aggravated by the uneven distribution of resources and productive potential, and by the differential impact of modernity upon different regions within a state. This has led to an obsessive fear of domination on the part of the less developed groups, and an understandable opposition by more affluent groups to the dilution of their higher standard of living by continued association with "depressed areas" with which they have no link other than the historical accident of common colonial rule (shown, for example, in the separatism of Katanga). In those instances where a region with a comparatively rich—or poor—endowment coincides with the area inhabited by one defineable group (e.g., the Ashanti in Ghana and the Yoruba in Western Nigeria), the economic interests of the respective groups strengthen the predisposition of leaders to appeal to "tribal" identity and separatism.

"Tribalism" has been identified by many observers of the African scene, both academic and popular, as the major obstacle to national unification in the new states. This is a gross oversimplification of the complex process of integration in Africa and reflects the loose and indiscriminate use of the term "tribe" (as well as the persistence of the notion that the tribe is Africa's only form of social organization) in much discussion of that continent. To be sure, there are many tribes, in the strictly anthropological sense, in Africa. Moreover, the number of persons in Africa who are still living in, or have only recently come from, predominantly tribal societies is undoubtedly larger than in any other major region in the contemporary world. Yet there are other types of human aggregation and ethnic grouping in Africa that can be called tribes only in the sense that Toynbee refers to all nations as tribes. Many large African ethnic groups, such as the Hausa, who number more than ten million, or the Somali, who number more than two million and occupy an area nearly the size of Texas, would be called nationalities or nations, if located in Europe. The distinction made here between tribes and nontribes in Africa is not a frivolous semantic quibble; it is essential for any sound understanding and analysis of such phenomena as political separatism, irredentism, and regional nationalisms found throughout the continent.

Once these observations are made, it would be incorrect to conclude that genuine tribalism is an unimportant factor in African politics. The general trend for national leaders to condemn any manifestation of tribalism—which, following the loose language of non-Africans, they also use to denote ethnic differences—is fair evidence that it must still be a relevant factor. The size of the ethnic group concerned is an important variable. The fact that Governor-General Nnamdi Azikiwe of Nigeria (an Ibo), Tom Mboya of Kenya (a Luo), and President Kasavubu of the Congo (a Mukongo) are identified with large ethnic groups is highly significant in the politics of their respective countries. On the other hand, the tribal origin of such men as President Nkrumah of Ghana, Kenneth Kaunda of Northern Rhodesia, and President Nyerere of Tanganyika, is an irrelevant consideration in their countries because the ethnic groups concerned are small or have never constituted a threat to other groups. Again, for a variety of historical, economic, and geographical reasons, certain groups bifurcated by international boundaries are the source of considerable instability, both within and between new states (e.g., the Ewe, between Ghana and Togo, and the Somali, between Somalia, Ethiopia, and Kenya.) Yet other divided groups of not dissimilar size and of equally variant social structure (e.g., the Yoruba, between Nigeria and Dahomey, and the Hausa, between Nigeria and Niger) have so far not created a political problem of any kind. It is not the multiplicity of tribes within a state that is necessarily an obstacle to the creation of a broader nationality—in fact, the larger their number and the smaller their size, the better. It is rather the large ethnic groups—the Foula in Guinea, the Ashanti in Ghana, the Yoruba in Nigeria, the Baganda in Uganda, and the Bemba in Northern Rhodesia—that complicate the task of building a national entity. Thus, although the internal stresses and strains of the new states are very profound indeed, the extent to which tribalism is a contributing cause varies considerably and makes generalization difficult.

Even in those situations in which tribalism, ethnic origin, and regional nationalisms are the source of continual internal tension, we should bear in mind that neither stability nor democracy requires complete uniformity or homogeneity. As R. H. S. Crossman has argued, "The stability of any democracy depends not on imposing a single unitary loyalty and viewpoint but on maintaining conflicting loyalties and viewpoints in a state of tension." Indeed, it is not impossible that, provided a measure of national unity is achieved, the tribal and sectional pluralism of African states could make dictatorship less possible by providing countervailing power centers which cannot be coerced and regimented into a single authoritarian system. Ironically, however, one of the factors nudging several African leaders towards greater authoritarianism, as will be noted subsequently, is the constant threat (real or imaginary) that dissident tribal, ethnic, or regional groups pose to the integrity of the new states. This has been particularly true in the Sudan, Ghana, and Guinea. In Nigeria, however, it could be argued that the tensions between the three regions, each the political core area of a major cultural group, and each unable either to dominate or to separate from the others, has created a structured, multiparty system that is largely responsible for the fact that, at the federal level, Nigeria is unquestionably the most free and open polity in independent Africa.

Social and economic developments that are gaining momentum and could minimize the disruptive effects of tribal or regional separatism include the expansion of the wage earning and commercial sectors of the economy, greater social mobility, and the appearance of a new generation of leaders who are more emphatically "national" in outlook. In short, those historic processes which have been integrative elsewhere are also at work in Africa.

A second obstacle to national integration in the new states is the tension between the forces of traditionalism and modernism. Here two issues should be distinguished: (1) the extent to which traditional social systems are a deterrent to the modernization of the economy and societies, and to the integration and democratization of the new political systems; and (2) the character of the relationship between traditional elites (chiefs, emirs, elders) at the head of the indigenous political systems and the modern secular political elites controlling the new states. The popular view that there is an inherent opposition between traditionalism and modernism is false; traditional systems have varying capacities to accept and assimilate modern innovations. Many societies are inherently resistant to change; others, like the Buganda Kingdom, have been able to "traditionalize" innovation with great ease and rapidity; still others, like the conservative and authoritarian Hausa emirates, can be effectively employed by the new secular elites as instruments for economic development. Yet a capacity to accept or to facilitate modernization in the economic and social spheres—thereby furthering the modernizing objectives of the new states—does not necessarily mean that the traditional society concerned will readily accept integration into the new national society. The Baganda of Uganda, and the Chagga of Tanganyika, for example, have been able to absorb modern innovations very rapidly; yet each presents a separatist threat to the political unity of the new states of which they are a part. Indeed, the very capacity of a traditional system to adapt means a capacity to persist—which is exactly what most centralizing, Jacobin-minded national elites do not want.

The extent of the cleavage between traditional and modern elites in the new states has varied considerably in different countries. The problem has been most pronounced in former British and Belgian dependencies, where under the policy of indirect rule, traditional elites were recognized, given status, and used not only as agents in the colonial administrative process, but also as imperial instruments to counter and negate the nationalist activities of the rising educated elites. In a few areas (Nyasaland, Northern Rhodesia, and Western Nigeria), close links were established during the agitational period between radical educated nationalists and traditional rulers. In other instances (Northern Nigeria, Mauritania, Sierra Leone, and the Cameroons) the conservative educated elite governing the new state has close family ties with important elements in the traditional elite. In most cases, however, suspicion and hostility of varying intensity has characterized the relationship between the two sets of elites.

The secular nationalist elites have, with the few exceptions noted, inherited central power, and have used that power progressively to curtail, neutralize, or extinguish the residual authority or influence of the traditionalists. Even in such cases as Nyasaland, where the relationship was fraternally cordial, or Northern Nigeria, where the educated sons of the traditional aristocracy assumed control over the regional government, the same process of centralization at the expense of the traditionalist elites has occurred. This has been most dramatically demonstrated by the recent action of the regional government of Northern Nigeria is removing from office two of the area's most powerful emirs (Kano and Gwandu). Although this general trend toward centralization is everywhere evident, in several of the new and emergent states the acute tensions between the two elites have yet to be resolved.

A third source of conflict in the new states is the persistence after independence of the gap between the comparatively affluent governing class and the mass of the people, but most particularly the clerk-teacher-artisan class. One of the most striking, and vulnerable, aspects of the social structure of colonial societies was the yawning gulf between the standard of living, perquisites, and social status of the members of the alien governing elite and of the indigenous subaltern clerk class whose aspirations and frustrations were particularly intense. In most African states, there has been little change since independence in the size and nature of the gap, or in the atmosphere of tension, fear, and envy between the two categories separated by it. The only change has been that the nationalist veterans of the agitational period, themselves recruited mainly from the clerk class, have been catapulted into the offices and homes rapidly vacated by the departing alien governing class.

Plans for economic and social development and for increased educational opportunity are all directed towards the creation of a social structure in which these gross discrepancies will be eliminated. But these are "long haul" measures, and over the next decade one can anticipate little change unless drastic measures are taken. In the meantime, two related post-independence trends operate to intensify the disaffection and political explosiveness caused by the gap. One is the growing discontent in those new states where saturation has already begun to be reached in the upper stratum of the social structure, A new generation of secondary school and university graduates, arriving on the scene in ever increasing numbers, is acutely aware that it will undoubtedly not have the opportunities of the present generation to climb rapidly to high positions of power and affluence. Moreover, in the government service—the source of most prestigious jobs—these graduates are compelled to accept junior positions, working under persons with little education and training, and frequently of very limited capacity. As the rate of upward mobility is progressively curtailed, discontent in the government service could assume proportions equalled only by the frustration felt by junior African clerks working under Europeans during the colonial period.

A second, and politically even more explosive, category of disaffected persons is the primary "school leavers," one of the most serious social—and, in due course, political—problems the governing elites of the new states may have to confront. For most of these states, independence meant the launching of vast new programs of educational development. Ironically, despite the almost limitless needs for trained manpower, the economies of the new states, and the number of post-primary educational facilities, are not expanding at a rate sufficient to provide career opportunities for the tidal wave of primary school leavers now commencing to hit the job market. The unemployment levels in this category are alarmingly high in many urban centers. The school leavers flocking to the cities create a high potential for mob action, and constitute a social category vulnerable to political manipulation by rival groups. Indeed, it is this very category which provided the mass base for agitational meetings and nationalist demonstrations in the pre-independence quest for power by the present governing elites.

Internal Organizational Weakness. The weakness of central authoritative institutions, and the limited development of an indigenous bureaucracy, army, and police force are among the more arresting internal structural characteristics of the new African states. They are a reflection, as already noted, of European colonial systems that neither anticipated nor desired early termination. Africanization of higher administrative, technical, and managerial positions was not seriously pursued until the very last "crash program" phase of colonial rule. Ironically, the departure of experienced personnel, and their replacement by raw recruits with limited training and experience, has been occurring simultaneously with a great expansion in the scope of government and a staggering increase in the demands made upon it. It is indeed truly remarkable that the fragile administrative structures of the new states have thus far avoided complete collapse.

That they have not has been due to several ameliorating factors. One is that despite the headlong rush towards full Africanization, many senior colonial officials have remained on in key roles, in some cases on pension, in most instances on contract. Although acutely sensitive to the pressures for Africanization, leaders of African governments have very realistically faced up to their administrative unpreparedness and weakness, and have agreed to generous arrangements to cover personnel willing to remain on for a transitional period. Former colonial powers have also made generous provision for financial assistance and career guarantees to maximize the retention or recruitment of experienced administrators and technicians. The French government, for example, has recruited and subsidized a large number of *counseilleurs techniques* for all former French dependencies that have requested them. Moreover, upon conclusion of their service to the African governments, these advisors are assured careers in the French home civil service. The United Nations Organization and its specialized agencies and the large American foundations have also provided substantial financial and technical assistance for the establishment of institutes of public administration and accelerated in-service training programs. The African governments themselves have tailored their scholarship programs to ensure that the products from universities or technical training institutions, both in the home countries and abroad, will be channelled into the most critically short categories. Finally, a significant number of those Africans who have entered the higher civil service have had extensive experience as clerks in the administration during the colonial period. This latter fact has tended to be undervalued. Certainly their presence has provided a measure of continuity.

The strong post-independence drive for rapid Africanization in the new states has undoubtedly resulted in a decline in efficiency and probity in government. Moreover, there is bound not to be a normal age spread within the administrative hierarchy. Europeans of various ages, at different rungs in the career ladder of the higher civil service, have been replaced by Africans all of roughly the same age. When all positions are Africanized, there could be virtual stagnation for nearly a generation, because of the absence of normal attrition and the consequent "promotion freeze." Thus there is a danger of an acute shortage of career outlets for the upcoming generation. Only the development of new and attractive careers in both government and the private sector could prevent the political instability such a situation would create.

Military establishments have been the last of the authoritative structures of government to be created in sub-Saharan Africa. Among the new states, only the Sudan, Senegal, and the Congo could claim at the time of independence to have a national army of any significance. This very fact illuminates the internal organizational weakness of the new states. In each of these three countries, the military establishment has played a decisive role in the political life of the country since independence. It has had more than a little impact upon the thinking not only of national political leaders, but also of the new cadres of army officers commanding the small but expanding national armies in other new states. Given the serious internal tensions, and the comparative fragility of other authoritative structures and central institutions, national armies are obviously destined to exert a profound influence on the future course of internal political development. (The fragility of the central institutions of the new states is strikingly revealed by the fact that it required no more than a platoon of disgruntled soldiers to overthrow the Olympio government in Togo and establish a successor regime.)

Each of the new sovereign states, large or small, is seeking to create some type of national military establishment of its own. States like the Sudan and Senegal inherited seasoned military units already bearing the name of the country concerned; in other states, such as Ghana, Nigeria, and Tanganyika, leaders have had to build a national force from segments of former interterritorial forces fragmented in the process of independence (e.g., the West African Frontier Force and the King's African Rifles); still others have started with nothing at all. Whatever the colonial legacy, the new states confront three internal problems of considerable political significance: the problem of ethnic balance in recruitment, the problem of civilian supremacy, and the problem of intra-service unity and discipline.

During the colonial period, the pattern of recruitment for defense forces primarily reflected imperial needs and security calculations, but also the fact that men from certain tribes or ethnic groups were predisposed to seek military careers and made better soldiers to boot. Thus, for example, the majority of recruits in Nigeria and Ghana came from the northern areas of those two countries, partly because in the eyes of the British government those areas were politically more reliable, and partly because men from northern ethnic groups actively sought life in the colonial defense forces. Again, in Kenya and in Uganda, the number of Kikuyu and Baganda soldiers is insignificant; yet the Kikuyu and the Baganda are numerically the largest, and politically the most important, ethnic groups in those countries. This same pattern of differential recruitment for African military—and police—units prevailed throughout colonial Africa. This has meant that the governing elites of the new states have been confronted with a gross imbalance in the ethnic and regional composition of the national armies they are seeking to create.

The imbalance was confined mainly to enlisted ranks, because of the reluctance of the colonial powers to create an indigenous officer corps. The 25,000-man *Force Publique* of the former Belgian Congo, for example, had no indigenous officers at the time of Congolese independence—which, incidentally, accounts for much of the chaos that followed. In the post-independence crash program to create a corps of African officers, leaders have faced the problem of ethnic imbalance in another form: Because of regional differences in the availability of secondary education, the recruitment of officer cadets for military schools on the basis of merit alone would obviously favor candidates from ethnic groups in the educationally more developed regions. This ethnic imbalance in the composition of the new national armies has been a matter of grave concern to the governing elites. President Nkrumah of Ghana, for example, was confronted at independence with an army composed predominantly of northerners, yet it was in the north that his personal position, as well as that of his party, was least secure. He was forced to retain expatriate officers in top command positions after independence while enforcing the principle of ethnic and regional balance in recruitment, and maintaining a special concern with the political orientation and reliability of the new officer corps.

As national armies become stronger in Africa's new states, it is doubtful whether the Anglo-American principle of civilian supremacy over the military will prevail. It is certainly an element in the colonial legacy, and it is also part of the ethos of military academies such as Sandhurst, where a sizable number of the new African army officers have received their training. Yet the model is not untarnished (e.g., the French Army in Algeria), and in any event, much of tropical Africa, particularly those areas under French and Portuguese control, was ruled in a quasi-military fashion with military officers carrying their titles (e.g., *"commandant du cercle"*) while occupying higher administrative positions. Moreover, an increasing number of African officers are receiving their military training in Soviet bloc countries, or from Soviet personnel in African countries.

It could be argued that the civilian elites now in the process of creating the new armies are in a position to devise a variety of safeguards to ensure civil primacy, but these can hardly remain once the military emerges as a semiautonomous structure. In fact, there are many elements in the situation which invite or compel army officers to use their organizational strength to seize or seek control over government: the puritanical impulse to cleanse the country of the corruption of civilian leaders; the fragility and impotence of civilian-controlled structures to modernize the society, to preserve national unity, to maintain internal security, or to attain development goals; and, of course, the simple age-old impulse to enjoy power. Whatever the motive, African peoples, accustomed by colonialism to bureaucratic authoritarian government, and desirous of rapid modernization, might well be attracted to army rule, if only for a transitional period.

National armies in Africa's new states are regarded not merely as standby forces for defense and internal security, but as integral parts of the whole national modernization effort. The extent to which they can serve constructively in this heroic task, either as adjuncts of civilian power or as controllers of the government, will depend upon the degree of internal unity and discipline they can achieve. Experience in the Sudan, Senegal, and the Congo, however, has demonstrated that the cohesiveness of the African army can be seriously threatened not only by ethnic conflicts, but also by tensions between senior and junior officer groups, and by rival factions within the army that have ethnic, ideological, or constituency links with rival factions in the governing party or competing groups within the society. The fact that the new armies are being developed on a crash-program basis, and therefore lack strong service traditions, maximizes the likelihood that tensions within the society will be reflected in the

ranks of the army, particularly in the absence of a countervailing
and restraining ethos of professionalism. Thus, military rule in
Africa would not necessarily mean political stability, much less
accelerated modernization.

Smallness in Scale. Africa is the continent par excellence of
the "micro-state." The majority of its political entities (25 out of
45) have populations of less than 3 million. Only three countries
(Nigeria, Egypt, and Ethiopia) have populations in excess of 20
million. The political fragmentation of the colonial period has
altered very little in the transition to independent statehood.
With few exceptions, African leaders in each of the artificial
entities created by colonialism have sought and attained separate
sovereign statehood under the slogan "independence first, then
unity." This has occurred despite the artificiality of colonial
boundaries, the unintegrated character of the societies embraced
within those boundaries, the brevity of colonial rule, and the
strong ideological commitment of African leaders to the idea of
African unity.

The reasons for the continuation of Africa's political fragmentation are many and varied. They include the disinclination
of the colonial powers to combine neighboring territories, or to
regroup them along more rational lines (although colonialism did
reduce the number of separate units from more than 700 to
under 50); the many practical considerations that made it expedient for African leaders to seek independence within the
confines of the existing territory, and particularly to "territorial-
ize" what in origin was a general racial nationalism; the need
to inculcate "national" loyalties and to protect "national" interests once independence has been won; and the rapid and inevitable development of vested private and group interests once
a sovereign unit has been created. In all these respects, of course,
Africa is not unlike other former colonial continents; its only
claim to uniqueness is that it has more land, is more sparsely
populated, and was divided up into more units.

The argument for relatively large political entities is usually
made on the grounds that this encourages economic growth and
the maintenance of international peace. The political fragmentation of a region into a multitude of micro-states is not only

a deterrent to economic growth, but maximizes the likelihood of interstate conflicts. Economic development is impeded because of the obstacles to mobility of goods and services, and because a disproportionate share of the national income must be diverted to government and administration. The probability of interstate conflicts increases, because there are a greater number of interacting sovereign units, each with its own national interests and army. As one contemplates the emerging pattern in Africa, it becomes clear that these general propositions are applicable to its array of new micro-states.

However, several ameliorating factors should be taken into consideration. In the precarious post-independence period, the new elites are highly vulnerable, and smallness in scale makes it easier for them to cope with the awesome problems of administering, unifying, and developing the societies of which they have charge. Also, federation or unification would not necessarily result in greater economy; it might mean simply that another higher and over-arching set of expensive governmental structures would be established, as has happened in the only two examples thus far—Somalia and Cameroon. Moreover, African states are working on a number of functional economic relationships and collective security arrangements to minimize the disadvantages of fragmentation. It is possible that economic necessity and ideological predisposition will lead to new patterns of cooperation. Finally, we should be ever mindful that many African states are "micro" only in terms of the size of their present population. Science, technology, and improved standards of living all point to an impending population explosion in Africa.

The Consummation of Freedom

The single most important factor serving to explain post-independence political developments in the new African states is their burning drive to consummate freedom. African leaders are agonizingly aware that legal independence has not substantially altered the fact that they are heavily dependent on the rest of the world. President Sekou Touré has stated the case very eloquently:

The anticolonial struggle was not brought to an end on September 28, far from it! It has merely been taken up again, more powerfully than ever, under its double aspect of the struggle against the remnants of the colonial regime.

To African nationalists neocolonialism does not mean the imposition of new forms of alien control from outside Africa; rather, it is the persistence of residual European influence in Africa itself. Moreover, it is not direct political control or influence that is the irritant, but the omnipresent cultural influence of the West, which saturates all aspects of life, and daily reminds the African of the ignominy he suffers for having blindly aped all aspects of an alien system, and for continuing to depend upon that system. As Touré put it, the demand is for "integral decolonization":

> When we say "Decolonization" we mean we want to destroy the habits, conceptions and ways of conduct of colonialism. We are determined to replace them with forms that are Guinean forms, conceived by the people of Guinea, adapted to the conditions, to the means, to the aspirations of the people of Guinea.

Although Touré has stated the argument more bluntly than other leaders, he is unquestionably the apostle of a new generation of African nationalism.

The practical political implications of this impulse to consummate the "African revolution" go far beyond mere Africanization of the civil service. They involve increasing state intervention into the schools and universities, to ensure Africanization of the curriculum, and into the economy, to maximize local control and initiative. They necessitate a self-conscious eclecticism in the adaptation of inherited political forms and in the fashioning of new procedures and institutions. Not only will the altered forms be something that can be called uniquely African, or Ghanaian, or Guinean, but the ideology and the rationale underlying the new forms will be identified as distinctly African. This is seen not only in such vague concepts as "African personality" and "Negritude," but more importantly, in such notions as "African socialism." It will be several decades before this psychological revolution is consummated; in the meantime, the powerful quest for cultural identity and pride that it reflects must be accorded a political significance it has often not received.

The One-Party Trend

The dominance of the one-party system is the most distinctive political feature of all newly independent states in sub-Saharan Africa. There are only two exceptions: the Republic of the Sudan, where the ruling military power has outlawed all parties, and the Federation of Nigeria, which has in effect three competing one-party regional systems, none of which has been, or is likely to be, able to control the whole. Elsewhere, there is either only one party by law (Mali, Guinea, Ivory Coast, and Chad), or one party overwhelmingly dominates the system. In all cases where competing parties existed at the time of independence, there has been a seemingly inexorable consolidation of control by one dominant party. Moreover, the process of consolidation is continuing in all of those states where it is not completed, and in those states on the threshold of independence, there is every indication that the same process is in motion. There is no evidence that any significant change will be made in this pattern in the predictable future.

There is one major explanation for this remarkable phenomenon: the extraordinary—indeed virtually limitless—power possessed or inherited by the majority party at the time of independence. This party may have already legally secured a monopoly over the political system (e.g., the *Parti Démocratique de Guinea* [PDG] in Guinea and the *Parti Démocratique de Côte d'Ivoire* [PDCI] in the Ivory Coast), or it may have controlled only slightly more than half of the votes in the most recent pre-independence elections (e.g., Togo and the Cameroons). In either event, the end result has tended to be the same. The task of consolidating power has been relatively easy in the former countries. Majority parties in the second category, that is, those who had not been able to preempt the political arena or monopolize nationalist symbols prior to the transfer of power, have had greater difficulty, but eventually their overwhelming predominance in the system has become nearly as complete.

A majority party that is the legal successor to a departing colonial regime inherits, or by default acquires, almost unparalleled power and freedom of action once it becomes the government of the day. It inherits the full panoply of legal powers and statutes, of coercive and punitive procedures, carefully developed by a colonial regime that was, as previously noted, bureaucratic authoritarianism in its purest form. It is also legatee to the enormous powers possessed by a government in a society in which virtually all services (roads, communications, schools, hospitals, water supplies, and scholarships), and most good jobs, are under the control of the governing party. The discriminatory use of these latter powers is among the more decisive elements responsible for the phenomenon known as the "vanishing opposition." When the power of deprivation of services and patronage is insufficient to persuade opposition elements to cease activity and to join the governing party in a vast *parti unifié*, or united front, then the more classical forms of persuasion or neutralization—imprisonment of opposition leaders, harassment by contrived allegations, censorship, and curtailment of political liberties —can be, and in several instances have been, employed.

The governing party in the immediate post-independence period not only inherits the massive legal powers possessed by the former colonial regime, as well as the vast patronage powers of the government of a welfare state, but it also functions in a virtual institutional vacuum. As we have noted, other central authoritative structures are weak, fragile, or nonexistent. The bureaucracy is in a state of violent transition, armies are either in an organizational state or are nonexistent, and national legislatures and parliaments have not yet had the chance to develop into significant central institutions. Because of the internal organizational weakness of other potential power centers, governing political parties have tended to emerge by default as the single authoritative structures in the new states.

Endowed with such comparatively unfettered power, the leaders of dominant parties have moved progressively toward the one-party system, in response to a variety of factors and pressures. One of these is the character of the opposition. In all but a few instances, opposition groups have tended to fall into one of three categories, each of which could reasonably be regarded as a threat to the integrity or independence of the new state: (1) groups identified closely with the interests of the former colonial power or its agents (e.g., the Conakat Party in Katanga); (2) groups based upon tribal, ethnic, or regional sentiment; and (3) groups linked with hostile regimes or movements in neighboring states. Thus, acceptance of the idea of a "loyal opposition," fundamental to the Western concept of democracy, has been difficult, because most opposition movements have ultimately sought support from "disloyal" sources.

Another consideration furthering one-party rule is the magnitude of the task of modernization. Most African leaders would support Walt Rostow's assertion that "The building of an effective centralized national state has been almost universally a necessary condition for [economic] take-off." In their eyes, the monolithic single party is the only structure *in being* which will enable them to overcome internal disunities and create a stabilized political community, mobilize the human and material resources of their country, and otherwise attain those basic preconditions for economic growth. As in all developing areas, authoritarianism —whether of the Communist, Kemalist or "guided democracy" variety—offers many attractions as a means for accelerating the pace of modernization and economic development, and for integrating and stabilizing the new national societies.

Single-party rule also maximizes the likelihood that the present governing elite will be able to perpetuate itself in office. This is, of course, a timeless and universal impulse among all ruling groups. In the contemporary African context, however, the wide gap in the social structure intensifies the struggle of the elite to remain on top and to resist at all costs the long fall back to the meager and drab existence of the clerk class, whence most of them have come.

These are a few of the considerations that help to explain the marked trend toward single-party regimes in the new states. Since most of the present generation of African leaders have been exposed to Western political values, and are hypersensitive to the fact that they are being judged by Western democratic standards, they have made a special effort to justify and to rationalize the one-party system. In addition to the various practical considerations discussed above (i.e., the disloyal character of opposition movements and the imperatives of modernization), party theoreticians have argued that the single party is a distinctive institutional pattern expressive of African culture. The argument is that in traditional African democracy there was no concept of an opposition within a society; a person was either an integral part of the society or an alien. Moreover, decision-making was a process of "talking it out" until unanimity was reached, a tradition African Marxists have hailed as supportive of the principle of "democratic centralism." The latter also argue that in traditional African societies there are no classes; hence, Marxism in Africa means "African socialism"—a heresy with which Moscow and Peking find it difficult to cope. Obviously, however, given the cultural pluralism of pre-colonial Africa, one can find a traditional cultural analogue and justification for any type of political system, ranging from the most egalitarian democracy to the purest form of despotism.

African apologists or rationalizers of single-party government seek to validate it on other than traditional grounds. For African Marxists—and most leaders in French-speaking Africa, and not a few in English-speaking Africa, are declared Marxists—the single, monolithic Party, reaching from the Central Committee of the Political Bureau down to the smallest village cell, needs no rationalization. It is the only valid form of political organization in a mobilization regime. Democracy, they claim, is found within the Party. A second and less doctrinaire argument is that in developing societies there exists a singularity of focus upon, and commitment to, agreed national goals; therefore, competing parties are an unnecessary luxury, diverting national energies and confusing the national will. In balance, whatever the theoretical defense, it is clear that for the predictable future the notion of a formal opposition party in Africa's new political systems will continue to be regarded either as unwelcome or heretical.

COLONIAL AND EUROPEAN SETTLER OLIGARCHIES

One of the characteristic features of British colonial policy in the past has been the willingness to devolve political power into the hands of resident white settlers, in those territories where the size and demands of the white community made such action necessary or expedient. This policy was largely founded on the belief that white British subjects had the right to responsible local government wherever they might reside, and that they would be as objective and humane as colonial officials in carrying out the burdens of trusteeship for the African masses. The European minorities in the Republic of South Africa and in Southern Rhodesia were the beneficiaries of this policy. In 1910 and 1923, respectively, they were given responsible government—South Africa as a Dominion (in 1931 it became fully independent), and Southern Rhodesia as a "self-governing colony."

Since the acquisition of internal self-government, the European oligarchies in these two countries have consolidated their positions of control over the African community through a long series of legislative enactments. Such measures have included the delimitation of separate European and African areas, laws to control the movement and residence of Africans, a legalized industrial color bar, the denial of African representation or participation in the central organs of government, and systems of "direct" European administration. Their positions were made even more secure by instituting stringent systems of social control and employing a variety of both subtle and overt devices designed to prevent or frustrate any serious challenge by the African community. In most of these measures, Southern Rhodesia has tended to follow the lead of the Republic of South Africa.

Southern Rhodesia. The political systems of Southern Rhodesia and South Africa are essentially similar in that they are oligarchical, are based upon the fundamental assumption of white supremacy, and receive the support of the overwhelming majority of Europeans in the two countries. Beginning in 1953, however, there was a naive hope among some persons that Southern Rhodesia might be progressively democratized, and its racial caste system broken down, as a result of its being a constituent unit of the new Federation of Rhodesia and Nyasaland. The constitution of the Federation was based on the principle of interracial "partnership," and provided for African participation in the central organs of government. From the very beginning, however, the Federation was destined to fail because of the violent opposition of Africans in Nyasaland and Northern Rhodesia. The rapid growth of nationalism and the rise to power of a new generation of militant leaders finally compelled the British Government to agree, early in 1963, to a dissolution of the Federation and to the ultimate independence under African leadership of the two northern territories. These developments provoked an equally violent reaction from the European oligarchy in Southern Rhodesia, manifested immediately in the victory at the polls of the Rhodesian Front Party—a European right-wing racist movement—over the United Federal Party, the so-called "pro-partnership" group. Throughout 1962 and early 1963, the Southern Rhodesian government banned all African nationalist organizations and enacted sweeping new security laws. The British agreement to secession by Nyasaland and Northern Rhodesia provoked an immediate demand for independence by the European oligarchy in Southern Rhodesia, and the threat of unilateral action if Britain refused. Thus, by mid-1963, Southern Rhodesia had emerged as one of the several racial tinder boxes of European-dominated southern Africa.

The Republic of South Africa. Although the European oligarchies in both Southern Rhodesia and the Republic are determined at all costs to preserve their supremacy, the Republic is in an infinitely better position to do so. It is comparatively wealthy, it has industrialized rapidly, possesses its own munitions industry, and more than 3 million Europeans call the country their home. The ruling oligarchy is relatively secure in its power, and is employing the entire machinery of the state to perpetuate a political system that is undemocratic in fact as well as in constitutional theory. Three points deserve consideration: the question of democracy within the oligarchy; factors affecting the stability of the present system; and the long-run prospects for a progressive democratization of that system. There can be little question that, except for certain features, the political process within the white oligarchy has in the broadest sense been democratic. One of the exceptions is the lack of open dissent and discussion within the ruling Nationalist Party. The special history and psychology of the Afrikaner community has produced a strong determination on the part of its leaders not only to create the impression of monolithic unity, but by various subtle measures to enforce such unity within the ranks of Afrikanerdom. This has further accentuated the historic tendency for membership in each of the two major parties to be predominantly of one nationality.

Other features, far more disquieting in the eyes of critics, are found in the actions of the Nationalist Party leadership since it came to power in 1948, namely, the lack of respect for normal constitutional restraints in carrying out certain aspects of its apartheid program, the "Afrikanerization" of the higher civil service and key posts in the foreign service, army, and police, and government intrusion into the realm of higher education. Critics maintain that these measures have led to what is in effect an Afrikaner dictatorship, not only over the non-European majority but also over the non-Afrikaner elements in the oligarchy. Sympathizers stress the basic agreement within much of the European community on government policies, including in particular the maintenance of white supremacy.

Most persons outside the Republic of South Africa now regard the situation as one pregnant with impending disaster. Yet, there is the possibility that a measure of sentimentality leads to an underestimation of the strength of several elements of police state stability in the present system. The strongest of these is the extraordinarily stringent system of social and police control over actual or potential African political leaders and dissident Europeans in particular, and over the non-European community in general. Backed by a comprehensive array of "security" acts, the authorities have been able to immobilize nationalist-minded African leadership and to make it virtually impossible for meaningful, united, and sustained political action to be organized in the non-European community.

The stability of the present regime is further strengthened by its policy of building up the traditional, largely rural, Bantu sector. Whether intended or not, this has the effect of sharpening existing cleavages and hampering unity of action between the African rural mass and the more nationalistic and educated urban leadership. Moreover, many policies of the present government have either the active or tacit support of a majority of the

Europeans, and whatever organized liberal opposition exists is politically weak, if not impotent. In sum, from a short-run standpoint the present regime is stable.

The prospects of an ultimate racial holocaust are made virtually certain by the intransigeance of the overwhelming majority of Europeans regarding the principle of white supremacy; the fact that most politically-minded Africans have passed the point of no return and will not accept any arrangement other than majority (i.e., African) domination; and the determination, and increasingly the capacity, of independent African states to give ever-increasing assistance, ranging from refuge and operational bases for guerrilla groups to military training and supply. The tragedy is that there is no higher or external legal authority, such as that of the United Kingdom Government over Kenya, or of the United States Government over the American South, that could enforce progressive democratization.

Portuguese Africa. Portugal was the first, and is now the last, major colonial power in Africa. Until the outbreak of the nationalist rebellion in northern Angola, in 1961, the Portuguese system gave the appearance of being remarkably stable, albeit an authoritarian stability. Even the limited successes of the rebellion, however, revealed the basic weakness of the Portuguese system. The fact that there had previously been no overt nationalist movement in Portuguese territories is explained by the thoroughgoing policy of repression and exile for dissidents, the extremely limited opportunities for higher education, and the lack of contact between most Portuguese Africans and "free" political systems. Since 1960, however, the emergence of independent states on the northern borders of Angola and Mozambique has transformed the situation. Dar-es-Salaam has become the headquarters for resistance groups organized for agitational and guerrilla activity in Mozambique, and Leopoldville performs a similar function for Angolan groups. The independence of Nyasaland and Northern Rhodesia will unquestionably lead to an acceleration of such resistance activity. The African leaders of all the neighboring independent states are publicly committed to a policy of support for the resistance groups.

The Portuguese response to these unexpected challenges has

been characteristically Portuguese: a few paper reforms legally abolishing the status known as *Assimilado* (after 300 years no more than 0.3 per cent of the Angolan population had achieved that status in any event), new economic development plans, and a new labor code; but there is little visible evidence of the radical transformation in approach and reform the situation demands. On the contrary, existing systems of social and police control have been tightened, and security forces and the number of white settlers from metropolitan Portugal have vastly increased. The point of gravest concern is that the Portuguese system will collapse precipitately like the Congo before any serious steps will have been taken to prepare even a handful of Portuguese-speaking Africans to handle the awesome tasks of government. Like Southern Rhodesia and South Africa, Portuguese colonialism in Africa not only imposes upon the liberal West one of its most agonizing moral problems, it has created a situation so pregnant with disaster that a peaceful solution, or one that does not leave a residue of racial bitterness that can affect the West's relations with Africa for generations to come, appears impossible.

IMPLICATIONS FOR AMERICAN POLICY

America cannot have a monolithic policy in Africa. Our major objective of democratic and stable political systems, although apparently hopelessly unrealizable in the predictable future, remains applicable throughout the continent. But we must pursue this objective through variant policies adapted to the different political situations.

In the new and emergent African states, we must be sympathetic to and understanding of the actions of leaders and governments related to the quest for the consummation and consolidation of African independence. We must be tolerant of the various forms of government and economy in Africa, recognizing the special circumstances that make their forms different from our own, and possibly necessary during a transitional period. We should also realize that the goals of democracy can be achieved through different types of institutions and cultural forms.

We must recognize that there are limits to which the political systems of the new states can be constructively assisted by external agencies. The political system of every independent country reflects a unique alignment of internal forces, and a distinctive way of making decisions and maintaining order. Moreover, the leaders and peoples of the new states are understandably sensitive to outside judgment on the way in which they manage their affairs. This does not mean that we must withhold comment or censure in cases of authoritarian excesses; it does mean that we should ensure that our judgment is free from ethnocentrism and historical prejudice, and make certain that it is based on facts and is not premature.

The major direct contribution that both the private and public sectors of American society can make to assist the political development of the new states, and yet not be vulnerable to the charge of intervention, is to expand opportunities for higher education and professional training for Africans, particularly in the fields of public administration and political economy. This would improve the qualifications of the new political and bureaucratic elites, and thereby increase their capacity to cope with the many critical problems of nation-building and development discussed in this chapter.

We must categorically affirm our complete opposition to the continuation of the colonial and European oligarchies of southern Africa, but at the same time offer to facilitate and assist in every way possible the painful process of adjustment required. Through private diplomatic channels, as well as in the United Nations, we should apply the greatest possible pressure for reform upon the governments concerned. The problems of transition in these areas are staggering, but the costs and lessons of the Congo tragedy should remind us of the painful consequences of inaction. It should also impress upon us the paralysis our government will inevitably suffer when racial conflagrations in these areas finally erupt and invite or compel external intervention. The Katanga imbroglio revealed with stark clarity the existence in American society of powerful forces that oppose our government's pursuit of a positive and creative policy in situations where the survival of a dominant white minority, or substantial

American private economic, or national strategic, interests are involved. Katanga was the catalyst which activated and joined together a melange of ultra-right and oppositional fringe groups (e.g., anti-United Nations, anti-foreign aid, pro-isolationist, pro-white supremacy, pro-big business), backed by a well-financed Katanga lobby with a surprising influence in prominent congressional circles. Yet Katanga is but an eye-opener to the far greater domestic opposition our government will confront once intervention in South Africa becomes an immediate policy issue.

3. Changing External
Pressures on Africa

VERNON McKAY

> I and my party are well aware of the realities of our time. As we
> would not have British masters, so we would not have Russian
> masters, or any masters for that matter. It is not our intention to
> substitute one imperialism for another.

Kwame Nkrumah made this emphatic statement on October 24,
1953, some three and a half years before the independence of
Ghana. Eight years later, after the quelling of an incipient plot
in Guinea, President Sekou Touré asked Moscow to recall the
Russian ambassador. "Guinea is an independent country and
intends to remain independent," Touré declared. Other African
leaders are a little less emphatic than the Presidents of Ghana
and Guinea, but the new African states are no longer pawns to
be manipulated at will by external pressures. In fact, they are
now demonstrating their ability to exert pressure on their former
metropoles and on the two great powers, the United States and
the Soviet Union. With less and less of its past power to dispose
of Africa's problems, the West has found it necessary to learn how
to deal with Africans.

Where the late 1940's and much of the 1950's witnessed a bi-
polarized world, the 1960's are increasingly pluralistic in nature.
The rise of some forty African and Asian states to independence
since the end of World War II is a major factor in this dispersion
of power. External pressures, influences from outside Africa, were

74

in large part responsible for the rapid end of the colonial period and the rise of Africa in world politics. These pressures include: (1) the shift in world power centers from Western Europe to the United States and the Soviet Union, (2) the growing principle of international accountability for colonial peoples, (3) the Asian revolt against the West, (4) the pressure of Communism, (5) the pressure of the United States, and (6) the new colonial policies adopted in Western Europe. The combination of nationalist forces within Africa and these external pressures gave strength through mutual support to political development, which therefore progressed more quickly than anyone expected.

Yet a largely independent Africa is still subject to external pressures, as are all states, weak or strong, in a world growing smaller. External influences described here include some that were strong shortly after World War II, but which have since declined in strength, such as those emanating from India. Other pressures have maintained themselves and even increased, such as those from the United Nations and from new African policies in the Soviet Union, the United States, and Western Europe. It is my purpose to describe these mutually interacting pressures and responses and to evaluate their possible effects on Africa's geopolitical orientation.

Whether Africa's emerging states will turn away from the Western world to become Soviet satellites, will identify themselves with the neutralists of Asia, or will develop their own ideological patterns—these alternatives will not be determined by the Voice of America, the Voice of Moscow, of Cairo, nor any other outside voice, but will be decided by Africans, who have already begun to shape the destiny of their continent. In making their decisions, nonetheless, African leaders will have to take the views and actions of the outside world into account.

THE PRESSURE OF THE UNITED NATIONS

The United Nations has been described as a mirror which reflects the rise of African issues. It is now evident, however, that the U.N. is far more than a mirror. It has a direct impact on Africa which has mounted steadily for more than a decade.

Political Impact of the U.N.

Among the many U.N. organs that deal with African problems, the most intensive study was carried on in the Trusteeship Council through its annual examination of conditions in seven trust territories, containing about 20 million people, or 10 per cent of the continent's population, and 802,744 square miles, or 7 per cent of its area. In addition to questioning representatives from trust territory governments, the Council examined thousands of written petitions, granted oral hearings to Africans, and sent its own visiting missions into the territories. Beginning in 1948, these missions toured each territory several times.

The impact of the United Nations in stimulating political agitation is clear. In the trust territories, the widely heralded visits of the Trusteeship Council's missions conveyed to the people the feeling that the outside world wanted them to advance. For example, the coming of the first visiting United Nations mission to the Ewe area in 1949 gave local politicians a unique opportunity to arouse mass interest in the abortive Ewe and Togoland unification movement. The Tanganyika African National Union (TANU), led by Julius Nyerere, grew rapidly after 1954, when a visiting mission angered the British by affirming that self-government was within the reach of the people of Tanganyika much earlier than the twenty to twenty-five years the same mission suggested for the Belgian trust territory of Ruanda-Urundi, thereby encouraging Tanganyika nationalism by giving Africans new confidence in the validity of the demands made by their nationalist leaders. The U.N.'s close scrutiny also tended to restrain the inclination of British authorities to restrict political agitation. British policy favored gradual evolution toward self-government, but the slow pace of political progress in Tanganyika had to give way to the combination of international pressure and nationalist demands.

Another U.N. activity that has helped to stimulate politics in the trust territories is the practice of granting oral hearings to enable petitioners to express their grievances in person at the United Nations. By the end of 1961, the Trusteeship Council had granted 41 appeals for oral hearings, and the General Assembly had granted 177. Although they rarely got what they asked for in New York, these petitioners stimulated much political excitement at home. (Several of them later became prime ministers or presidents, including Abdullahi Issa in Somalia, the late Sylvanus Olympio in Togo, and Julius Nyerere in Tanganyika).

Outside the trust territories, evidence of U.N. stimulus to political activity is less tangible but nonetheless real. As no visiting missions may regularly enter other areas, and no regular channels for petitions are available (except for the inhabitants of South-West Africa), items for discussion in the General Assembly must be formally proposed by states rather than individuals, and must be approved by a majority of U.N. members before being placed on the agenda. Nonetheless, Algerian, Moroccan, and Tunisian nationalists in North Africa waged from the beginning a persistent campaign for U.N. help. France contended that North African questions were outside the Assembly's competence, and refused to participate in certain Assembly debates. French anger at U.N. intervention at first stiffened the French position, and nationalist leaders were punished with jail or exile. Once again, however, the combination of nationalist demands and international pressure proved too difficult for long resistance. It is often argued that the French did not capitulate

TABLE 1

African and Asian Membership in the United Nations

Year	Total*	Africa†	Asia‡
1945	51	3	7
1950	60	3	13
1955	76	4	18
1958	83	9	19
1960	100	25	20
1962	110	32	20

* Many of the countries in the "total" column vote for anticolonial resolutions regularly, but do not belong to the Afro-Asian group.

† Excludes the Republic of South Africa.

‡ Excludes Japan, Israel, and Turkey.

because of U.N. pressure, but it cannot be denied that the sympathy of world opinion expressed through the U.N. was a continual encouragement to the nationalists to struggle until the French gave in.

Proliferation of the U.N. Activities

U.N. activities in Africa have expanded widely in the past few years. This is no doubt in response to the expansion of noncolonial members over the colonial powers; whereas prior to 1957 the ratio was 52 to 8, it is now 72 to 10. A particularly revealing development affecting Africa is the Assembly's resolution of November 26, 1957, recommending that the Economic and Social Council "give prompt and favorable consideration to the establishment of an Economic Commission for Africa." This resolution, adopted by a vote of 78 to 0, with Belgium abstaining, marks a sharp reversal in the attitude of the colonial powers and the United States, which had opposed earlier proposals for an Economic Commission for Africa. At the time of these earlier proposals, the colonial powers were launching the six-power Commission for Technical Cooperation in Africa South of the Sahara (CCTA), and it was argued that a U.N. Economic Commission would duplicate CCTA efforts, though it was then little more than a name. But by 1957, the CCTA had built up a widespread organizational network in many fields of economic and social cooperation, had admitted Ghana and Liberia to membership, and had invited other African states to join, so that a U.N. Economic Commission for Africa would seem even more repetitious and unnecessary. But the 1957 proposal came from Ghana (supported by Egypt, Ethiopia, Liberia, Libya, Morocco, the Sudan, and Tunisia, as well as twenty-one non-African cosponsors), while earlier proposals had been made by non-African states. The United States boarded the bandwagon early, and the United Kingdom, after abstaining in the Fourth Committee, switched to an affirmative vote in the plenary session of the General Assembly with the weak explanation that it did not consider the resolution mandatory on ECOSOC.

The U.N. Secretariat has also helped to expand U.N. activities affecting Africa. Over the years, Secretariat officials have produced voluminous and invaluable documentation on Africa. It has not been an easy task, partly because of the difficulty in obtaining accurate and up-to-date information, and partly because of the conflicting pressures exerted on the Secretariat by colonial and anticolonial powers.

The 1957 Assembly also voted for U.N. supervision of the 1958 elections for the Legislative Assembly of French Togoland, an unusual and important step that helped to prepare the way for the termination of trusteeship. In later assemblies, many Afro-Asians attempted to pass a resolution that would call for a U.N.–supervised referendum in Algeria, and the U.N. did supervise the plebiscites in the northern and southern sections of the British Cameroons in 1960.

Later expansions of United Nations activities were frequently combined with a growing tendency to insist on African solutions for African problems, with Africans regarding the U.N. as a vehicle for this purpose. This is evident in the predominantly African composition of the U.N. Advisory Committee on the Congo; in the large number of African contingents which originally participated in the United Nations military presence in the Congo; in the work of the Special Committee of Twenty-four set up by the General Assembly to study the implementation of the 1960 Assembly's Declaration on the Granting of Independence to Colonial Countries; and the United Nations Commission appointed to advise on the problems of Ruanda-Urundi.

The evolution of the U.N. and the expansion of its machinery have taken place in an increasingly emotional atmosphere. Time and again, the depth of feeling of both colonial and anticolonial delegates has affected U.N. discussions even on technical and procedural questions. Lest the wrong impression be conveyed, however, a word of caution is in order. These emotions, while deeply felt, are expressed relatively seldom in open debate. One who attends a session of the Trusteeship Council, or even of the less-restrained Trusteeship Committee of the General Assembly, usually finds the proceedings quite prosaic and tedious after the novelty has worn off. In the art of "trusteemanship," much time is spent by delegates in carefully calculated maneuvering to put their opponents at a procedural disadvantage. Both the colonial and the anticolonial groups have their private meetings behind the scenes where their strategy is planned. The anticolonials, with the advice of friends in the Secretariat, maintain constant pressure to extend the system of international accountability. But they are not so emotional that they cannot beat a coolly rational retreat, if they consider it desirable, when they push the administering authorities to the point of boycotting U.N. machinery.

The system of international accountability, even when its excesses angered and disillusioned them, continually prodded the administering authorities to reappraise and perfect their colonial policies and methods. Even the African inhabitants of South-West Africa have benefited in material ways, despite the South African government's rigid defiance of U.N. resolutions. Perhaps U.N. criticism has the indirect psychological effect of provoking governments to further action, if only to prove their integrity to themselves.

THE PRESSURE OF INDIA

With the birth of many African states, India's influence on events in Africa waned, and initiative in the anticolonial struggle, particularly concerning South Africa, passed to the more militant African states. India remains an example to many African states, however, both in its anticolonialism and its mode of development.

India is a target of European antagonism partly because of the presence of about 850,000 Indians in Africa, partly because of India's policy of championing the fight of colonial peoples for freedom, and partly because of the widespread belief that India has imperialistic ambitions of its own in Africa. Nearly half a million of Africa's Indians live in South Africa, while most of the remainder live in the three East African countries of Kenya, Tanganyika, and Uganda. In retaliation against South Africa's discriminatory racial laws, India in recent years has closed its diplomatic post in the Republic, has embargoed South African trade, and has attacked South African policies in the United Nations. Indian citizens have given financial and other encouragement to African-Indian political movements. A representative in the Indian Parliament once said, "I wish India was in a position to declare war on South Africa here and now." In 1953 Europeans in Kenya and the Rhodesia were angered by statements of Prime Minister Nehru tacitly approving Mau Mau, and attacking the British proposal to establish a Central African Federation. In a foreign policy debate in the House of the People, on September 15, 1953, however, Prime Minister Nehru described the official policy of India as follows:

> We have been accused of interfering in the affairs of other countries in Africa. We have also been accused of some kind of imperialist tendency which wants to spread out in Africa and take possession of those delectable lands which now the European settlers occupy. As a matter of fact, this House knows very well that all along, for these many years, we have been laying the greatest stress on something which is rather unique . . . we have rather gone out of our way to tell our own people in Africa . . . that they can expect no help from us, if they seek any special rights in Africa which are not in the interests of Africa . . . we have told them: "We shall help you naturally, we are interested in protecting you, your dignity or interests, but not if you go at all against the people of Africa, because you are their guests, and if they do not want you, out you will have to go, bag and baggage."

During the 1950's, the Government of India took a number of steps similar to those of the United States and the Soviet Union, although on a smaller scale, to improve its knowledge of and contacts with Africans. With a staff recruited from Africa and Britain, as well as India, and including a director, five readers, and two African-language lecturers, the University of Delhi opened a School of African Studies in August, 1955, to give a two-year postgraduate diploma course. Planned for 30 students, it had 17 in its first year. In the same month, an Africa and Asia Study Group organized a visual exposition on Africa, and a similar study group was later formed in Delhi. An African Society of India was also formed along the lines of the learned societies in Europe and America. By the end of 1959, it was estimated that the number of African students in India had risen to 350, mostly from East Africa, about ninety of whom were attending the University of Delhi.

Indian policy on African issues is particularly interesting in the United Nations. In this forum, the attitudes of Indian delegates have varied all the way from the moderate and reserved approach of Shiva Rao, an early Indian representative on the Committee on Information from Non-Self-Governing Territories, to the eloquence and showmanship of Krishna Menon. When India was first elected to the Trusteeship Council, Menon enlivened its prosaic proceedings with his colorful oratory and gestures as he warmed to his themes. As he once told the Council, "Our responsibility is to criticize, make suggestions, and probably to make noise—we are conscious of the last factor."

Much attention was given to racial discrimination and economic underdevelopment, but the paramount concern of Indian representatives was for the political advancement of dependent peoples to self-government: "Self-government is more important than good government—and there will be no good government without self-government." With this general theme as a guiding star, well-prepared Indian delegations questioned the reports of the administering authorities on the trust territories with minute care. No device to cloak colonial authority escaped them. If there was a legislative or executive council in the territory, they wanted to know how many Africans were on it. If there were Africans, were they nominated or elected? Was African representation proportional or communal? If not proportional, why not, and when would it be changed? If there were Africans in the civil service, how many were in senior posts? What were they paid? Could they disagree with official policy? Year after year, such questions were addressed to the special representatives who were sent from each territory to the Trusteeship Council to answer its questions. Indian delegations also expressed a consistently strong dislike of administrative unions, arrangements which provided for certain common administrative services between a trust territory and an adjacent colony under the administration of the same metropole.

Another basic Indian policy, consistently pursued from session to session, was to bring steady pressure for the continual expansion of U.N. activities affecting Africa. India also played a prominent role in all United Nations efforts on the three South African agenda items—South-West Africa, apartheid, and the treatment of peoples of Indian origin in South Africa. The last problem, the item of most direct interest to India, naturally aroused bitter Indian feeling long before the United Nations was born.

Indian Motives

India was motivated to take a leading role in African affairs for several reasons. First, India had a great desire to play a leading role in world affairs, and Africa represented a valuable component of the "third force" with which Nehru sought to moderate the Cold War. Second, Indian leaders were still smarting under the racial humiliations of the colonial relationship which they had themselves only just escaped. Third, the Gandhian tradition of nonviolence remains strong in India, and takes the form of Nehru's sincere desire for peaceful change. There is no evidence of Indian imperialism in Africa in any of these factors. Indian emigration to South Africa has been banned for fifty years and highly curtailed in the rest of the continent for a decade.

When so many African states attained independence in 1960, India became more conscious that anticolonialism was not enough to sustain its foreign policy. The leading role of Indians in the Afro-Asian movement, which Nehru held at the Bandung Conference of 1955, had already declined by 1957, when Nasser welcomed the first Afro-Asian Peoples Solidarity Conference in Cairo. The many all-African conferences since 1958 bypassed India altogether. Within the U.N., Africans not only took over the leadership of the anticolonial struggle, but even came into conflict with India over certain African issues. The moderate position of India on such items as the French Cameroons elections in 1960, and the attempt to impose strong U.N. sanctions on South Africa, irritated African leaders. Furthermore, India has been placed in the unwelcome position of having to choose between different factions in the Congo and to support one side or the other in the Morocco-Mauritania dispute. Its prestige among Africans received a sudden boost, however, when India invaded Goa and two other Portuguese territories, in December, 1961. African opposition to the use of force to settle international disputes was far outweighed by a long-smoldering resentment against Portugal, not only for its obdurate resistance to change but because of its brutal suppression of the rebellion in northern Angola.

Although India needs technicians for its own development program, it has a valuable opportunity to provide Africa with skilled technicians who are familiar with the problems of underdeveloped countries and who do not cost as much as Western experts. It has already made a small beginning, through bilateral agreements to provide technical experts for air force training in Ethiopia and Ghana, and it has supplied teachers, doctors, and administrative and technical personnel to other African countries. As a country which maintains democratic freedoms along with a high degree of government economic planning, India could serve as a useful example for Africans.

PRESSURES FROM EGYPT AND ISLAM

Nasser's Ambitions

Egypt is another state attempting to influence the shape of things to come in Africa. Egypt is involved both in the Pan-African and Afro-Asian movements, and in the related Pan-Arab and Pan-Islamic movements; these multiple interests sometimes conflict.

For many centuries, Egypt has had links with the North African coastal area through Islam and the Arabic language. It also has a long-standing geographical interest in northeastern Africa because of its lifeline in the waters of the Nile. It is only in the past decade that President Nasser has brought the area south of the Sudan to Egypt's attention. In his 1955 book, *Egypt's Liberation: The Philosophy of the Revolution,* he wrote that Egypt cannot "remain aloof from the terrible and sanguinary conflict" between 5 million whites and 200 million Africans:

> We cannot do so for an important and obvious reason: we are in Africa. The peoples of Africa will continue to look to us, who guard their northern gate, and who constitute their link with the outside world.

In an odd note reminiscent of Rudyard Kipling, he added that "we will never in any circumstances be able to relinquish our responsibility to support, with all our might, the spread of enlightenment and civilization to the remotest depths of the jungle." This mixture of paternalism and ignorance of African conditions has been considerably mitigated since 1955, though it is apparent that Egypt's sponsorship of many African "liberation" movements was based on chimeras and the lack of a true appreciation of political conditions in various African territories.

In the three zones of Egyptian interests propounded by Nasser, Africa took second place, after Egypt's Arab concerns, but before those of Islam. The attention paid to Africa in Egypt has increased greatly since the early 1950's. In addition to its strongly anticolonial (and sometimes just anti-Western) posture in the United Nations, Egypt has served as a refugee center for many African nationalists, and has in addition subsidized African liberation movements in exile. Both Tunisia and Morocco had offices in Cairo before independence, and Egypt remained the most militant sponsor of the Algerian nationalists; early stages of the November 1, 1954, uprising were planned in Cairo by Ben Bella and his fellow revolutionaries. Egypt's continuous aid to the Algerian rebels was certainly one of the considerations that led the French to participate in the Suez adventure of 1956. In addition, African bureaus were set up in Cairo by African nationalists from Cameroon, Uganda, Kenya, Somalia, South Africa, the Federation of Rhodesia and Nyasaland, Niger, Chad, Mozambique, Nigeria, Zanzibar, and other African countries. The African Association was started in 1955 to group together the different national bureaus and to provide aid, advice, and propaganda for the African cause and Egyptian influence.

The most dramatic early step in Egypt's bid for leadership in

Africa was the widely publicized Afro-Asian Peoples Solidarity Conference, which met in Cairo at the end of December, 1957. Including a number of exiles and refugees, the conference was attended by nearly 500 delegates representing the "peoples" rather than the governments of more than 40 African and Asian countries. After a week's discussion, dominated by Soviet delegates and their followers, the conference adopted a series of anticolonial and anti-Western resolutions. A ten-member permanent secretariat, headed by an Egyptian, was established in Cairo, and was given, officially, a $29,000 annual grant by Egypt. However, Nasser was reportedly surprised and uneasy at the Soviet domination of the conference, and Egyptian influence in the movement was further weakened at the Second Afro-Asian Peoples Solidarity Conference in Conakry, in 1960, where the Guineans, together with the Soviets, sought to minimize Egyptian influence in the movement.

In addition to its active role in the Casablanca and the Afro-Asian solidarity movements, Egypt has (1) increased its diplomatic posts in Africa; (2) granted scholarships to several thousand African students for study in Cairo; (3) established an Institute of African Studies at Cairo University; (4) sent many Egyptian teachers, technicians, and officials to Libya, the Sudan, Somalia, and other countries; (5) employed Radio Cairo not only for broadcasts in Arabic, English, and French, but for a Voice of Africa program in at least 9 African languages for a total of nearly 9 hours a week in 1962; (6) made loans of $5 million at 2.5 per cent to the Somali Republic, in December, 1960, and to Guinea, in May, 1961, and agreed to construct complete factories for Mali; and (7) used a clandestine Radio Cairo program, The Voice of Free Africa, for inflammatory broadcasts to the south, exhorting Africans to drive out the "white dogs" of the Western oppressors, and branding the United States as the banker of the sterling bloc and therefore another of Africa's masters.

Islamic Expansion

In addition to this Pan-Africanism, Egypt is involved in the wider Pan-Islamic movement. More than 80 million Africans are

Moslems, and half of these are Negroid peoples south of the Sahara. Since its penetration of the Sudan, more than a thousand years ago, Islam has successfully adapted itself to African customs, and is still expanding. Africans from the Sudanic belt have attended Islamic institutions in Fez and Tunis for centuries, but Al-Azhar University in Cairo is the main attraction. Its graduates have helped to develop numerous African Moslem religious brotherhoods, both traditional and reformist, as well as a number of modern Moslem clubs, centers, leagues, associations, and congresses which foster Islamic cultural, economic, and political activities.

The annual pilgrimage of thousands of Africans to Mecca is another unifying force. It not only renews the African's sense of Islamic solidarity and his pride in belonging to a universal religion, but it often exposes him to the anti-Western fervor of many an Arab propagandist. In the Republic of the Sudan, the last census included about half a million Nigerians, many of whom were stranded and poverty-stricken pilgrims—a situation which led the Nigerian Government, in January, 1962, to refuse pilgrimage passports to applicants without the money deemed necessary to cover the cost of a round-trip ticket to Mecca.

The idea of Islamic solidarity propounded by the Pan-Islamic movement of the nineteenth century led to the organization, in 1954, of the Islamic Congress, proposed by Saudi Arabia and supported by Pakistan, Egypt, Syria, Yemen, Indonesia, Iran, Afghanistan, and Morocco. The Islamic Congress grants scholarships, mostly for study in Egypt, and contributes to Moslem cultural centers and Koranic schools in Africa and Asia. In January, 1956, it also established an Islamic Health Organization.

Egypt tends to use the Pan-Islamic idea for political purposes, but it is difficult to measure the political utility of Pan-Islam, since its objectives, as enunciated from Egypt, are so vague. Nasser himself has categorically repudiated the idea of an Islamic Federation of African and Asian states where the Moslem faith predominates.

Appeals to Moslem solidarity and the greatness of Egypt will continue to be sufficient to bring prestige and influence to Egypt.

But the rapid increase in conversions to Islam noted in the last few years in sub-Saharan Africa is laying the foundation for possible future political projects and pressures.

THE PRESSURES OF THE SOVIET UNION

Many of the alleged facts about Communism in Africa are based on fifth-hand information that comes to us via the world of rumor and cocktail gossip, and then through the newspapers. Because the turmoil in postwar Africa proved ideal for Communist exploitation, many observers jumped to the false and dangerous conclusion that it was caused by Communists. It was a false conclusion, because Africa's protest movements were primarily a natural reaction to foreign domination. It was dangerous, because confusion over the causes of political agitation handicapped the West's ability to develop an effective policy. In fact, by overemphasizing Communist penetration of Africa in the first ten years after the war, Westerners only helped it with free and unnecessary publicity.

Although Soviet Communism had relatively little to do with the development of nationalist sentiments in postwar Africa, since about 1958, it has had an increasing influence in African affairs and is operating efficiently to further that influence. Since 1960, the Soviet Union has adopted new tactics, extended its diplomatic, economic, and cultural missions in Africa, and taken advantage of the opportunities provided by the new states on the continent.

It therefore becomes more important than ever to understand the nature of Soviet activities. There is, of course, a distinction between Communism as an international movement and the Soviet Union as a great power. We shall be concerned primarily with the latter, insofar as their interests and influence do not overlap. By 1961, it became clear that the influence of the Soviet Union as a great power would rise in Africa in the next decade. Whether this would turn Africans more and more to Communism was another question.

Channels of Soviet Penetration

The duality of Soviet policy must not be forgotten. On the one hand, the Soviet Union attempts to foster Communism in Africa, while on the other, it seeks to promote its interests and influence as a great power. Thus it is useful to survey briefly both the governmental and nongovernmental channels through which Soviet influence and Communism penetrate Africa.

Diplomatic and Consular Posts. The year 1958 marked the beginning of an important expansion of Soviet government activities regarding Africa. In September, a new department to deal with African affairs was established in the Foreign Ministry. Within the next three years, the diplomatic, consular, and trade posts not only of the U.S.S.R. but of the whole Soviet bloc were substantially increased throughout the continent. By January 1, 1962, the bloc had about eighty posts in Africa—quite a jump from 1954, when there were only Soviet diplomatic missions in Ethiopia and Egypt, and a Czech consular mission in Cape Town.

Trade Missions. Beginning about 1956, and mounting noticeably in 1958, Soviet bloc trade missions also entered Africa. By 1961, more than eighty-five trade delegations of one kind or another had negotiated numerous trade agreements between African and Soviet bloc countries.

In 1960, United States exports to Africa totaled $761 million, and imports totaled $535 million, while Russian exports amounted to $94 million and imports to $148 million. For the Russians, however, this was a notable increase over the 1956 figures, when U.S.S.R. exports to Africa totaled only $24 million, and imports $29 million. U.S. trade, meanwhile, remained at about the same level. Soviet bloc trade, it should be noted, is almost entirely state trading under barter, credit, or payments agreements, while U.S. trade flows through private channels.

While Czechoslovakia led the bloc in exports to Africa in 1956, the value of U.S.S.R. exports was almost twice that of the Czechs in 1960. Egypt, which accounted for more than two-thirds of all bloc trade in 1956, accounted for slightly over half in 1960. By 1960, China's trade with Africa had reached sizable proportions, mounting to $78 million in imports from

Africa and $49 million in exports. In both 1956 and 1960, Soviet and bloc imports exceeded exports.

The expansion of Soviet bloc trade with Africa was accompanied by the gradual expansion of Soviet aid, in the form of loans or credits, as shown in Table 2.

TABLE 2

Soviet Loans or Credits to Africa

Date of Loan	Recipient	Amount of Loan *(in millions of dollars)*
1958	Egypt	275
1959	Ethiopia	100
1959	Libya	28
1960	Guinea	35
1960	Ghana	40
1960	Congo (Leopoldville)	3.7
1961	Sudan	22
1961	Tunisia	28

Communist Party. The Communist Party has had little success either in the old colonial Africa, where European administrators took the necessary steps to keep Communists out and hold Communist propaganda to a minimum, or in newly independent states, where strong African leaders are willing to deal with Moscow, but not to permit the growth of local Communist opposition. A Soviet writer has asserted that the combined strength of Communist parties in black Africa increased from 5,000 to 50,000 during 1960 and 1961; Western sources generally give a considerably lower figure. But counting Communists in Africa is largely guesswork.

In mid-1962, there were six Communist parties in Africa officially recognized as such by the Communist world. These parties included most of Africa's Communists. Of the four in the northern part of the continent, it was estimated, in 1958, that the Algerian Party had 5,000 members; Tunisia, 1,000; Morocco, 1,000–1,500; and Sudan, 1,500 members and approximately 4,000 sympathizers. The other two parties were in South Africa (with an estimated 800 members and 6,500 sympathizers) and on the island of Reunion. Only the Party in Reunion has a legal existence. The Algerian Communist Party, composed mostly of Europeans, has doubtless lost a large percentage of its following with the European exodus in the face of Algerian independence. There are also a faction-ridden, severely repressed Communist Party in Egypt, and a "Titoist" Communist Party, established in 1960 in Malagasy, where most Communist efforts are directed toward an alliance of radical nationalist movements.

There are a number of indigenous parties of a Marxist-Leninist inclination which group a relatively small number of "like-minded Marxists." The *Parti Africain de l'Indépendence* (PAI) in Senegal, a party of intellectuals, was outlawed in 1960. Of similar stripe are the *Parti de l'Unité Gabonaise* (PUNGA) in Gabon, whose support seems to be largely among students and whose chief characteristic is not Marxism, but a strong aversion to President M'ba and his pro-French policies, and the *Parti de la Révolution Socialiste du Bénin*—a somewhat grandiose name for a small group of extremists from Togo and Dahomey.

There is also the so-called Communist Party of Kano, which appears to have gathered together some disillusioned former members of Northern Elements Progressive Union (NEPU), and the somewhat more important Nigerian People's Party, led by Gogo Nzeribe, which has aligned itself with the left wing of the Nigerian trade union movement, the NTUC. Some of the literature of the illegal terrorist wing of the *Union des Populations du Cameroun* (UPC) is Marxist-inspired, and the activities of the party allegedly Communist-supported; in the process of engaging in guerrilla warfare in parts of the southern Cameroons, it looked to the Chinese rather than the Russians as its mentor. The establishment of the Communist Party of Basutoland was made known in November, 1961; as yet there are no estimates of its strength.

Nationalist Parties. The political movements in British territories after World War II were predominantly nationalist efforts little influenced by Communists, despite the wooing of African students in England by British Communists. The neighboring French territories, however, offer several instructive examples of Communist efforts to penetrate African parties, particularly with respect to the UPC, the *Rassemblement Démo-cratique Africain* (RDA), and the PDG of Guinea, the latter originally a section of the RDA. French Communists influenced the RDA from 1946 to 1950, when that party broke its alliance with the French Communist Party in the French National Assembly and elsewhere. The illegal wing of the UPC was the only nationalist organization to remain under Communist influence. Since the independence of most of the African states (in those states where there is a single party system), any Communists or Communist sympathizers operate within the framework of these parties. Within the dominant mass parties of Ghana (CPP), Guinea (PDG), Mali (US), and some other African countries, there are individuals and factions with pro-Communist or pro-Russian sympathies. The distinction is not always clear, nor can it always be made, but it is important nonetheless.

Trade Unions. In mid-1962, African trade unions directly affiliated with the Communist-dominated World Federation of Trade Unions (WFTU) were small and in several cases illegal. They included the General Confederation of Cameroon Trade Unions (CGKT), which in November–December, 1962, was contemplating disaffiliation; the Mauritius Trade Union Federation; the outlawed Sudanese Workers Trade Union Federation (SWTUF); the four branches of the CGAT (*Confédération Générale Africaine du Travail*) in French Equatorial Africa (Chad, Gabon, Central African Republic, and Congo–Brazzaville), which refused in January, 1957, to affiliate with the *Union Générale des Travailleurs d'Afrique Noire* (UGTAN), deciding to maintain their affiliation with WFTU; the Confederation of Independent Indigenous Trade Unions of French Somaliland; and FISEMA, the trade union of the *Congrès de l'Indépendence de Madagascar* (AKFM). However, since 1956, the WFTU has been encouraging African trade unions aligned to the main nationalist party in each territory. Under the banner of leading the efforts for "unity" and "national integration," the Communists have also encouraged the growth of a single nonaligned trade-union federation for Africa and Asia; when this proved unsuccessful, they attempted to do the same on each continent. The Communists gave moral, and allegedly financial, support to the formation and establishment of the All-African Trade Union Federation (AATUF), an African trade-union international led by Guinea, Ghana, Mali, and Morocco, which insists that each national center cease all its affiliations with other internationals. Since very few unions are affiliated with the WFTU, this restrictive demand applies primarily to the large number of African trade unions that are affiliated with the International Confederation of Free Trade Unions (ICFTU).

The countries whose trade unions are members of AATUF tend to use these unions as arms of the state in foreign policy (with the exception of Morocco, where there is no link between the Union of Moroccan Workers [UMT] and the government), and these trade unions readily accept aid from the WFTU. AATUF, however, is neither a Communist front nor Communist dominated; disaffiliation with other internationals does not preclude "fraternal relations" with these internationals. Since it is the ICFTU that is dominant in Africa, this international receives the onus of being "imperialistic." The leaders of AATUF attempt to use the WFTU to their own advantage in gaining control over the African trade-union movement, and the WFTU attempts the same. To offset the aggressive proselytizing efforts of AATUF, the affiliates of the ICFTU, as well as those of the Catholic International Federation of Christian Trade Unions (IFCTU), met in Dakar in January, 1962, and established the African Trade Union Confederation (ATUC). The government-controlled Egyptian trade unions and the Egyptian-inspired and controlled Confederation of Arab Trade Unions (CATU) cooperated closely with the WFTU and its associated trade internationals, operating as a source of contact between Communist and African trade unions, up until 1959, when relations between Egypt and the U.S.S.R. became increasingly cool.

The Communists have also set up several trade-union organizations that function as fronts: among these are the International Trade Union Committee for Solidarity with the Workers and Peoples of Algeria, established in 1958 in Cairo, and a similarly named committee for the Workers and Peoples of South Africa, established in 1961 in Accra, both called for by WFTU conclaves. While these "committees" are Communist fronts, a number of trade unions from truly nonaligned countries, and some from Western-oriented countries, have participated in them. The Communist bloc also runs trade-union schools in East Berlin, Prague, Leipzig, and Budapest, as well as in Rome and Paris, where shorter courses are normally given. These schools draw trade unionists from a large cross-section of African countries, and their curricula are primarily devoted to the role of the trade unions in the political process of the developing countries.

Front Organizations. About forty "friendship associations" and other identifiable front organizations were operating in Africa in 1961. A Soviet Association for Friendship with the Peoples of Africa was created in April, 1959, and a year later a Chinese African People's Friendship Association, sponsored by seventeen Chinese organizations, was formed. These and other bodies give financial assistance to enable Africans to attend meetings of such Communist front groups as the World Federation of Democratic Youth (WFDY), the International Union of Students (IUS), the World Federation of Teachers, the Women's International Democratic Federation, and several others.

The Congress of Democrats in South Africa is a good example of a local front organization. A different and more significant type of nongovernmental organization for the dissemination of Communist propaganda is the Afro-Asian Peoples Solidarity Conference, which held its first meeting in Cairo at the end of 1957. The fact that this was a conference of peoples rather than governments enabled the Soviet representatives to be even more unrestrained than usual. They not only promised to support independence movements and approved confiscation of Western investments, but they made a lavish offer of economic aid without strings to all Asians and Africans. Despite words of caution from Nasser to Egyptian delegates and despite efforts of delegates from Ghana, Tunisia, Ethiopia, the Sudan, and India to moderate its anti-Western tone, the Conference adopted a battery of resolutions condemning NATO, the Eisenhower Doctrine, the Baghdad Pact, nuclear weapons, and other Western innovations.

Perhaps the major Soviet gain was the foothold the Russians obtained to carry on their activities. The Conference voted to create an Afro-Asian Peoples Solidarity Council, to meet at least once a year and to have a permanent secretariat in Cairo with an Egyptian secretary general and ten members, including representatives of the Soviet Union and Communist China. The Afro-Asian Peoples Solidarity Conference was originally suggested and organized by the World Peace Council, another Communist front organization, but it should be noted that the Soviet Union never really established the control it desired over the Conference and Council.

African Students. In the early postwar years, only a small number of African students studied behind the Iron Curtain. Many thousands, however, attended universities in Britain and France, where they were more or less systematically cultivated by British and French Communists. Many of these potential African leaders were contacted by young members of "cultural associations" with innocuous names, who arranged sight-seeing tours for them, invited them to meals, and sometimes paid their expenses to student conferences in Prague, Warsaw, or Moscow. In London, when the inroads the Communists were making by such tactics were discovered not long after the war, members of the Fabian Bureau attempted to counter them by developing their own program for colonial students.

Within the Soviet Union, the Russians appear to be having occasional difficulties with African students, just as the United States, India, and other countries do. Nonetheless, the Soviet Union, like the United States, is expanding its facilities for African students. The People's Friendship University (now renamed Patrice Lumumba University) was established in February, 1960, in Moscow, for students from underdeveloped areas, with plans for 500 students in 1960–61 and an ultimate capacity of between 3,000 and 4,000 students. In March, 1960, it was reported that East Germany, offering "Red Fulbrights" on a large scale to Africans and Asians, was financing 2,000 students from 40 countries in its universities; new students were required to attend a six-month course in special schools for foreigners in Leipzig to learn the German language, as well as the principles of Marxism-Leninism.

The number of African students in Soviet bloc universities appears to have doubled in the academic year 1960–61, reaching an estimated total of nearly 1,200. This figure does not include industrial trainees, but covers those enrolled in institutions of higher education for at least one semester. These figures also do not include Egyptians, about 150 of whom were studying in the Soviet Union, and approximately the same number in other bloc countries. This is a large and significant increase, but it should be noted for purposes of perspective that a far greater number of African students were attending universities in the Western bloc during the same period; there were 2,831 African students enrolled in the colleges and universities of the United States, from 7,000 to 9,000 in France (40 per cent of whom were in secondary schools), and 17,000 in the United Kingdom.

Cultural Exchanges. In addition to diplomatic and trade missions, the Soviet bloc has also stepped up the sending of a wide variety of cultural missions to Africa. Many cultural agreements have been signed providing for exchanges and cooperation in science, the arts, drama, sports, broadcasting, and cinematography. In 1960, the number of cultural delegations traveling through Africa increased, and about two dozen Soviet exhibitions were held in nine African countries between January, 1960, and May, 1961. Seven Soviet bloc athletic teams had visited Ethiopia, Morocco, and Tunisia between 1957 and 1959, and in 1960, they concentrated on West Africa, mostly soccer teams like the Moscow Dynamos, who played a return match against the Ghana Black Stars in Moscow in 1961. The years 1960 and 1961 also witnessed an increase in exchange visits by Soviet and African women's and youth organizations. It has been estimated that a total of about 500 delegations traveled to and from the Soviet bloc in 1960, a substantial increase over the total of 177 in 1957, 202 in 1958, and 389 in 1959.

Soviet Radio and Press. The radio war in Africa mounted in 1958, although Soviet radio broadcasts had been heard as far south as South Africa for many years. The expansion of broadcasting to Africa was slow until 1958 when, on April 19, Radio Moscow began 15-minute-a-day programs in both English and French on three different meter bands. By October, the time for broadcasts beamed to Africa was reportedly tripled.

By the end of 1961, bloc broadcasting to Africa reached a total of 200 hours per week—a rise of over 100 per cent since the beginning of the year. To this figure must be added 10 hours per week partially beamed to Africa, and 166 hours per week of Arabic-language broadcasts. The other bloc countries also stepped up their radio propaganda to Africa. Radio Peking, which is said by many Africans to provide the clearest reception, expanded its broadcasting 80 per cent by increasing its English output and by initiating French and Swahili programs. The European satellites —excluding Albania and Hungary—more than tripled their output to Africa in English and French.

Soviet themes are also widely disseminated through Communist or Communist-oriented newspapers and periodicals, about twenty of which are published in Africa and the Malagasy Republic. Other magazines and printed materials are brought in from bloc countries and sold cheaply in Africa. The attractive Soviet Information Center in Ethiopia has distributed Soviet journals and other materials to selected individuals and organizations for some time. The large increase in bloc diplomatic and consular posts in Africa in 1960 and 1961 opened the way for a much wider dissemination of Communist propaganda.

The United Nations. During the first fifteen years after World War II, while Soviet penetration of Africa was curtailed by colonial governments, Russian diplomats found the United Nations a particularly valuable forum for spreading anticolonial propaganda and subverting the Western alliance.

The double-barreled technique of Soviet delegates is (1) to exaggerate, oversimplify, and distort African problems, and (2) constantly and deliberately to repeat the same themes, sometimes even with cynical humor. Although the tears of the bear often looked like those of the crocodile, even to anticolonial delegates who shared some of the Russian views of Africa, the general effect of Russian extremism was indirectly to encourage other anticolonial members to move toward a more extreme attitude toward the colonial representatives. For example, this tended over a period of time to embitter and confuse Trusteeship Council issues and debates.

In the long run, these persistent tactics helped to build up the image of the Soviet Union as a friend who always fought for colonial peoples. Conversely, the more conscientious, though not necessarily correct, position of the United States led it into numerous negative votes and abstentions which were often insignificant in individual cases, but over the long run built up an opposite image of the United States as a defender of the colonial powers, if not of colonialism. As African issues spread throughout U.N. machinery, Russian tactics in the Trusteeship Council were carried over into other U.N. organs, notably the General Assembly, where the Soviet Union could get more publicity in portraying the United States as a supporter of colonialism.

Whether the U.N. will be as useful to the Soviet Union in the future remains to be seen. Soviet opportunities for exploitation of the colonial issue may diminish as colonies disappear, although several thorny problems still exist, notably the Portuguese colonies and South Africa. Moreover, the strong African bloc in the U.N. has occasionally been irritated by Soviet tactics and now wants to lead its own fights.

A Tactical Shift in Communist Ideology

The basic tenet of Communist ideology on Africa is the familiar thesis of Lenin that imperialism is the highest stage of capitalism, which carries with it the implication that the destruction of capitalism and colonialism are but two aspects of one and the same task. This is a powerful idea among Africans anxious to rid themselves of colonialism, and it still handicaps the West today. A second important Soviet theme is the systematically distorted portrayal of Africa as a land of oppressed peoples suffering under colonial slavery. And a third is the contention that a new step in the imperialist struggles for Africa is a greedy American drive for the economic, political, and military expansion of United States interests.

These three Soviet propaganda themes have been relatively consistent. A fourth doctrine merits special attention because new Soviet tactics led to its modification in 1955. This was the ironical and contradictory picture of the "national bourgeoisie" of Africa. Committed by doctrine to the principle that revolutionary leadership must be in the hands of the working class, the Communists found that in Africa, as in other colonial areas, the workers and peasants had not developed to the point of being able to assume such leadership. The Communist appeal, therefore, had to be directed at the nationalist-minded bourgeois intelligentsia. This troublesome problem was discussed in 1950 by the leading Soviet Africanist, I. I. Potekhin, in an article in *Soviet Ethnography* entitled "The Stalinist Theory of Colonial Revolution and the National Liberation Movement in Tropical and South Africa." Potekhin warned that the African bourgeoisie "supports the revolutionary movement of the masses of the people only with a view to taking advantage of the fruits of the revolution and seizing political power for the suppression and enslavement of the masses of the people of its own country." He cynically argued, however, that these reactionary nationalistic elements could be used in "the special strategic stage of the colonial revolution, the stage of the nation-wide anti-imperialist front when the national bourgeoisie still supports the revolutionary movement."

The sardonic implication was that African nationalist leaders would be due for liquidation after the Communists were through using them. Potekhin even went on to name some individuals he had in mind. He branded Gold Coast Paramount Chief Ofori Atta, and Bamangwato Chief Seretse Khama, as "feudal or semifeudal lords," and said that the Nigerian nationalist leader, Nnamdi Azikiwe, followed "the ideology and policy of petty bourgeois national reformism," a "colonial edition of the reactionary American philosophy of pragmatism" (evidently a reference to Azikiwe's American education). "Zik" 's fellow nationalist, Nwafor Orizu, was also labeled a national bourgeois leader who attacked British colonial policy but "at the same time advocates the preservation of the bases of capitalism."

Egypt's President Nasser was referred to in the 1952 *Large Soviet Encyclopedia* as one of "a reactionary group of officers connected with the United States." When Prime Minister Nkrumah was turning a cold shoulder to Communist influence in the Gold Coast before independence, his administration was attacked for representing "the interest of the reactionary section

of the bourgeoisie and not the workers." President Tubman of
Liberia was described in the 1954 *Large Soviet Encyclopedia* as
"an agent of American monopolies" heading a government of
"landlords and capitalists." King Idris of Libya was branded "the
stooge of the English." Ethiopia was called a feudal society under
the domination of American imperialism. And in a 1955 book,
Potekhin declared that the African National Congress started as
a "feudal summit, the tribal chiefs . . . a feudal comprador
organization collaborating with imperialism."

By 1955, however, the Communists evidently felt the need to
reverse or at least modify the Party line in order to facilitate their
efforts in Africa and elsewhere. In May, 1955, the Party's
theoretical organ, *Kommunist,* declared that "serious mistakes
have occasionally been committed in appraising the role of the
national bourgeoisie of the countries of the East in the anti-
imperialist movement." After the Twentieth Party Congress, in
February, 1956, Potekhin and other Soviet scholars and theorists
therefore began to reverse themselves. African leaders were
praised rather than reviled, and it was contended that colonial
peoples may find more than one road to socialism. In October,
1956, Potekhin wrote in *Moscow News* that "a great popular
independence movement has surged up throughout the continent," and "a national bourgeoisie . . . has made its appearance and is claiming its place in the sun. . . . In every
colony there are political leaders of ability and energy: Nkrumah,
Azikiwe, Jomo Kenyatta and others." A related item of propaganda guidance issued by the Central Committee of the Party
warned against the indiscriminate branding of certain small
states at the United Nations as U.S. satellites only because their
official representatives sometimes are "compelled to vote contrary
to their own conviction under the pressure of American diplo-
macy."

However, when African states moved quickly toward independence, at the end of the 1950's, and the Chinese Communists
became a significant force in world politics, the opportunist "soft"
line swung back toward the earlier position. The Soviet attitude toward the "national bourgeoisie" hardened. This was
evident in the declaration issued by the 1960 Moscow Conference

of eighty-one Communist Parties, and was reemphasized in the program adopted at the Twenty-second Soviet Communist Party Congress in October, 1961. The latter document brands national bourgeoisie leaders as "the reactionary circles of the local exploiting classes," who serve as "allies of imperialism." Although the 1961 program retains the line that the choice between capitalism and socialism is "the internal affair of the peoples themselves," it expresses a vigorous confidence that the national liberation movement will not end with the gaining of political independence, but will, with Soviet aid, move onward to complete the "anti-imperialist, antifeudal, democratic revolution" by establishing a "national democracy." Nonetheless, this 1961 doctrine symbolizes a real difference between the Stalinist and Khrushchev regimes, because the "national democracy" appears to be a new concept—a kind of way station on the road to the "peoples democracy."

This emphasis on the growing class struggle is evidently designed to combat the view of those African leaders, including Guinea's Sekou Touré, who have asserted that classes do not exist in Africa. Potekhin challenges this trend in a 1960 booklet, *Africa Looks Ahead*. He attacks the theory of an "African socialism" that denies the existence of classes in Africa. He acknowledges that "the process of class formation" is still unfinished, but contends that Marxist-Leninist theory is nonetheless applicable to African conditions, where one does find "feudalism of the patriarchal type" and "an African petty bourgeoisie" which now has new opportunities for development in independent African states. The peasant communes of Africa can nonetheless, if power is in the right hands, "serve as the connecting link for a direct transition to socialism," enabling Africa to bypass the capitalist stage of development.

These propaganda shifts during the African revolution illustrate the difference between long-range Soviet ideology and short-range propaganda tactics. The renewed emphasis on the role of the working class indicated that the old line was reversed only while nationalist leaders were in the actual process of winning their revolutions. When the new states began to resist Communist penetration, however, Soviet theory regarding the inevitable betrayal of the revolution by the national bourgeoisie seemed to be confirmed.

THE PRESSURE OF THE UNITED STATES

Both in the period of the struggle for independence and in this predominantly post-independence era, the United States has been and remains inescapably committed to a moderate and responsible policy toward Africa, which contrasts sharply with the unrestrained Soviet tactics. Since the many aspects of American influence are elaborated elsewhere in this volume, they need only brief mention here.[1] Our government brings pressure to bear through diplomatic persuasion; through our votes on African issues in the United Nations—even when we abstain; through the Voice of America and other propaganda media; through our educational exchange program; and through economic and technical assistance to Africa totaling about $2.5 billion from World War II through 1961. Many thousands of Americans —journalists, teachers, students, scholars, technicians, clergymen, philanthropists, Congressmen, businessmen, labor leaders, Negroes, Vice-Presidents Nixon and Johnson and, on numerous occasions, G. Mennen Williams—have made their way through much of Africa in the past few years. In the last few years, also, the operations dealing with African affairs have expanded rapidly in order to meet the needs and problems of the new states of Africa.

The mingled irritation and uneasiness Europeans feel at American pressure is well reflected in the attitude of André Siegfried, who once suggested (*Figaro*, Feb. 7, 1949) that the United States, by fomenting colonial revolts, was as dangerous a revolutionary force as the Soviet Union. While this may overstate the case somewhat, the decolonization process which had brought twenty-eight African states to independence by the end of 1962, twenty-three alone in the two-year period 1960–62, has resulted in the retreat of European predominance and an obvious increase of American (and Russian) influence in Africa. And

[1] See also Appendix.

though American policy was slowly evolving through the 1950's with respect to accepting the pre-eminence of African interests in Africa, the Kennedy-Rusk-Williams team of 1961 not only carried forward these new trends in Africa but injected a valuable New Frontier spirit into our relations with African leaders. The role of the United States in the Congo crisis, its essential support for the U.N. policy, as well as its own participation and the pressure brought to bear on its NATO allies, was perhaps the most pronounced indication of the vigorous concern of the Kennedy Administration with African affairs.

The Pressures from the West: Eurafrica

The barrage of criticism from the outside world since World War II, accompanied by increasingly vehement African demands, prompted the major colonial powers to adopt new tactics. The old negative tendency to resist premature African demands was replaced by a new form of pressure—a positive effort to offer inducements that would persuade Africans to remain in the Western fold once they obtained self-government.

These new influences included the granting of several billion dollars by European taxpayers for development and welfare programs; the British decision to move the Gold Coast rapidly to self-government, with Nigeria and other territories to follow; the concessions made by France in the effort to persuade the people of West and Equatorial Africa to accept a new form of autonomous relationship; the British attempt to induce Kenya and the Federation of Rhodesia and Nyasaland to adopt a multi-racial pattern of political evolution; and the Eurafrican movement to include non-self-governing territories within the new European Economic Community.

The idea of Eurafrica was born between the two world wars, but did not begin to acquire significance until after World War II. Its advocates had economic, political, and military motives. Certain leaders in weakened European countries began to conceive of a Eurafrica formula as a means of maintaining European political influence and prestige in African territories attaining independence. Another political motive was the belief that Eur-africa might save Africa from the Soviet threat.

The postwar emphasis on Africa's military importance was a new departure in geopolitical theory. Early geopoliticians, who stressed the role of geography in determining the politics of nations, paid little attention to Africa. The experience of World War II, however, led to a new appreciation of Africa's strategic importance, partly because North Africa served as one of the springboards for the defeat of Germany. The military importance of North Africa was particularly stressed by French writers. General de Montsabert, a French officer, contended in April, 1953, that in current military concepts Eurasia and Eurafrica had replaced the separate continents of Europe, Asia, and Africa.

The military considerations prompted a number of postwar efforts to develop Eurafrican defensive arrangements. A notable African Defense Facilities Conference met at Nairobi in August, 1951, to review ways and means of facilitating communications and the movement of troops and military supplies in eastern and central Africa. Britain, France, Belgium, Italy, Portugal, Southern Rhodesia, and South Africa were the main participants, with Ethiopia also represented and the United States having an observer present.

Although the emergence of independent African states killed any prospects of a Eurafrican defense organization, it did not entirely destroy the possibility of some kind of a Eurafrican economic organization. Despite similar psychological obstacles, economic cooperation and organization were more promising because of the intense aspirations of African leaders for economic development of their new countries. In the beginning, at least, many of the new states were willing to participate in the Common Market of the European Economic Community (EEC) which went into effect on January 1, 1959.

The basis for linking the overseas territories to the Common Market is found in Article 79 of the European Coal and Steel Community Treaty, extending to all members the preferential measures with respect to coal and steel enjoyed by any member in its own overseas territories. Other plans for Eurafrican economic cooperation can be found in the Overseas Working Group of the OEEC and in the Strasbourg Plan of the Consultative Assembly of the Council of Europe.

Under the provisions of the Rome Treaty of March 25, 1957, the six nations of Little Europe "'established among themselves a European Economic Community" (EEC), based on a Common Market to be gradually implemented over the next 12 to 17 years. The possibility of linking the overseas territories to the Community was raised at an early point in the Treaty negotiations, and eventually became a condition of French agreement. Articles 131 to 136 relate to the association of "non-European countries and territories which have special relations with Belgium, France, Italy, and the Netherlands." Specific arrangements for this association are spelled out in an accompanying five-year Implementing Convention. A development fund provided for a total of $581.3 million, to be contributed to the development of the overseas territories over a five-year period.

The Common Market, it will be noted, covered French, Belgian, Italian, and Dutch territories, but did not include British, Portuguese, and Spanish territories or the independent states. The early hostility of Africa's independent states to the Common Market again revealed a conflict between psychological and economic factors. In the United Nations General Assembly in the fall of 1957, a heated discussion arose over the possible effects of the European Economic Community on non-self-governing territories. A controversial resolution on the subject was opposed by Western Europe and the United States. The American Delegation contended that (1) it would be premature to attempt to deal intelligently with possible future effects of the Common Market; (2) the Common Market would "prove to be a contribution to the economic development of the African territories concerned, on a basis of equality and mutuality of interest"; and (3) the details of the operation of the Common Market still remained to be worked out and the General Agreement on Tariffs and Trade Organization (GATT) was the only proper forum for the discussion of these details.

The anticolonial group, however, would accept none of these arguments. They contended, among other things, that (1) the Common Market might have an adverse effect on infant industries in Africa; (2) links with the metropole might make African territories suffer during economic declines in Europe; (3) the Common Market would hurt the trade of non-self-governing territories outside the European Economic Community, and might have an adverse effect on the economies of African states bordering the Common Market territories; (4) the reduction of tariffs in African countries might jeopardize African fiscal structures; and (5) the Common Market would discourage investment from countries outside the European Economic Community. In addition to the economic contentions, the anticolonialists placed heavy stress on certain political arguments, that (1) the Common Market was a violation of the right of self-determination in that the non-self-governing territories were not consulted regarding their association with the European Economic Community; (2) the absence of any provision regarding freedom of movement in the associated countries and territories of workers from member states might bring a flood of Europeans into Africa; and (3) the Market was incompatible with the principle of paramountcy of indigenous interests, set forth in Article 73 of the United Nations Charter.

In an attempt to refute these arguments, the administering authorities asserted that (1) the arrangement would open up a market of 180 million people; (2) African countries could establish their own tariffs; (3) the investment fund would bring new capital; (4) Africans were consulted about the establishment of the Treaty and would be regularly consulted in the future; (5) it was untrue to say that the association of non-self-governing territories in the European Economic Community would keep them from attaining independence; (6) to discuss the matter was a violation of Article 2 (7) of the U.N. Charter; (7) it was a bad precedent for the U.N. to discuss treaties before they were ratified; and (8) the anticolonial attitude in this case was a threat to the principle of regional cooperation.

With the exception of Guinea, however, all the former French colonies and trust territories have maintained their association with the EEC since independence, as have Somalia, the Congo (Leopoldville), Burundi, and Rwanda. British negotiations with the EEC for full membership in 1962 opened up the possibility of association for former British colonies and remaining dependencies. Uganda, Tanganyika, and Kenya, as well as Ghana and Nigeria in West Africa, all rejected the idea of association; Sierra Leone indicated that it would consider association. At the end of 1962, however, the three East African territories were ready to negotiate with the EEC on a bilateral basis for entry of certain of their products.

During 1961 and 1962, the associated African states negotiated with the EEC for a new convention of association, more in keeping with their independent status. Under the new convention of association, agreed upon in late 1962, the 18 independent associated countries would receive $730 million over the next 5 years, while the remaining dependent territories would receive $70 million. Under the new convention, the privileged arrangements that the former French territories had with France, whereby France bought all their crops in guaranteed quantities and at prices well above world markets, are to disappear. Of the $730 million in aid, $500 million is to go into general development and $230 million is to be used to ease the awkward transition between the old guaranteed prices and those on the world market.

The present tenor of African nationalities, with its emphasis on neutralism and positive nonalignment, has largely vitiated the military aspects of Eurafrica. Events have also demonstrated that political influence—a slippery concept that is difficult to measure in any case—is not necessarily linked to institutional arrangements. On the other hand, the economic aspects of the European-African relationships have a more clearly discernible impact. Although far short of constituting a Eurafrican community, these arrangements have an economic value that most of Africa's present leaders are unwilling to ignore.

THE SHAPE OF AFRICA'S POLITICAL FUTURE

The immediate future of Africa is that of a continent of independent states, each working out its own destiny under African leadership. The formal structure of these African states will tend to follow the line of the metropolitan countries to which they have in the past owed their allegiance. Similarly, the boundaries of each of these new nations will have the characteristics of the boundaries of the separate colonies or subcolonies organized by the metropolitan countries during the colonial period. Each of these countries will be "independent," in the limited meaning of that term in modern world affairs. That is, each will select its own governors, determine its own internal organization, and establish its own external relations. The basic question for the future is, however, the dual one of the character of the relationship between the political structure and the economic system, and the relationships that these independent nations will develop with the major powers.

A Communist Africa? Our knowledge of other areas indicates that people don't just "go Communist." Force rather than ideology is the ultimate determinant of Communist success. What is needed is a hard core of Communist intellectuals with efficient political machines, backed by armed force. In most of Africa, it is doubtful whether the Communists can develop this kind of position, at least in the foreseeable future.

Perhaps American policy should therefore be based less on the fear that Africa might go Communist, and more on the conviction that the influence of the U.S.S.R. as a great power will inevitably rise in Africa. Khrushchev's new "keep smiling and keep them neutralist" tactics seem flexible enough to achieve far more for Soviet power and prestige than the doctrinaire Stalinist call for Communist revolutions. This Madison Avenue "soft-sell" technique becomes all the more effective when combined with the $531.7 billion of Soviet loans (through 1961), distributed among eight African countries, normally with an interest rate of only 2½ per cent.

A Democratic Africa? In his *Modern Democracy,* Carl Becker pointed out that democracy has flourished for a relatively short period in history, and only in societies which (1) were either small in size or had means of communication sufficient to create the necessary solidarity of interest and similarity of information over large areas; (2) were economically prosperous, or at least had a certain measure of economic security; and (3) had a citizenry capable of understanding inevitable conflicts of interest and willing to reconcile divergent opinions. These conditions are not likely to exist in most of Africa in the foreseeable future. Though the old African tribal chiefs-in-council were often quite democratic, the political units now emerging are not small groups of tribesmen who know and understand each other; they are relatively large states made up of many peoples with differing customs, traditions, and languages.

Numerous observers are now advancing the somewhat ingenuous contention that Africa will be democratic if one does not insist on too strict a definition of democracy in the "Western style." A variation on this theme holds that benevolent despotism will be necessary in the new democracies during a "transition period" while society is readjusting itself to cope with the problems of the new freedom. However, this does not fit Becker's definition of democracy, the essential test of which is that "the source of political authority must be and remain in the people and not in the ruler." Almost all of the new leaders in Africa envisage their leadership as tutorial in nature, their mission that of educating their people, not of responding to their desires. Regardless of our feelings about this kind of political system, it may be well for the West to recognize this fact.

Pan-Africanism and Nationalism

The first loyalty of Africans is to Africa; it is to the forces inside Africa—African nationalisms and Pan-Africanism—that we must look if we are to understand the shape of Africa's future politics. Born of a common subjugation and discrimination, and nurtured by a common struggle to freedom, Pan-Africanism has evolved since its inception in 1900 at the hands of American Negroes and West Indians until the movement was taken over by Africans after World War II. Chiefly a movement of English-speaking Africans, Pan-Africanism found its prime advocate in Kwame Nkrumah of Ghana. The French territories, grouped together in the two vast federations of French West and French Equatorial Africa, are more recent converts.

While Nkrumah has pressed for the political unification of all African states, most other African leaders have been a little reticent in their desire to surrender their recently acquired independence. All African leaders give at least lip service to Pan-Africanism, but most envisage pan-national cooperation rather than political unification in the immediate future. Numerous groupings of African states have appeared in the years since 1958, including the Guinea-Ghana, then Guinea-Ghana-Mali Union, the *Conseil de l'Entente* (the Ivory Coast, Dahomey, Niger, and Upper Volta), the Mali Federation, the Brazzaville group (all former French colonial territories save Mali and Guinea), and, in East Africa, the Pan-African Freedom Movement of East, Central, and South Africa (PAFMECSA). The two most important groups that have emerged, aside from the Brazzaville group, are the Casablanca and Monrovia groups. Disputes over policy in the Congo, and the right of Mauritania to independence, crystalized divisions between African states into their present form, and various issues such as Algerian independence (where the dispute was one of form rather than substance) have led to the maintenance of these groups. In early 1963, however, prospects for a merger of the two groups seemed promising.

But even if a single group should emerge, it is unlikely that this will result in any more than international cooperation within an institutional framework such as the Inter-African and Malagasy Organization. It would appear that there are too many obstacles to political unification on a federal or even confederal basis: Africa's vastness, coupled with the rudimentary state of its transportation and communications, its cultural and historical diversity, its differing colonial heritages (notably the different European languages with which they have been endowed and are forced by circumstances to maintain), competitive economies, and the personal ambitions and rivalries of various African leaders. There are also real differences in outlook among African states as to the nature of post-colonial links and relations with the former metropole; this conflict can perhaps be seen most clearly in the arguments of the associated and nonassociated states over the EEC. But perhaps the most important obstacle to Pan-Africanism lies in the particularistic nationalism of each territorial entity. The questionable economic viability of many of these states has been insufficient to bring about federations, and the recent dispute over a soccer game, for example, which led Gabon and the Congo (Brazzaville) to break "athletic relations," is an augury of the unfortunate possibilities of a provincial nationalism. On the other hand, the efforts of the Brazzaville group to bring about a reconciliation between the two states speaks well for African cooperation.

One key to understanding these Pan-African manifestations lies in the "feelings" they inspire. One of Ghana's intellectuals believes that the common people of British and French West African territories feel a sense of unity, despite the personal rivalries of some of their leaders. A variation of this idea has been expressed by James Baldwin, a peripatetic American Negro who was an observer at the first International Congress of Negro Writers and Artists, in Paris, in September, 1956. As the Congress debate wore on, he wrote, it became clear

> that there *was* something which all black men held in common, something which cut across opposing points of view, and placed in the same context their widely dissimilar experience. What they held in common . . . was the necessity to remake the world in their own image, to impose this image on the world, and no longer be controlled by the vision of the world and of themselves held by other people. What, in sum, black men held in common was their ache to come into the world as men. And this ache united people who might otherwise have been divided as to what a man should be.

The congress Baldwin described was a cultural conference at which declarations of political views were supposedly out of order. But Alioune Diop, the opening speaker, referred to it as a kind of second Bandung.

The questions discussed at the Paris Congress revealed some of the political undertones of cultural Pan-Africanism: "What are the essential qualities and enduring values of our Negro-African inheritance? How can it best be developed and renewed? How can we be ourselves? How can we make use of European ideas, institutions, and techniques, without becoming their prisoner —without ceasing to be African?" The conference ended with a resolution to engage "all black men in the defense, the illustration, and the dissemination throughout the world of the national values of their people." As Diop expressed it in his final remarks, black men must define themselves "instead of always being defined by others."

In view of the determination of African leaders to resist all foreign domination, Americans should develop a more relaxed attitude designed to show that we respect the right of Africans to make up their own minds. A relaxed attitude does not imply a do-nothing policy. It means that in our educational exchange, information, technical assistance, economic aid, and other activities, we should be intelligent enough to make generous provision for Africa, but humble enough to avoid pushing our own ideas. It means thinking less about what Africa ought to have and more about what Africans are likely to want. We must not succumb to cynicism if new states fall short of democratic ideals. Africa has already proved that we must expect surprises and learn to roll with the punches. We must further realize that our power to influence the course of events is limited, and that today's policy may be out of date tomorrow. And the American people must learn to appreciate that the peoples of Africa are not inferior, but only different. In the thoughtful words of an unusually perceptive observer, the missionary-explorer David Livingstone, Africans are "just such a strange mixture of good and evil as men are everywhere else."

ECONOMY

4. The Character and Prospects of African Economies

ELLIOT J. BERG

After the winning of political independence, two problems move to the center of the African stage: political integration and economic development. The two are obviously related. Leaders of the new states know they cannot create modern nations without the resources that economic development makes available. They must build more roads, schools, and hospitals, not only because their people want these things, but because without them there can be no national construction, no replacement of local feelings by wider allegiances.

The immediate post-colonial years in other parts of the world, particularly in Asia, were not notable for economic achievement. Many observers see a desperate decade or two ahead for Africa, or at best a period of stagnation. Obstacles to rapid growth in Africa are enormous, and there are many question marks about African ability to overcome them. But the picture is not without its brighter features, and the pervasive pessimism which characterizes much contemporary discussion of Africa's economic future is not altogether justified by the facts.

In this paper we will examine some important factors in Africa's economic prospects. The focus will be on internal factors. The basic question of future price trends for African commodity exports is not considered, partly because it is discussed elsewhere in this volume, partly because the pace of Africa's economic advance will depend more on internal factors than on terms of trade changes.

The Pattern of Economic Development

The Brevity of Modern Economic Contacts

The modern economic history of Africa is extremely short. Except for North Africa, which had long been in economic contact with Europe and the Middle East, Africans lived in near economic isolation from the outside world until very recently. South of the Sahara, there were only four points of contact with the outside as late as 1880: the ancient trans-Sahara trade between the western Sudan and North Africa; European trading posts on the western coast of Africa; Arab settlements on the east coast; and the European settlements on the southern tip of Africa.

Goods and ideas had trickled into Africa for hundreds of years through these points of entry, but they had little impact on the lives of most Africans. South Africa had moved further in the direction of intensified contact than other areas, although before diamonds were discovered, in 1869, it was not much different from the rest of Africa. Subsistence agriculture occupied many of its white residents; in the 1870's, sheep raising was their predominant income-earning activity. Penetration inland had taken place only to the depth of some 150 miles.

West Africa, with its ancient trans-Sahara trade, had in some ways a more intensive experience with money economy than had South Africa. Important commercial centers such as Kano, scattered throughout this part of Africa, impressed European explorers in the early eighteenth century. The West African slave trade also led to the development of active monetized sectors, towns like Whydah (in Dahomey) and Lagos (in Nigeria). African trading groups were to be found all along the coast in the late 1800's; by 1860, peanuts were exported from Senegal, and rubber and palm products from Ghana and Nigeria. Trade in East Africa was probably less substantial than in West Africa. Though Livingstone saw evidence of trading activity in addition to the slave trade, markets were generally less prevalent in East and Central Africa than in the West, and experience with the money economy appears to have been much less intensive.

By 1880, then, Africa was a continent of subsistence production—that is, production for self-consumption rather than for sale in markets. European dealings with Africa for over three centuries were based mainly on the trade in slaves and did not require European movement beyond the coastal areas; they failed to work any fundamental transformation in African societies. When the European powers carved up Africa, they found economic systems that had undergone few changes in basic structure for as long as men could remember. Until 1900 or so, occupation of the area, political consolidation and the establishment of settled administrations absorbed most of the colonizers' energies. But from the turn of the century, economic matters began to claim major attention.

The Growth of the Money Economy

It is widely believed that not much happened in African economic life until after World War II. The report of the International Bank Mission to Nigeria, for example, speaks of the "leisurely pace of the pre-war economy." But development before World War II was hardly leisurely either in Nigeria or in other African areas. Indeed, the rate of economic change and growth from 1900 to 1930 was relatively rapid by most criteria. World War I slowed it down somewhat, and the depression of the 1930's even more. But the performance of most African economies over a period of some 60 years has been remarkable.

It is hard to measure long-term rates of growth because long series of national income data exist for only a few countries. Between 1911 and the mid-1950's, the national income of the Union of South Africa grew at a rate of about 4.5 per cent a year. In the Congo, from 1920 to the mid-1950's the rate was over 4 per cent a year. For a shorter span of time, the years 1923 to 1939, it has been estimated that Kenya's economy expanded at a rate of about 2.7 per cent a year in real terms. For at least these countries, then, the rate of economic growth over the past few decades has been among the highest in the world.

Export statistics indicate a similar rapid expansion in much of Africa. In the decade before World War I, the value of exports doubled in French West Africa and in Nigeria, more than quadrupled in Ghana, Kenya, and Tanganyika, rose over sixfold in Nyasaland, and increased more than tenfold in Uganda. Even more impressive is the expansion of the 1920's. The value of exports rose by at least 200 per cent in most of the continent during the 1920's. It doubled in Ghana and Nyasaland, tripled in Northern Rhodesia, Uganda, and Tanganyika, quadrupled in Kenya, rose five times in French Equatorial Africa and the Belgian Congo, about eight times in French West Africa, and over fifteen times in Nigeria.

The buoyant expansion of the 1920's came to an abrupt halt at the end of the decade. The Great Depression dealt Africa a staggering blow; export prices plummeted and the pace of economic change slowed markedly. The 1930's were a decade of retrenchment in most parts of the continent, at least during the first half of the decade; government services were cut, employment fell, land brought into production for the market was turned back to the subsistence sector.

The rhythm of growth of the 1920's was recaptured and in many cases exceeded after World War II. The years between 1947 and 1960 represented for most of Africa a period of tremendous economic expansion. The export sector paced the advance. In value terms, exports in many African countries were between ten and fifteen times greater in the late 1950's than they had been in the late 1930's, whereas general price levels rose only about three times over the same period. Investment also increased markedly after 1946. In French Africa, for example, more public capital assistance was received from France between 1947 and 1958 than in the previous fifty years of the French presence. While the rate of increase was perhaps more spectacular here than in some other areas, it was impressive in most, and Africa as a whole did better than underdeveloped areas generally. Rates of gross capital formation—the proportion of national income invested in fixed capital—exceeded 40 per cent in the Rhodesias during some years, were in the neighborhood of 30 per cent in the Belgian Congo throughout the early 1950's, and were less than 15 per cent in only a few countries. These capital formation rates, moreover, understate the true rate of investment in most cases, since they generally exclude peasant investment in cash crop agriculture.

Three main factors account for the rapid rate of growth of the postwar decade. First, world prices and market conditions were generally favorable for Africa's exports, despite some weakening of prices in 1954 and in the late 1950's. High world prices created greater private incomes for both export crop growers and wage earners, and larger flows of income which could be taxed away (through export duties and marketing board surpluses) and used for development purposes. Secondly, high earnings and optimistic expectations (as well as the inflow of European immigrants into white-settler Africa) led private individuals and business firms to undertake new investments, and encouraged the reinvestment of earnings by established firms. Finally, a new urgency to development arose due in part to the "New Deal" which typified postwar colonialism. The most notable examples were in the Belgian Congo, where more than a billion dollars were invested under a ten-year plan (1950–59), and in French West Africa, where public investment during the years 1947–57 (mostly provided by metropolitan France in the form of grants) reached nearly a billion dollars (1956 value). In the Congo, as in English-speaking Africa, most investment came from internal sources, though the British colonies in Africa were helped by grants from the half-billion dollar Colonial Development and Welfare Fund established in 1946 and by U.K. government loans.

Beginning about 1958, a new and less hopeful phase began for many African countries. Prices of some of Africa's chief exports (notably coffee and cocoa) fell sharply, and rates of growth of export earnings declined; in some cases export earnings stagnated or even fell. Political independence or turbulence had inevitable effects on capital flows. In the Congo during 1959 and in 1960 there was a massive hemorrhage of private capital, and South Africa in 1959 was also shaken by large-scale capital flight. In East Africa and Southern Rhodesia there were the same tendencies, though on a smaller scale. Everywhere the enthusiasm of private capital for African investment has diminished. The result of all this has been a general slowing down of economic growth in the past several years, though continuing increases in the volume of exports have in most countries offset price declines and maintained the level of export earnings. Considering these price movements and the fact that the years since 1957 have witnessed political transformations of unparalleled magnitude, it is remarkable that the economic transition has been as smooth as it has.

Forms of Development

Economic development took different forms in different parts of Africa. Everywhere, however, it involved either the activation of unused resources or the transfer of resources out of subsistence agriculture into money earning activity. The two general models of economic development into which most African countries fit are:

1. Economies whose base is either mining or European agricultural production. In these countries development occurred by the relatively large-scale inflow of capital from abroad into mining and agriculture. Generally non-African settlers are found in these countries (although not invariably; in the Congo, for example, there was a substantial European agricultural sector but few real settlers). In these countries, the African has entered the money economy primarily as a wage earner. Typical of this group are the countries in North Africa, South Africa, Northern and Southern Rhodesia, Kenya, the Congo, and the Portuguese areas.

2. Peasant-producer economies, where development has been by African peasant production of cash crops for export. In these economies there are relatively few large-scale expatriate enterprises, few or no European settlers, and relatively few African wage earners. The role of the European in these countries has been essentially that of a trader or administrator. Most of West Africa and Uganda fall into this category.

These categories are simplified models. Not all countries fit easily into them. Guinea, for example, has a mineral export sector of growing importance since 1960; of its chief export crops, coffee is produced by African peasants, bananas by European and Levantine planters. Tanganyika, similarly, has a relatively large plantation sector (sisal), but its coffee is peasant-grown. Liberia's rubber is mainly produced on expatriate plantations, but there is a growing African planter group.

Despite such cases, the broad distinction is useful, and reflects a number of important factors. The proportion of Europeans tends to be substantially greater in the mining-expatriate agriculture economies. South Africa, of course, has the greatest number of Europeans—about 3 million; Southern Rhodesia had 270,000 Europeans (in 1960) to 3 million Africans; Northern Rhodesia, 73,000 to 2.4 million Africans; the Belgian Congo (in 1959), 110,000 to 13 million Africans. Elsewhere (with the exception of Angola, which had 110,000 Europeans and 4.5 million Africans in the late 1950's), the proportion of Europeans is much smaller: in Ghana, 7,000 to 7 million Africans; in Nigeria, 15,000 to 50 million Africans; in Nyasaland, 9,000 to 2.9 million Africans. Senegal, with almost 50,000 Europeans to 2.3 million Africans, and the Ivory Coast, with almost 15,000 to 3 million, are the peasant-producer countries with the highest proportion of Europeans.

Capital investment throughout most of the colonial period was concentrated in the mining expatriate agricultural economies. According to Professor Frankel's calculations (*Capital Investment in Africa*), South Africa was the site of some 42 per cent of the total foreign investment in Africa south of the Sahara between 1880 and 1936. The two Rhodesias received another 18 per cent, the Belgian Congo 11 per cent, Kenya and Uganda together about 4 per cent. Ghana and the French West African territories received less than 3 per cent each.

The incidence of wage earning is substantially greater in the mining-expatriate agricultural economies. In South Africa and Southern Rhodesia, over one-quarter of the resident African population is in "modern" paid employment; in Kenya, Northern Rhodesia, and the Congo the proportion is about 10 per cent; in most of the rest of the continent it is below 5 per cent; and in Nigeria and the former territories of French West Africa it is about 2 per cent (or 4 per cent, if we include Africans working for African farmers).

The figures of national income distribution are probably the clearest indications of the differences between the two groups of countries. In South Africa, Northern Rhodesia, Kenya, and the Congo, less than one-third of the total money income generated in the late 1950's was African income; this indicates the large portion of total market activity in the hands of non-African factors of production. In Nyasaland, Uganda, and most of the West African countries, African incomes are about two-thirds of total money income.

Finally, the countries differ in the proportion of African income derived from wage-earning. In South Africa, the Federation of Rhodesia, and the Congo, between 65 and 90 per cent of the aggregate money income accruing to Africans comes from wages. Even in Kenya, which is mainly agricultural, over 80 per cent of African money incomes in the late 1950's was earned through wage employment; in Nyasaland, in 1958, about 65 per cent. In Uganda, on the other hand, only about 25 per cent of African money income is derived from wages, and in Ghana, probably less than 20 per cent.

These differing forms of development have some obvious consequences for Africa's future. The economies that rest on a mining and European agricultural base are generally richer, more industrialized, and have had higher rates of capital formation in the recent past; their national output has in general grown faster than that of the peasant-producer economies. They also have generally denser networks of social overhead capital. At the same time, the "enclave" character of these economies is more marked and they are politically less developed. The peasant-producer countries have a more even racial distribution of income, a wider participation of Africans in economic decision-making, and more political experience. Peasant-producer economies are thus in one sense more resilient: They are less exposed to withdrawal of expatriate skill and capital; they are more "African." At the same time, their economic institutions are less complex, and hence more manageable.

CHARACTERISTICS OF AFRICAN ECONOMIES

Despite great diversity, most African economies share certain common characteristics. They are mainly agricultural economies. They all have large subsistence sectors. They are all "open" and most are specialized in the production of a few export commodities. In the modern sector of the economy non-African capital and skills predominate; the continent is particularly poor in trained human resources. Economic development has been unevenly distributed geographically within countries. Most of Africa, finally, remains relatively underpopulated.

The Primacy of Agriculture and the Dominance of the Subsistence Sector

In most African countries, between 80 and 90 per cent of the population is found in rural areas engaged in agriculture. As column (2) of Table 1 shows, agriculture accounts for between one- and two-thirds of national output, except in the Central African Federation, where it is only 20 per cent, and in South Africa, where it is 12 per cent. Mineral production rivals agriculture only in the Rhodesias, the Congo, and South Africa while manufacturing generates 10 per cent or more of the national income only in South Africa, Morocco, Tunisia, Southern Rhodesia, the Congo, and Kenya.

Within the agricultural sector, subsistence farming remains the predominant activity. According to United Nations' estimates, in the late 1940's over 70 per cent of the land under African cultivation was in subsistence crops, and less than 10 per cent in crops wholly for export. Estimates for the late 1950's still indicate that more than half of the African agricultural area is devoted mainly to subsistence farming, though there are very wide differences between countries: In the peasant-producer economies of West Africa, well over half of the cultivated land is probably now given over to production for the market.

What is true of land resources is equally true of labor. Most Africans spend most of their time bound up in the village econ-

TABLE 1
Gross Domestic Product by Industrial Origin
(in per cent)

	Year	Agri-culture	Of which Subsistence Agriculture	Mining	Manu-factur-ing	Con-struc-tion	Trans-port and Commu-nication	Com-merce	Services (including Public Utilities)
	(1)	(2)	(3)	(4)	(5)	(6)	(7)	(8)	(9)
Senegal	1959	27		2	9	4	4	27	28
Ivory Coast	1960	54		1	4	4	5	32	1
Ghana	1958	60–65	30–33	4	3	4	15	29	8
Nigeria	1958	63	30–33	1	2	11	15		8
Sudan	1958/9	58			2	8	14		19
Ethiopia	1959	62	50		2	3	5	13	15
Congo (Leopoldville)	1958	31	12	16	10	4	9	7	23
Federation of Rhodesia and Nyasaland	1958	20	9	14	12	8	6	16	24
Kenya	1958	42	25	1	10	4	8	13	22
Uganda	1956/9	67	27	1	4	3	3	10	12
Tanganyika	1958	65	41	4	4	3	7	7	11
Tunisia	1955/58	32		4	11	4	8	20	20
Republic of South Africa	1959	12		13	25		8	12	31

Source: *Economic Bulletin for Africa*, II, No. 2 (June, 1962), and national accounts, various countries. Totals of more than 100 per cent are due to rounding.

omies. In the continent as a whole, there are probably no more than 10 million Africans who work for wages during any part of the year. Only in southern Africa is there more than 10 per cent of the population engaged in modern wage-earning employment. In most of the continent, the greater part of these wage earners are migrant workers, only temporarily in paid employment, who return to the villages after a spell as wage workers.

The continuing predominance of the subsistence sector is indicated in column (3) of Table 1, which shows that in most African countries subsistence production accounts for between a quarter and a half of total output.

Export Orientation and Specialization

African economies are "open" or export economies in which a substantial proportion of what is produced for sale is exported and many non-food consumer goods are imported. Only the northern and southern tips of the continent, with their relatively dense European populations, have well developed internal markets. Elsewhere, between 25 and 60 per cent of marketed production is exported.

These countries tend to send abroad only a narrow range of goods, almost exclusively raw materials in unprocessed or semiprocessed form. Thus Senegal, Mali, and Niger are almost totally dependent on peanuts, which make up over 80 per cent of the value of their exports. Cocoa and coffee provide 75 per cent of the Ivory Coast's export earnings, cocoa over half of Ghana's. Copper exports are 90 per cent of Northern Rhodesia's sales abroad. Some countries have a somewhat more diversified list of export commodities: Nigeria (peanut products, palm products, cocoa, tin); the Congo (copper, coffee, cotton, cobalt, tin); Southern Rhodesia (tobacco, asbestos, gold). And some other areas have brought new exports into production in recent years: Liberia (iron ore, in addition to rubber); Guinea (processed bauxite, in addition to coffee, bananas, and iron ore); Gabon (manganese and iron ore, in addition to wood products). But most African economies remain very narrowly based.

The Predominance of European Capital and Skill

Except in the agricultural sectors of the peasant-producer economies, the African role in modern economic life has been restricted to the provision of unskilled and semiskilled labor, petty trading, and some handicraft production. In the private sector, the entrepreneurial role, management, and high-level technical skills—all of these have been the near monopoly of non-Africans. This was true everywhere until very recent years, and remains true in much of East, southern, and Central Africa.

The private non-agricultural sector of most African economies consists of a cluster of expatriate enterprises, usually large in size, small in number, and international in character, surrounded by a constellation of smaller enterprises—small manufacturers, transporters, and trading firms—sometimes African in management but most commonly managed by members of immigrant communities—Syrians, Lebanese, Greeks, Levantines, and Asians (particularly in East and Central Africa). Thus in the Congo several dozen large, diversified firms (and through financial control, one firm in particular—the *Societé Générale de Belgique*) centralize control over a large segment of the modern economy. In Northern Rhodesia, two mining groups are in control of the copper-belt copper mines. In Liberia, Firestone and a dozen other firms (mainly American) are dominant. In the rest of West Africa, a handful of great trading firms (some of which have become more diversified organizations with interests in mining and manufacturing) control the channels of external and, to a lesser extent, internal trade (The United Africa Company, the *Societé Commerciale Ouest Africaine*, etc.).

The "commanding heights" in the money economy, then, are occupied by expatriate organizations even in peasant-producer countries, while in the mining and European agricultural economies the capital and management of the basic producing units are also non-African in origin.

Thus, positions of skill and decision-making responsibility in the private sector have until very recently been occupied exclusively by non-Africans. The situation was not much different in the public sector, until a decade ago. In Nigeria, for example, of the more than 3,000 senior posts in the civil service in 1951, less than 700 were held by Africans. Changes in this respect have come quickly in the past few years. As of the beginning of 1961, some 90 per cent of the senior civil service posts (those usually requiring some college training) in Western Nigeria were held by Africans. In Ghana, the proportion was comparable, though slightly lower. In French-speaking areas and in East, Central and southern Africa, the rate of Africanization has been much slower. In Senegal, in 1961, there were still some 1,500 French technical assistance personnel in the country, and in Kenya and Tanganyika less than 20 per cent of the senior posts of the civil service were held by Africans in 1961. In West Africa and the ex-Belgian Congo, Africans do most skilled work below the foreman level, but in East Africa many of these jobs are held by Asians, and everywhere expatriates fill many if not most of the lower level supervisory jobs—even in Ghana, in 1960, 300 out of that country's 900 foremen were expatriates.

Uneven Geographical Development

Within most African countries, the geographical pattern of economic development has been exceedingly uneven. It is a continent dotted with islands of modern economic development. In West Africa, for example, the region extending some 200 miles inland has moved rapidly into the money economy, whereas the vast interior regions (where most of the people live) have been relatively little touched by modern economic advance. The interior territories of French-speaking West Africa and the northern regions of Ghana and Nigeria have lagged behind the coastal areas both economically and socially. This pattern appears throughout the continent. The Buganda area in Uganda is well ahead of the rest of the country. The Gabon Republic, in ex-French Equatorial Africa, is much richer than the other parts of that area; two provinces, Leopoldville and Katanga, generated most of the income arising in the ex-Belgian Congo. In Northern Rhodesia, there is the copper-belt, and not much else; European farming areas straddle the railway, but most of the rest of the country remains untouched by modern communications and by modern economic activity. In white-settler Africa generally, economic development has largely bypassed the "native Reserves."

Relative Underpopulation

The African continent below the Sahara in general does not have any serious population problem. There are some areas where population presses on the land (parts of Kenya and Tanganyika, Ruanda, Burundi, Nigeria), and population growth is almost everywhere high, probably about 2 per cent a year. But land remains relatively abundant in most of the area.

It is not generally very good land. About one third of Africa's land mass is desert or semidesert, and much of the area is infested with tsetse fly, which makes it uninhabitable for men and beasts. Great areas are not well-watered. But even when account is taken of the low carrying capacity of African land under present technological conditions, it remains true that the continent is not overpeopled.

Thus, despite occasional famine in certain areas and chronic malnutrition in many, there is little rural misery of the kind found in much of the Middle East and parts of Asia. Recent publications of the Food and Agricultural Organization have claimed that in the decade of the 1950's, food consumption per capita declined in Africa. This is a dubious proposition; it rests on scattered and altogether unreliable estimates of food-production trends in the subsistence sector. Bad crop years in North Africa and flood and drought in Tanganyika in 1961 did lead to some difficulties in those areas. But there is no convincing evidence that the ordinary African today eats less food than he did a decade or two ago, and there is a great deal of evidence that some portions of the population are eating a more varied and abundant diet than ever before.

THE ECONOMIC PROSPECTS: VIABILITY AND GROWTH

The question is often raised about the new African states: Are they economically "viable"? Strictly speaking, the question has little meaning. Almost any political unit can be viable if viability means mere capacity to survive economically. In African conditions, with only scattered population pressure and an economy still largely subsistence-oriented, this is no real concern. If, however, by "viability" we mean something more—the capacity of an economy to maintain a customary or expected level of income, or to increase it—then clearly a number of African countries are not presently viable, and some may never be able to become so.

It is easy to be gloomy about the economic prospects for the new Africa. All the old obstacles and restraints to development remain: an ungracious nature and a delicate agriculture; an imperfect commitment to money-earning in the villages; inadequate transport facilities in a large land mass; uncertain resource endowments; low levels of money income, and hence limited domestic sources of saving; uncertainties about price prospects for African exports on world commodity markets. To these have been added new and different problems: administrative inadequacies arising from rapid Africanization in the face of terrible scarcities of technical and administrative abilities; political turbulence, with consequent capital flight or hesitancy of potential private investors; the new costs of sovereignty; some tendencies towards economic adventurism by new governments.

On top of all this, independence or its approach has unloosed powerful new ambitions. This can be seen in the new development plans which have sprouted in the post-independence period: Senegal hopes to find $370 million in investment resources over the years 1961–64, $200 million of which is public investment. Mali's Four-Year Plan anticipates investment of $250 million. Guinea's Three-Year Plan, founded in 1960, involves planned investment of $155 million; Nigeria's 1962–67 plan counts on $1.8 billion, and Tanganyika's Three-Year Plan on $67 million. Ghana's new Seven-Year Plan aims at government expenditure of $1.4 billion.

All of these plans have two features in common: They involve capital expenditures at rates substantially greater than that occurring in the recent past, and they rely on outside aid for at least half of their total investment resources. The Tanganyika plan is particularly illuminating. A World Bank Mission to Tanganyika in 1960 recommended a plan of $47 million. The Tanganyika government regarded this as too conservative, and increased its size by over 40 per cent. At the same time, Tanganyika counts on external loans and grants for more than 80 per cent of total planned expenditure.

Most of the new plans mention increases in real income of 3 to 5 per cent per capita per year. This is a substantial growth rate. Since population is increasing at a rate close to 2 per cent a year in most of the continent, and more in a number of countries, it means increasing aggregate income by between 5 and 7 per cent a year. Such a rate of economic growth is not impossible; output in Germany, Austria, Japan, Israel, Greece, and the Eastern European Communist countries grew at a rate of more than 6 per cent a year during the decade of the 1950's. In Africa, the Rhodesias and Nyasaland, during the latter half of the 1950's, had income growth of 6.8 per cent a year in the aggregate and 4.1 per cent per capita. But these are uncommonly high rates of growth. The Congo, during the extraordinary boom of the 1950's, expanded its output at an aggregate rate of over 5 per cent a year, or 2.5 per cent per capita. And total real output in Nigeria during the 1950's increased at about 4 per cent a year, which is a rate much closer to average African performance during these years.

To maintain, much less increase, these rates of growth during the decade ahead will be a strenuous task. In weighing the prospects, it is essential to emphasize that inter-country differences are very great: The economic prospects for the Upper Volta, Chad, or Nyasaland are hardly comparable to those of the Ivory Coast or Northern Rhodesia.

OBSTACLES TO GROWTH

The Scarcity of Trained Manpower

The experience of the Congo, left at independence without a single African doctor, lawyer, engineer, or army officer, dramatically brought the African manpower problem to world attention. Many African countries are better endowed with high-level manpower than was the Congo in 1960, but in all of them there exists a critical need to develop the skills and raise the level of education of their people. In all of Africa below the Sahara, there were in 1958 not more than 10,000 Africans studying in universities at home and abroad, and 6,500 of these came from Ghana and Nigeria. In the same year, only a few other countries had more than 200 students in universities. Since 1958, the rate of intake into universities has markedly increased, but a recent report on Nigeria stated that even if an educational program (which is far beyond Nigeria's present financial possibilities) were introduced, it would be more than a decade before that country could meet its normal needs for trained manpower from domestic sources. During the decade of the 1960's, Nigeria would have to import almost 7,000 man-years of secondary-school teachers—and Nigeria is educationally one of Africa's most advanced countries.

The problem of university-trained people is most striking, but the principal bottleneck is on the secondary-school level. In all of sub-Saharan Africa there were in the late 1950's only about 8,000 Africans graduating from general academic secondary schools, of which about 40 per cent were in Nigeria and Ghana alone. Vocational and teacher training school graduates swell the number, but it is still true that in the late 1950's more people graduated from Chicago's high schools than from all the high schools of Africa.

This scarcity of trained human resources is a major constraint on rates of economic development in Africa. It means that African governments lack the administrative ability to execute large and complex development schemes, and that governments and private firms must continue for years to import expensive foreign manpower. It means also that African countries must devote substantial resources to education and the development of skills. Although investments in education are productive, they involve reductions in investment in fixed capital. Investment in people, moreover, yields little increase in the output of society in the short run, at the same time that it adds a great and growing budgetary burden in the form of teacher salaries and school maintenance costs.

Until recently, primary education has received most attention, and this has created delicate problems of imbalance in educational systems. For the thousands of youths now graduating from primary and junior high schools, there are few places in high schools. Nor are these boys able to find the clerical jobs once open to primary school graduates. They thus remain idle, living with relatives and friends in town. To an important extent this is a transitional problem, due to the rapidity of change; but until agricultural employment or unskilled manual work is accepted as suitable for literate men, a serious potential social problem will exist.

There is something more. Relatively large portions of public revenues are already being devoted to education. In the southern regions of Nigeria, to take the most striking example, almost half of total government current expenditures now go to education. Few African governments spend less than 15 per cent, and in all of them the proportion is rising rapidly. Now a great step forward must be taken in the area of secondary and higher education, at potentially staggering cost. It has been estimated that in one West African country (Senegal) the total cost of turning out a primary-school graduate is about $350, whereas the cost of a secondary-school graduate (boarding school) is over $6,000. This illustrates the problem: At a time when most African budgets are already groaning under educational expenditures, tremendous new demands will arise due to the increase in secondary education.

Capital Scarcity

In order to increase money income in any country, it is usually necessary that the individuals or enterprises in that country set aside some portion of their current incomes for investment. This is not the only way that capital formation takes place. Every time an African farmer plants a cocoa tree or clears a new piece of ground for planting, capital formation occurs, even though it involves no "saving" in the conventional sense. But the setting aside of a part of current money income is basic to development.

In the postwar period, we saw earlier, many African countries experienced high rates of capital formation because of favorable world prices for African exports, loans and grants from colonial powers, and high rates of reinvestment of earnings by private companies in some of the countries. But for these rates of capital formation to continue and to increase, it is necessary that savings of Africans provide a larger portion of investment funds. The capacity to draw off significant amounts of savings from the domestic economy, however, is limited by the low level of African money incomes. Per capita average annual money incomes are less than $100 in most African countries, between $100 and $200 in some, and over $300 only in the Republic of South Africa.

Though these figures should be used cautiously, they are useful in indicating the difficulty of raising local resources for the financing of economic development. These difficulties are often exaggerated. In British Africa and the Belgian Congo, the respectable rates of capital formation over the postwar period were in large measure financed from domestic sources—in British Africa, mainly through levies on the export earnings of peasant producers. It is also true that, compared with peasant producers of export crops, much of the African population tends to be undertaxed, particularly the higher level African civil servant group and comparable employees in the private sector. Nonetheless, even with higher rates of taxation and with continuing levies on export crop growers, the possibilities for financing development from domestic sources are restricted by low levels of taxable money incomes.

Furthermore, it is worth emphasizing something that is often forgotten: A major economic problem in Africa is to induce men to shift their energies from "leisure" (non-income-earning activities) and subsistence production to income-earning activity. The possibility of higher levels of consumption is one of the major instruments for accomplishing this, so that potential incentive-destroying effects of taxation in the agricultural sector must be guarded against. The failure of Ghanaian cocoa output to expand more during the 1950's, for example, is not unrelated to the high rates of taxation imposed through marketing boards and export duties on the cocoa industry. Even the taxation of higher-level

African employees is subject to the restraint created by the existence of an international market in high-level manpower; high taxes on incomes of African technicians can add another element to the bundle of inducements that already encourages them to take jobs in other countries.

The Difficulties of Agricultural Development

Agricultural development is the key to general economic growth. Since most Africans are agriculturalists, and since land is relatively plentiful, expansion of agricultural incomes is the main way open to expand the local market. Furthermore, expansion and diversification of agricultural output is essential to any basic improvement of African health and welfare since, though adequately fed in terms of calorie intake, most Africans are badly fed. In particular, they lack protein, which reduces their general resistance to disease. The production and consumption of more protein-rich foods is thus indispensable for an improvement in the general health and well being of the majority of people.

Obstacles to increasing the quantity and diversity of agricultural production are formidable. First, African soils generally tend to be exceedingly delicate; it has been estimated that only about 10 per cent of the total land area of the continent can be cultivated without special attention. The lush forest areas, once regarded as endlessly fertile, are susceptible to leaching of chemical nutrients and to massive erosion when cleared and exposed to burning sun and hammering rain. This is equally true of the wooded prairie in the savannah regions, of which much of the interior consists.

Second, cultural or social factors obstruct agricultural change and growth. Under traditional forms of land tenure arrangements, land is held "communally"; it is also held in unconsolidated pieces; and where matrilineal inheritance patterns exist, fathers pass their improved land (cocoa farms, for example) to nephews, not sons. These patterns of landholding and inheritance tend to reduce incentives to improve land and, more important, lack of clear-cut ownership claims exposes land titles to uncertainty and makes it difficult to establish systems of agricultural credit.

Third, economic and technological obstacles exist. Foremost is the scarcity of transport and marketing facilities. The essential motor for the expansion of agriculture must be an increase in effort by villagers now devoting themselves to subsistence production, or to nonproductive activity. This cannot come about until there are ways for villagers to get their crops to market at relatively low cost, and marketing facilities which will allow villagers to purchase consumer goods conveniently and cheaply. While in some parts of Africa both transport and markets have been provided, particularly in the last decade, in many countries vast areas remain isolated. The presence of adequate transport is particularly significant with respect to the marketing of local foods; these tend to be heavy in weight and without low-cost transport, the return from their sale is not sufficient to stimulate production. Improved transportation, therefore, is a prerequisite to agricultural development.

Wider use of mechanization in agriculture is another frequent prescription. Experience with mechanized agriculture, however, has revealed serious pitfalls. Many African soils contain widespread rock formations, are particularly hard in texture, or have dense underlying root systems—all of which make the use of tractors and plows extremely hazardous. Visitors to the site of the famous Tanganyika Groundnut Scheme, where many of these difficulties were encountered, said it resembled a battlefield, strewn with wrecked and abandoned equipment. Some kinds of functions, moreover, are not readily performed by agricultural machinery perfected in industrialized countries; one of the major problems in large-scale African agricultural projects, for example, is the digging out of tree stumps, but no machine has yet been designed which can adequately perform this job. There is furthermore a great deal that is as yet unknown about the effects of mechanization on African soils. It is not even known whether continued plowing in tropical heat and moisture leads to declining fertility through oxidization of organic matter.

The economics of mechanized agriculture raises other questions. Operating costs of machinery are very high. Wear and tear in physical terms is great. There are few skilled drivers available, particularly drivers aware of the subtleties of machine maintenance. Maintenance costs for machinery are thus exceedingly high, partly because skilled labor costs so much, and partly because repairmen must often be brought long distances to repair damaged machines.

Finally, despite some growth of agricultural research and extension services, there is still a vast ignorance about much that is relevant to agricultural development: the nature of African soils, the long-term effects of plowing, the suitability and economics of fertilizer use. This lack of knowledge is one of the major factors blocking the expansion of African agriculture.

The Colonial Heritage

A number of obstacles to expansion arise from the peculiar set of ideas and practices passed on to Africans by the colonizers. This is a many-sided issue which can only be touched on here. But it is at least as important as most of the questions so far considered.

One feature of this heritage is an all-pervasive paternalism in economic matters. Everyone recognizes that in political terms a colonial system is profoundly authoritarian. What is not always equally recognized is that colonial economic systems, with a few exceptions and some differences in degree, are equally authoritarian. To an astonishing extent, economic policy in most of Africa has been paternalistic, *"dirigiste,"* anti-individualistic. As often as not, African peasants have been told what to produce, when and how to produce it, to whom and at what price it must be sold. Colonial internal economic policy in most African countries was typified by a passion for "order" and "organization" on the part of the officials responsible for economic policy. The freely competitive market was in general regarded with a sour eye. To colonial administrators it was a symptom of economic disorder to have two sellers where there might be one, or to have spirited competition between railways and roads; it was a symptom of conspiracy when retail prices rose. Markets had to be "organized" and the flow of commodities and labor "regularized."

The paraphernalia of state controls flowered almost everywhere, ranging from price supports and marketing boards to sales quotas, price controls, monopolistic allocations of sales and purchases, regulation of entry into trade and industry, provision of "rations" as part of wage payments, and compulsory "deferred saving" schemes of various sorts in the wage sector.

Economic controls were often ineffective for their explicit aims. But whatever their effect in determining the pattern of development, the world view from which the attempts at controls arose had important effects in shaping African economic attitudes. For one thing, it slowed the growth of a sense of responsibility among Africans. The competitive market, whatever its shortcomings, is a great educator; the countless decisions demanded of individuals in a market economy provide a training ground for the growth of a sense of individual responsibility. In Africa, traditional economic policy under colonial rule made the emergence of this sense of responsibility much more difficult than it would otherwise have been. It is probably no accident that English-speaking West Africa, where economic paternalism rested with a lighter hand, is characterized by a general vitality of economic behavior distinctive in the continent.

Perhaps a more significant consequence is that African elites bring to their new political responsibilities little warmth for or understanding of the operation of the market mechanism, and an implicit faith in the efficacy of economic controls. There are of course many other reasons why this is so, but the colonial economic tutelage is one of the more important ones. It is in part for this reason that so much African thinking on economic policy runs in terms of state enterprise, state control over production and marketing, "suppression of intermediaries," and so forth. The motives underlying these policies may be different, yet in one fundamental sense at least they represent a continuation of the past: They reflect skepticism and distrust of individual initiative in the free market. Having seen so little of it in the past, few African leaders are disposed to try it now.

Another aspect of the inheritance in attitudes relates to employee behavior in the wage-earning sector. In the colonial period, African wage earners, whether of low place or high, regarded their employers as separate and distant—as "they." This was of course hardly irrational. Non-Africans were in fact in control of almost all private and public economic power and decision-making. The colonial situation with its vast gap between the managers and the managed thus stunted the growth of a sense of common enterprise. This was reflected in careless work performance, cheerful neglect of the ordinary rules of machine maintenance, and a general lack of personal commitment to craftsman-like ideals. In the post-independence period this has led to serious problems on state-run enterprises, the railway system in Guinea having had particularly severe difficulties of this kind. For this reason, pleas for a "decolonization" of work habits have arisen.

Another facet of the colonial heritage is the wage structures left to independent African states. Where the supply of trained and educated manpower is scarce, the wages of trained people tend to be very high in comparison to that of unskilled workers. This is simply a matter of supply and demand, the demand for skilled and educated manpower is great while the supply is sparse. This would be enough in itself to create a very "wide wage structure." This natural situation is exacerbated in Africa because the educated people were lacking and it was necessary to pay the rates obtainable in European countries for skilled labor, plus some premium to compensate for the so-called discomforts and hazards of service in Africa. These already handsome base salaries were matched with a whole range of attractive fringe benefits—housing allowances, car allowances, long vacations in Europe, etc. This caused no particular problem so long as there were few or no Africans in comparable positions. As the colonial era came to an end and more and more Africans began to assume responsible positions, African replacements began to demand the same privileges which it was politically necessary to grant (with somewhat fewer fringe benefits). Table 2 suggests what this meant in terms of the wage structure. In these West African countries, a university graduate entering the civil service receives something in the order of five times the wages of the lower-paid civil servant; in the United States, the ratio is about 1.2 to 1.

TABLE 2

Civil Service Salary Structures

Monthly Rates in United States dollars, 1958

	Lagos (Nigeria)	Accra (Ghana)	Abidjan (Ivory Coast)
Primary or Middle School Graduate, Entering Rate	26.60	25.70	67.00
Secondary School Graduate	35.00	37.30	162.00
University Graduate	140.00	158.00	240.00

The consequence of this has been that as African governments assume power, one of the first tasks they find themselves faced with is that of "taming" civil servants. Civil service salaries are often taking enormous portions of the budget and it therefore becomes necessary to bring civil service wages, indeed the wages of all highly skilled people, into line with the general level of wages in the country. In most cases, it is the abundant fringe benefits that are aimed at; in 1962, the Ivory Coast, for example, eliminated housing allowances for senior civil servants. But the market forces of supply and demand tend to keep the highly skilled wage up, and habits of the past as well as political factors tend to restrict the possibilities for reductions.

Another aspect of the colonial heritage, peculiar to ex-French Africa, is a heavy dependence on direct subsidies from the metropole, especially since the end of World War II. The substantial development programs of the postwar years were financed almost wholly by France. The total of French grants and loans (most of it was in the form of grants) for investment purposes between 1947 and 1958 amounted to about 700 billion French francs. (Changes in the value of the franc and difficulties in finding an appropriate rate of exchange make it hard to put a meaningful dollar figure on this total; converted at the exchange rate of the mid-1950's—350 francs to a dollar—it comes to about $2 billion). It made possible a rate of capital formation in French Tropical Africa estimated at close to 20 per cent of national income. It also bred in some French-African political leaders an unwillingness to come to grips with some of the hard problems of financing development from internal sources.

Moreover, French Africa has traditionally been more intimately bound up in trade relations with the metropolitan country than other African areas. In the postwar period, some 70 per cent of total African trade has usually been within the franc zone. Because of high tariffs and exchange controls, Africans in these areas have been forced to buy consumer and capital goods from high-priced French suppliers, but as a counterbalance, African producers have enjoyed over most of the postwar period a protected market in France where they sell their crops at higher prices than could be obtained in the open world market. Over most of the past decade peanuts have enjoyed a price advantage between 10 and 30 per cent, and coffee about 20 per cent. This dependence has grown greater, not less, since political independence. With the collapse of the world coffee market after 1958, the French granted to the Ivory Coast, the main franc zone producer of coffee, a high degree of protection: Coffee from the Ivory Coast sold in France in 1961 at about twice the price that could be obtained on other world markets. All of this means that French African producers have grown up in a kind of hothouse atmosphere, isolated from the rigors of world competition.

Economic Ideologies

It was noted above that African thinking on economic policy has been in part shaped by the economic experience of paternalism under colonial rule. Even more important in determining economic policy is the "socialism" that so many African leaders proclaim. "Socialism" of one variety or another is indeed the dominant post-independence ideology. There are many reasons for its prevalence: the identification of capitalism with "exploitation" and with colonialism; the ideological tendencies absorbed by African students in metropolitan capitals, particularly in Paris; the belief (expressed by President Nkrumah, for one) that capitalism is "too complicated" for Africa; the view that socialism is more compatible with the communal traditions of African society.

African varieties of socialism are generally extremely vague. Only one thing is clear about them; they are heretical. For Mr. Senghor of Senegal, socialism is a mixture of Marxism, Christian humanitarianism, and Negritude. President Sekou Touré of Guinea, who has been most articulate in these matters, rejects a basic tenet of orthodox Marxism—the class struggle; in Africa, he says, there is only one major conflict—between the colonizers and the colonized. All Africans are united in this struggle.

"African socialism" expresses itself mainly in two concrete ways in the area of economic policy. First, with respect to agricultural development, interest tends to be placed on large-scale, state-run efforts, such as the state farms Ghana is experimenting with at the present time, and the rural enterprises envisaged in Guinea's planning. Secondly, and more important, there is an inclination to give the state a much greater role in internal and external commerce through the creation of state trading corporations. Ghana and Senegal have begun to make some halting steps in this direction, and in Mali state trading firms now control some 30 per cent of the total external trade.

This development has gone furthest in Guinea. Shortly after independence, Guinea set up state trading firms which were to monopolize the export and import trade. Though local retail trade was to remain much as before, it was not long before it, too, was under the control of the state monopolies. State retail outlets and widespread price regulations were introduced. The result was disastrous. Meat and fish disappeared from markets in Conakry, the capital city; fishermen sold their catches in neighboring Sierra Leone, where prices were better, and cattlemen from Northern Guinea shipped their animals across to Liberia. Mismanagement of state stores led to waste on a large scale. Soon corruption began to appear. By March, 1961, organized trading had practically ground to a halt. Conakry was badly provided with products of the interior; the interior lacked imported goods, which were piling up on the docks in Conakry. It was finally necessary to mobilize all available trucks in the country to bring goods to the countryside. Shortly thereafter the state trading agency was decentralized and private traders given a freer hand. But the damage was enormous, in morale as well as in money.

Certain conclusions emerge. The expanded role of the state demands trained personnel in large numbers. They are not present in most African countries, and are not likely to be present for at least a decade. Under colonial rule, the role of the state had been great; about half of the wage-earning labor force was employed by the state in most African countries. The operation of the state sector, even in its pre-independence size, is a task to strain all the meager resources in trained manpower which the African countries possess; to expand the role of the state into new areas is to place an intolerably heavy load on the cadre of trained men available and to invite trouble. Management of the economy under African conditions is exceedingly difficult, for reasons including the long frontiers over which smugglers can roam at will, and the universal difficulties of regulating the economic behavior of intractable peasants and crafty traders. The common tendency to give the state more than it can do with its present resources in manpower is one of the most ominous features of the African landscape.

Political Decomposition

One of the accompaniments of independence has been the breakup of political and economic units created under colonial rule. In 1960, the Belgian Congo was a centralized state with six administrative provinces. In 1963, some twenty states appear to be emerging in a Congolese federation with a central government of uncertain powers. In 1958, the eight territories in French-speaking West Africa and four in Central Africa formed part of the federations of French West Africa and French Equatorial Africa. In 1963, there are twelve independent states.

Economic disengagement has paralleled these political changes. The vast free trade area of French-speaking Africa broke up after 1958. The common currency, airlines, and research organizations of British West Africa have disappeared. The economic unit that was formed by the Central African Federation is undergoing changes as a result of the withdrawal of Nyasaland and Northern Rhodesia. Only in East Africa do the pre-independence economic institutions (a common market and the Common Services Organization) persist.

Although the real economic consequences of these changes are usually exaggerated, they have had several negative effects. First, with larger political units many public services could be provided more cheaply per person, and all could be manned more efficiently when government was able to draw on a wider labor market for its personnel. Secondly, the replacement of larger political units with smaller ones has entailed some competitive expenditure in the military and diplomatic fields, increasing the charges of sovereignty. Thirdly, in the larger political unit and the larger market associated with it, there may have occurred a larger volume of private investment than would otherwise have taken place. Manufacturing enterprises in Senegal, for example, were established with a capacity designed for a wider, all-French West African market. The same is true in Kenya, Southern Rhodesia, and Leopoldville Province of the Congo. Similarly, certain public investment decisions could be coordinated so as to reduce duplication of investment—notably in statistical and research facilities and in general administrative overheads.

These have been the general costs of the new political arrangements. There have been more specific costs for some of the individual states involved. As was to be expected, the relatively poorer states have suffered most. Formerly they relied on subsidies from their richer partners; many now subsist only with greater subsidies from abroad. This is particularly the case in the ex-French territories; presently the French government is financing not only the development expenditures of most of these states, but part of their ordinary expenditures as well. Dahomey is a good example. Its 1961 budget was in the neighborhood of $25 million, but only $18 million could be raised from local resources—just enough to cover the salaries of civil servants. The situation in Nyasaland is not much different. Once outside of the Central African Federation it will have to depend on Britain for the $8 million to $11 million annual subsidization it formerly received within the Federation.

The real or imagined advantages of larger economic units

and the fact that so many Africans give at least verbal support to Pan-Africanism account for the variety or organizations that have sprung up in the past few years aimed at bringing about closer economic cooperation: The Organization of African States, the Union of African and Malagasy States, the Ghana-Guinea-Mali Union, and others. The "Casablanca" powers have taken steps towards the formation of a common market and a common military command. But it is the eighteen ex-French states in the African Malagasy Union (UAM) that have gone furthest. They have created an economic organization (*Organisation Africaine et Malgache pour le Coopération Economique,* or OAMCE), a defense organization, a tourist organization, and a common airline. They are making efforts to extend their cooperative ventures in such areas as joint development banks, shipping lines, common diplomatic organization at the United Nations and elsewhere, and common recruitment of technicians.

These inter-African organizations notwithstanding, the main trend has so far been toward less rather than more actual economic integration. The old French African free trade area has been disrupted by unilateral commercial policies; the barriers between franc and sterling zone countries have not notably diminished—the lowering of barriers between Ghana and the Upper Volta in 1961 is the only exception.

There are a number of economic reasons why closer economic integration has not yet become more of a reality. First, cooperation between ex-French and ex-British African countries has been hindered by the continuing connection of the ex-French territories with the franc zone and the European Economic Community. The rules of the game within the franc area and the EEC preclude departures in monetary and fiscal policy and restrict action in the area of commercial policy; associated countries cannot, for example, form customs unions with nonassociated African neighbors. Secondly, French-speaking Africans desire to retain the privileges they enjoy through association with the EEC (economic aid and tariff preferences on tropical products), and this limits the extent to which they are disposed to cooperate with nonassociated African countries in economic matters. Finally, economic integration is not unambiguously advantageous for all combining states or regions. The record of the common markets or free trade areas with which Africa has had experience suggests the following observations. (1) A relatively rich agricultural country is not likely to benefit from economic union with its poorer neighbors, since it will have to help pay for the public services of the poorer partners, and not have much compensatory benefit in the form of larger markets for manufactures. This was the experience of the Ivory Coast in the old Federation of French West Africa, and to a lesser extent of Gabon in ex-French Equatorial Africa. (2) The advanced member state which has an industrial head start will benefit; its industrial sector will grow faster than that of its partners, and its income will rise faster. This is what has happened in Kenya (within the East African customs union) and in Southern Rhodesia (within the Central African Federation).

In both types of situation there is likely to be reluctance on the part of some states to continue the economic association; for example, the Ivory Coast has been the least willing of any West African state to join in closer economic arrangements with other states. There has been considerable grumbling in Uganda and Tanganyika that Kenya has gotten most of the benefits of economic union, while Uganda's and Tanganyika's industrialization has been slowed. Although there is probably not much substance to the latter charges, the fact that they exist is important.

All of this means that economic unification is not likely to be easy, at least in the near future. This in turn means that a number of the African states will remain "client" states forced to rely on outside help to maintain themselves. The French-speaking states of the interior (Mali, Niger, Upper Volta, Chad, Central African Republic, etc.), the small coastal states (Togo and Dahomey), the Central African states of Ruanda, Burundi, Nyasaland, the High Commission territories—these territories cannot be maintained at their present levels of living, much less develop in new directions, without support from somewhere. They will either continue as wards of the world community, or they will find their place within a wider African grouping of states.

FAVORABLE ELEMENTS

The list of pitfalls and obstacles to be overcome by African countries on their way to economic modernization is long. It is no surprise that there are many observers who see a dim economic future for most of the continent. But the scales are not without their counterweights.

Population

There is first of all the population factor. The fact that land exists in relative abundance in much of the continent is an advantage of great significance. Aside from reducing the harshness or misery of village life, the life that most Africans still lead, it means that the "population explosion" is less of an economic menace than elsewhere in the underdeveloped world. In parts of Africa, increased population may in fact stimulate the growth of income per head; it can increase the intensity of cultivation in certain areas and render certain investments (notably in roads) more economical.

Furthermore, the existence of adequate land tends to exercise a levelling influence on African societies, giving to most of these societies a relatively equalitarian cast. This is not true in some areas; in the hierarchical societies of the Sudanese belt of West Africa, and in parts of East and Central Africa, class structure tends to be fairly rigid. But sharp and durable division in traditional societies tends to be a function of land scarcity; where each man has access to land, such divisions form with difficulty. Related to this is the fact that most of Africa, unlike most of Asia and Latin America, lacks a landlord problem; there is no need to confront the economic and political dilemmas created by a system of landholding which leaves most of the land to the few.

Economic Structure

The economic structure of most African countries is such as to create an apparently high degree of resiliency, an ability to weather extraordinary economic and political upheaval. For example, partly because much of the wage-earning labor force in the continent consists of "migrant" or temporary workers, slowdowns in economic activities and urban unemployment, such as occurred after 1958 in many African countries, can be absorbed without inordinate shock. Men return earlier to the villages and fewer come out for employment. The rest are cared for by extended family members or by friends in town. In short, the absence of a large, permanently committed work force has prevented the emergence of a true proletariat of any size, and in a period of turbulence and change this introduces an element of flexibility which does not exist in many other parts of the world.

Similarly, the "enclave" character of some African economies has itself provided an element of stability in times of disturbance. In those countries where economic or political conditions deteriorated after independence, expatriate enterprises were able to maintain output. In Guinea, FRIA, the large bauxite processing firm, began production and expanded its output in the years following independence, at a time when the surrounding economy was faltering badly. And more striking still, many enterprises in the Congo, although sitting on a powder keg of potential inflation and civil disorder approaching anarchy, have managed to do surprisingly well; exports from the Congo in 1962 were only about 25 per cent below those of several years earlier—an extraordinary performance, given the political circumstances.

Quality of Leadership

The quality of African political leadership is another positive factor. This may seem a surprising statement. African leadership has been subject to considerable criticism, and even derision. There seem to be too many parades, too much conference-going, too great a diversion of energies to political exercises in general. African cabinet ministers are accused of living too stylishly, of moving too eagerly into the villas of their former overlords or building new and better ones, and of driving too often in shiny new Mercedes autos. Corruption and graft have been pointed to and, as the recent Coke Commission Investigation in Nigeria made plain, they have occurred on a large scale. Everywhere there seems to be a marked penchant for setting up unprofitable national air lines. Africa is filled with talk of rapid industrialization and forced draft growth, much of which seems unrealistic.

Yet the fact is that on the whole African political leadership is dedicated, honest, moderate, responsible, and intelligent. It is indeed a remarkably able leadership, far more responsible than might have emerged, given the pace of political change, the degree of training and preparation available to Africans in many parts of the continent, the nature of the colonial situation and the psychological scars it has left, and the political premium on radicalism. It is a leadership practically everywhere dedicated to rapid modernization; nowhere in the continent is there to be found a ruling group which aims at slowing the modernization process, as in other parts of the undeveloped world. Similarly, if corruption has appeared in a number of African countries, it is worth emphasizing that it rarely exists in Africa on a scale comparable to that found in many parts of the world, particularly in Asia. Vigorous efforts, moreover, are made to deal with it. In how many countries of the world could a Coke Commission fail to find dirty linen in abundance?

It is in the area of economic attitudes that, as we saw earlier, the most serious questions have arisen regarding the new political elites. Nonetheless, except in the Congo, moderation and restraint have so far prevailed even here. In fiscal and monetary policies, most African leaders (the Congo provides a notable exception) have roared like lions but acted more like lambs—partly, it is true, because they have had no alternative. Their development plans have in practice contained relatively little fat or waste. Showplace schemes are few. Industrial white elephants on the Asian scale are relatively unknown. The counsels of the cautious have most often been followed; transportation, education, agriculture, and public health have been at the center of public investment programs. Economists can look with justifiable concern at the growing current obligations required to maintain expanding educational systems, but these are responses to political pressures not easily contained. It is well to recall, moreover, that in the past four or five years more Africans have won access to secondary and university education than in all the previous years of the colonial presence, and that the rate of output of university graduates is already two or three times greater in some countries (Kenya for example) than was predicted only two or three years ago.

Finally, most African leaders have attacked with courage and vigor problems which all European observers have decried for decades. They are trying to reform work habits, and have urged more effort, responsibility, and dedication on all their people. They are preaching the virtues of manual labor in general and agricultural work in particular. They are pushing technical and vocational training. They spend little—usually less than 3 per cent of their budgets—on military expenses (except in Ethiopia). They have introduced, at least in a number of cases, tax reforms from which the colonial regimes shrank. They have for the most part adopted policies of wage restraint and have tried to breach the citadel of privilege in the civil service. They are trying to spread literacy and the gospel of modernization throughout their countries. Lethargic leadership is rarely a problem. Indeed, the real danger is that they will try to do too much, too quickly.

Resources

The fragility of African agriculture and the difficulties inherent in its improvement were described earlier. But the agriculture sector is not without its promise. First, it is essential to remember that the African villager has been an economic orphan, neglected for decades by economic policy-makers. Outside of the peasant-producer countries, and even there to a certain extent, he was given little encouragement and few of the instruments required for his entry into the modern economy. Transport facilities remain very rudimentary in most African farming areas. Marketing facilities are far from abundant. Price policies for export crops and consumer goods have often been such as to discourage the growth of incentives for the expansion of agriculture. In Central and southern Africa, hesitations to improve land arose from fears of European expropriation.

Second, the knowledge of African soils and general agricultural potentials remains rudimentary. Increased research will certainly open up new possibilities. At the same time, the widening of primary education may well increase the receptivity of ordinary villagers to new ideas for the development of money-earning agricultural activities within the framework of village society.

Third, and most important, African agriculture is at such a low stage of technology that relatively slight changes can have enormous impact. It is not in large-scale change of a revolutionary sort that the greatest future expansion can be anticipated, but in the small things—new seeds, new rotations, the application of known fertilizers, the use of hybrids and better strains, the control of plant disease through spraying, etc. Examples of such changes abound. In Ghana, the recent introduction and spread of capsid spraying on a wide scale has probably led to a 15 per cent increase in cocoa yields at low cost. In parts of southern Africa, animal fertilizer has vastly increased corn yields on nearly exhausted lands—in some cases by as much as 300 per cent. Experiments with chemical fertilizers in parts of West Africa have shown comparable results. There is enough evidence, moreover, to show that African farmers will adopt these changes when they are convinced of their efficacy. There is in fact general evidence that the African peasant is prepared to work small revolutions if he is given the means and the incentive. For example, in the Ivory Coast, where roads were slashed through the forest region so that African cocoa and coffee farmers could go to work readily and market their crop, coffee output tripled in ten years, making the country the world's third largest coffee producer. Kenya promises to give a similar testimony to peasant energy; in the last few years there has occurred remarkable expansion of African-grown export crop production, as a result of new attention shown some African farmers by the Kenya government.

With respect to non-agricultural resources, the variation in the continent is so great as to rule out brief or easy treatment. Bauxite is scattered throughout Africa, and potential water power is abundant—an estimated 40 per cent of the world's total. The potentials for aluminum production are therefore widespread. Rich iron ore deposits have been found in various parts of West Africa; manganese in Gabon and Ghana; iron in Liberia, Guinea and Southern Rhodesia; copper in Mauritania; oil in Nigeria, Libya and the Gabon. It would be risky to base future predictions on great mineral strikes now unforeseen: It is not certain that the African subsoil contains a great store of mineral wealth. But it is a fact that geological exploration is in its infancy in much of the area, and even places formerly believed to be geologically uninteresting have offered surprises. It was not, for example, until after World War II that rich new gold fields were discovered in South Africa—one of the best-prospected areas in the world. As late as 1950, it was the sober opinion of the most technically competent people that the Sahara was devoid of profitable minerals. And in the mid-1950's, Libya was cited in a United Nations report and in textbooks on economic development as an example of a country without resources, and hence a country which could not go anywhere; Libyan oil today flows abundantly.

One good mineral find is no guarantee of rapid growth. But it can provide a big push. In a land of 2 or 3 million people it does not take much of a mineral find to light up the future. And minerals hold out special hope because mineral exploration and exploitation is perhaps the only activity in Africa that receives sustained interest from private enterprise in the non-Communist world. African governments, moreover, whatever their ideological complexion, are increasingly disposed to encouraging private capital in this area.

The Size of States and Economic Development

Africa now has more nation-states per square mile than any other continent. This is a dubious distinction. We noted earlier some of the inconveniences it causes, but the existence of numerous small states instead of larger units is probably a much less substantial barrier to economic growth than is commonly supposed.

It is not at all clear that over-all growth is adversely affected by the kind of political and economic breakup that we have witnessed in Africa since 1958. The poorer countries suffer, but the richer ones gain—they are able to devote to their own development resources formerly allocated to their poorer partners in larger units. In these circumstances, over-all growth for the two areas together is retarded only to the extent that: (1) public and private capital flows to the separate states are smaller than they would be if the two states were joined together, and (2) the productivity of public investment in the poorer states is greater than the productivity of investment in the richer ones. The first possibility is likely, but there is little evidence that it has in fact occurred, and the experience of the Ivory Coast and Gabon (two of the best-endowed states in ex-French Africa) certainly does not bear it out; they have probably had more, not less, private and public investment since their separation from the former federations. The second possibility is most unlikely. In fact, the presumption would be to the contrary—that public investment in the richer area will almost surely, at present stages of development, yield greater returns than investment in the poorer area. A road in the Ivory Coast, for example, will tend to increase output more than a road in the Upper Volta. What this means is that it is not inconceivable that over-all incomes will grow faster in the absence of larger units than with them; but this income will be distributed differently.

Coordinated planning and investment policy—one of the major possibilities pointed to as an advantage in larger political units, is not demonstrably easier within such units than outside of them. This is particularly the case when the larger unit is a federation. It is thus not obvious that in federated Nigeria investment coordination occurs to any greater extent than in fragmented ex-French Africa. Within the common market area of East Africa, each of the three territories tries to lure its own new industrial investment.

The smaller size of markets, one possible consequence of economic separatism, is not necessarily a heavy burden. The effect of small market size on investment and growth depends on the way average unit costs of production vary with output. Put another way, it depends on the extent to which "economies of scale" can be realized by larger output. If a relatively large volume of output is needed before a plant can produce near its top efficiency, market size clearly sets sharp limits on industrial development. If, however, costs per unit of product do not fall much with larger outputs (once a relatively small volume of output is reached), then larger markets are not so vital. Now it is obvious that in some lines of production economies of scale are substantial—in steel or autos, for example. Economists are in disagreement as to the significance of scale economies in many lines of production, but studies in industrial countries suggest that in much manufacturing industry, and particularly in the kind of light manufacturing which presents the greatest possibilities for African countries in the near future, relatively small plants are not notably less efficient than large ones. It is, therefore, only under certain conditions that small market size due to political and economic fragmentation will retard industrial development: (1) if economies of scale exist in the production of specific goods which might be manufactured locally, and potential national markets are too small to absorb that volume of output which allows firms to produce near their lowest cost points, and (2) if at the same time these firms are prevented by tariffs or other means from marketing part of their output in neighboring countries because competing firms have been created there. While these are not unlikely circumstances, neither are they universal.

Finally, many of the more obvious costs of small state size can be dealt with without important political reshuffling—through common diplomatic representation, joint ventures in the banking and transport area, etc. Nor is it clear that the higher administrative costs normally attributed to small state size are avoided when political integration occurs; federation, which is the only realistic alternative in most of Africa, is not famous for low-cost administration.

None of this is to say that small state size is beneficial. It is simply that it is not obvious that such political arrangements need be serious obstacles, at least at present, to over-all growth. What political separatism does is to make clear the precarious position of the poorer regions of the continent. It also has the negative effects noted earlier. But none of these is of overwhelming significance.

Foreign Aid

The flow of foreign economic aid has not been reduced with independence; indeed, it has increased. The European Economic Community countries made available to African states associated with them a total of $580 million in the period 1958–62, and have since promised an additional $730 million for the period 1963–67. This is in addition to substantial bilateral aid: $675 million from France in 1962, $109 million from West Germany, $152 million from the United Kingdom, $45 million from other Western European countries, and $123 million from other sources (the International Bank, the United Nations, etc.). To this should be added the indirect aid from France in the form of price supports for exports; under EEC arrangements these are to be extended until 1967, though at lower levels, at which time they will be abandoned. The pace of United States aid has markedly increased in the past several years. Between 1946 and 1962 the United States provided a total of $1.7 billion of aid in all forms to African countries, but in 1962 alone U.S. aid in all forms amounted to more than half a billion dollars. The Soviet Union similarly has contributed to African assistance programs. Total Soviet and other bloc aid commitments between 1959 and 1962 amounted to $678 million, having grown from very little ($3 million) in 1959 to $236 million in 1962. The total foreign aid inflow to Africa in 1962 was close to $2 billion, which is more than the average annual aid during the booming 1950's. Thus the world community has continued to provide support on a large scale. Despite a certain restiveness among all aid-giving countries, it is not likely that Africa will be abandoned in the decade ahead.

AFRICAN ECONOMIC DEVELOPMENT IN SUMMARY

To set out these more hopeful facets of the African economic picture is not to underestimate the magnitude of the obstacles to African development, nor to ignore the darker trends and

tendencies which cloud the future. The specter of political turbulence, absent nowhere in the continent, is particularly ominous
in the states of East, Central and southern Africa. Political experience in these areas is slight, the ranks of African elites are
thin, there are acute tribal differences in some areas, and little
political consensus among existing parties. The price prospects
for some African commodities on world markets remain uncertain, even after discounting the endemic pessimism of economists
and African political spokesmen. The dangers of economic adventurism, particularly by overloading the state with tasks that
it is not now capable of performing, are real. The threat of
reductions in foreign economic aid, arising in part because of
dissatisfaction with the political dividends yielded by aid to
Africa, cannot be dismissed; the Clay Report, which urged
sharp curtailment of U.S. aid efforts in Africa, and some recent
trends within the Communist bloc which indicate similar Soviet
views, are not to be taken lightly. Finally, there is the danger
that African political leadership will not recognize the potentials
of peasant agriculture and will strike out in other directions;
this would put the development prospect in another light.

But the economic obstacles, the policy shortcomings, the er-
rors, the economic illusions circulating in the continent—these
have received wide attention. Other considerations of a more
hopeful nature are also present, and emphasis on these is needed
in order to put into better perspective the economic outlook for
Africa. For the prospects are by no means uniformly bleak. In
many important respects, they are better for Africa as a whole
than for either Asia or Latin America. Latin America must
contain and channel a rising storm of social revolution. Much
of Asia has population pressures and/or military and social
problems crippling to its development efforts. These are not
African concerns—at least not yet.

All of this means that it would be a tragic mistake if we in
the U.S., and in the West generally, began an economic withdrawal from Africa on the grounds either that the economic
or political returns are too small. In the long run, the economic
and political pay-off for our aid efforts may well be greater in
Africa than anywhere else.

5. The African Economy and International Trade

ANDREW M. KAMARCK

THE ECONOMIC IMPORTANCE OF AFRICA

Past Relations with the United States

Before World War II, Americans took little interest in Africa and—economically speaking—we were right to be indifferent. Africa was relatively unimportant to the United States as a supplier of industrial raw materials and unprocessed foodstuffs. According to United States trade statistics, our total imports from all of Africa were around $50 million a year, or about 2 per cent of total imports. (Our actual imports were somewhat higher, perhaps $100 million a year, since some came by way of Europe and according to prewar practice appeared in our statistics as imports from Europe.) As a market, Africa was also not important: Our total exports to Africa were only a little more than $100 million a year. American investments in Africa were very small. By World War II, a total of around $6 billion of capital from outside had been invested in Africa south of the Sahara. Of this, the United States share was under 3 per cent ($160 million). In North Africa, our stake was also comparatively tiny—we had only $40 million invested, mostly in Egypt.

By 1961, our total imports from Africa had grown to $670

million and had doubled in relative importance, but were still under 5 per cent of total United States imports. Our exports to Africa in 1961 were 8 times the prewar level, but around 4 per cent of our total exports to the world. Our total investments in Africa had gone up six-fold to around $1.4 billion, and were 2 per cent of our total investments abroad. The general picture of economic relations with Africa is as follows:

	Before World War II	1961
	(in millions of dollars)	
Annual Imports	100	670
Annual Exports	100	830
Investments	200	1,400

Africa supplies the bulk of our consumption of diamonds (industrial and gem), columbium, cobalt, corundum, pyrethrum, arabic gum, wattle bark and extract, palm and palm kernel oil; at least half of our consumption of cocoa, cloves, vanilla beans, extra long staple cotton, mahogany logs, long fiber asbestos; and around a quarter of our consumption of antimony, chrome, graphite, manganese, tantalum, goat and kid skins, papain, and canary seed.

In the world outside the United States, the two areas that are important for us as sources of raw materials, now and in the future, are the other countries in the Western Hemisphere and Africa south of the Sahara. Africa has largely supplanted Southeast Asia in importance to us. Since I work on Africa and not on the Western Hemisphere, I am sorry to have to say that the Western Hemisphere is still immensely more important to the United States than is Africa. Total United States trade with the Western Hemisphere is about ten times greater than with all Africa (Central America alone buys more from us than does the whole of Africa), and United States investments in the Western Hemisphere are twenty times greater.

The absolute figures on our trade with Africa and our investments in Africa look fairly impressive but are relatively not very important. The commodities we get from Africa are of course very useful, and even indispensable for some purposes, but it would be possible for the American economy today to get along without them. Our total spending on African commodities is barely more than one-tenth of one per cent of our gross national expenditures, and Africa buys about the same percentage of our gross national output.

The loss of the American imports from Africa would undoubtedly cause hardship to some industries, raise costs somewhat to others, and might cause heartbreak to girls who would have to get engaged without receiving a diamond ring—but one can scarcely claim that Africa is economically vital to us at present. We could get along without African commodities and African markets with an imperceptible ripple in our standard of living.

Trade with Europe

Africa's position vis-à-vis Western Europe is quite another matter. Western European exports to Africa are nearing $5,000 million a year; this is about one-fourth of the value of goods that Western Europe exports outside of intra-European trade. Western European imports from Africa are about $4,000 million a year, or about one-fifth of total imports from outside Europe. As poor as Africa is, she is a better market for Western Europe than is the United States. We provide more European imports than does Africa, but Africa is vitally important to Europe as a source of raw materials and unmanufactured foodstuffs.

This importance to Western Europe makes Africa indirectly important to us. The United States has spent around $30 billion since the war to help make Western Europe economically viable. To the extent that the economic development of Africa aids Europe, it also interests us.

The African economy also affects us in another indirect way. A large part of the economic development in Africa is complementary to or competitive with development in the other countries of the Western Hemisphere that are main suppliers of primary products: The prosperity of the copper producers in Chile (and the copper price in the United States) hinges on the expansion plans of the copper mines in Northern Rhodesia and the Congo. The ability of Brazil, Colombia, and Guatemala to buy American products already is strongly influenced by the policy pursued by African coffee planters. All this is true even though the bulk of the African output continues to be marketed in Europe and only marginal amounts come into the American market or supplant Latin American exports in Europe.

Future of United States–African Economic Relations

The real direct economic interest of the United States in Africa is in the future. Africa as a source of supply for raw materials and as a market for United States goods is destined to play a more important part in the American economy of the future. Basic changes, both in the United States and in Africa, will bring this about.

World War I changed us from a debtor to a creditor country. World War II resulted in perhaps as important a shift in our position in the world economy: from being a large net exporter of raw materials we have become a large net importer. We have outgrown our raw material base and are increasingly forced to look abroad for raw materials. We can scarcely call ourselves a "have-not" nation in raw material, but we have definitely become a "haven't-enough" nation. The United States consumes roughly half of the total industrial raw material output of the non-Communist world, and one-tenth of what we consume is imported. Our dependence on imports of raw materials is expected to continue to grow.

MAJOR COMMODITIES IN AFRICA'S INTERNATIONAL TRADE

It is this change in the fundamental position of the American economy that is increasingly making Africa of interest to us as a future supplier of industrial raw materials and unprocessed foodstuffs. Africa has been called "the continent God kept in reserve." It is becoming more and more necessary to find out what is in this reserve. Africa, the second largest continent, is large enough to make the chances good that needed resources can be found which may or may not be immediately exploitable.

By World War II, Africa had already become an important world producer of a number of commodities, and she continues to maintain or improve her position in these. She continues to produce around 90 per cent of the world's output of diamonds; two-thirds of the palm oil, sisal, and cacao; around half of the manganese and chrome ore; one-third of the antimony and phosphate; and one-tenth of the wool. In copper, her output has climbed (as has her relative position) to more than one-fourth of the world's total. According to figures cited by Sir Ronald Prain, chairman of Rhodesian Selection Trust, one of the two biggest African copper producers, Africa's known published reserves are estimated at about 60 million tons of copper content or just under one-third of the non-Soviet world's holdings. African gold output has gone up from 40 per cent of the world's prewar output to around 70 per cent now; in coffee the fraction of the world market supplied by her has tripled and is now 20 per cent of the total.

The strongest impulse to the development of Africa has been the interest in her mineral deposits. Diamonds and gold sparked and made possible the modern development of the Republic of South Africa; gold and copper of the two Rhodesias; and Katanga copper of the Belgian Congo. The African minerals provided, and continue to provide, the strongest attraction for outside capital. It is largely to the exploitation of her mineral resources that Africa owes the building of her ports, railways, and towns. In the immediate future, in addition to water power, the particular resources that have become of real interest to American and European capital are still mostly minerals: African bauxite, oil, uranium, manganese, and iron ore. Whereas most of the past mineral development has been in southern and Central Africa, some of these newly attractive resources are located in West Africa, particularly in the French-speaking countries. For the first time, this opens up for these nations the possibility of a more rapid development and one more largely financed from their own resources.

TABLE 1

Principal Exports and Imports in United States Trade with Africa, 1961*

(in millions of dollars)

Exports of United States Merchandise to Africa

Machinery	192
Foodstuffs	151
Autos, tractors, parts, and accessories	80
Textiles, semi- and finished manufactures	55
Chemicals and related products	40
Iron and steel and metal manufactures	26
Petroleum and products	19
Wood and paper	17
All other exports, including re-exports	84
Total	664

Imports from Africa for United States Consumption

Coffee	136
Cocoa	113
Uranium	87
Ferro-alloys, ores, and metals	52
Crude rubber	39
Nonferrous ores and metals	34
Precious stones	25
Wool, unmanufactured	25
All other imports	122
Total	663

* Excluding Egypt.

Source: U.S. Department of Commerce, "Trade of the United States with Africa," World Trade Information Service, Part 3, No. 62-27.

Hydroelectric Power, Bauxite, and Aluminum

Economically speaking, aluminum is crystallized electricity. The abundant supplies of bauxite in Africa and the abundant possibilities of producing cheap electric power make Africa a natural site for producing aluminum. A number of companies recently appear to have reached this conclusion.

African water power has become of great interest for the

future. For centuries, Africa was a coast line and not a continent, largely because the river highways into the interior (such as were used in opening up America) were interrupted by rapids and falls as the rivers tumbled over the edge of the African plateau on their way to the sea. These rapids and falls give Africa greater hydropower potential than any other continent. A French estimate is that Africa has hydropower sites with a capacity of 200 million kw. This is equal to both Americas (75 million kw. each) plus Europe (50 million kw.). With most of the sites where cheap electricity can be produced already utilized in North America and Europe, what was a handicap for Africa is becoming an important asset.

In the former Belgian Congo, the Le Marinel hydropower station in the Katanga, with 250,000 kw. capacity, is equal to the largest in Western Europe. Power from it is being used by the copper, cobalt, and manganese mines in the Katanga. The power grid in the Katanga is interconnected with that in the Rhodesias. Power from Le Marinel, about 300 miles to the north, and from the great Kariba dam on the Zambesi River, 300 miles to the south, are both used by the Northern Rhodesian copper-belt mines and refineries. In exchange, in 1960, when the mines of the Katanga were temporarily cut off from their own power stations, power from Kariba kept them going.

The Kariba power project, financed by the World Bank and a consortium of banks and mining companies, started producing at the beginning of 1960. Kariba, with an ultimate capacity of 1.5 million kw., will be one of the ten largest power producers in the world and has already created the largest man-made lake in the world in the heart of the Rhodesias. It makes abundant, reasonably priced power available throughout the Rhodesias until around 1970. Among other uses, it provides power for the copper-belt in Northern Rhodesia (which is half owned by a United States-controlled company) and North American-owned chrome and asbestos mines in Southern Rhodesia. It also opens up the possibility of new electro-metallurgical or electro-chemical plants being established in the area.

The Owen Falls dam at the Nile outlet from Lake Victoria, with an ultimate capacity of 150,000 kw., is producing power which is being used to process minerals from the copper mines at Kilembe in Uganda, while another part of it is being exported over a 300-mile-long transmission line to Nairobi industries in Kenya. There is still surplus capacity available, and the Uganda Government is building transmission lines to the west and north that will make electricity available to most of the people of Uganda.

Inga, on the Congo River, potentially the biggest power project in the world, is still on the shelf. Inga would use part of the enormous energy wasted in the 150 miles of rapids of the Congo River—which has an annual flow several times that of the Mississippi at its mouth—as it tumbles through the mountains to the sea. At the proposed site alone, the potential has been initially calculated at around 25 million kw. This is 10 times the size of Grand Coulee. It could produce about as much power as all of Western Europe now consumes and at a mere fraction of the average cost in Western Europe. But even bigger than the problem of raising the necessary capital is the question: Who would consume the power? Before the independence of the Congo, the Belgian government was actively exploring the possibility of getting American capital to help finance and American industry to set up plants to use power from a proposed first stage of Inga. This would generate about 1½ million kw., and has been estimated to cost around $300 million.

Export of bauxite began from the Gold Coast (now Ghana) during the war, and large deposits have been found. Export is still small, and plans for the future utilization of these deposits in making aluminum in Ghana have been postponed until after completion of the Volta scheme, now under way, which is initially to make aluminum from imported alumina. Exports of bauxite began from Guinea in 1952. A group of American (Olin Mathieson), French, Swiss, British, and German aluminum companies have constructed a plant costing more than $100 million at Fria in Guinea to produce around a half-million tons of alumina a year from Guinea bauxite.

Part of the Fria alumina output goes to Edea in Cameroun where it is converted into aluminum using hydropower. This plant produced the first aluminum in Africa in 1957 and now

produces about 47,000 tons a year, making Cameroun the thirteenth largest producer in the world. The Volta project in Ghana,
on which work began in 1961, will be considerably larger. This
project consists of a dam with a reservoir to hold about as much
water as Lake Kariba and a power plant with an initial capacity
of 590,000 kw. and eventually of 880,000 kw. Power from the
Volta project is to be used for Ghana's general needs and to
produce aluminum in a smelter with an annual capacity of
100,000 to 150,000 tons of aluminum. The power project, costing almost $200 million, is being financed half by the Ghana
government and the remaining half by the World Bank and the
U.S. and British governments. It is to be finished in 1966. The
smelter, which is to be owned by American aluminum companies (Kaiser and Reynolds), and to cost well over $100 million,
is being financed with the help of a loan from the Export-Import
Bank.

Other aluminum projects which have also been actively considered in the past were on the Konkoure River in Guinea and
on the Kouilou River in the former French Congo. Since the
African projects are almost inevitably enormous, the capacity
of the world aluminum market to absorb such large new supplies
of aluminum tends to be an important factor in determining
when they can be built.

It is still much too early to make any estimate of how important
African aluminum may become in the world picture. A study cited
by GATT (the international trade organization, the Contracting
Parties to the General Agreement on Tariffs and Trade) indicates that by 1970 about 750,000 tons of aluminum must be
imported into the industrialized parts of the world—a demand
that African aluminum might meet. This is equivalent to about
a quarter of present world production. The projects being considered in Africa fit into the Paley Commission's suggestion that
"as far as security considerations permit, lower-cost aluminum
production facilities in Canada and possibly those along the
northern coast of South America and in Africa should be included in the pattern of future development of United States
supplies."

To sum up the discussion on African hydropower: It is quite

clear that African resources are very large and would probably be economical by most tests. It is also true that investment in Africa bristles with difficulties. Nevertheless, a firm in any industry in the United States or in Europe that is a consumer of large blocks of power (such as the aluminum, electro-chemical or electro-metallurgical industries) must now consider seriously either the possibility of investing in Africa itself or the likelihood that its competitors will take advantage of cheap African power.

Oil and Gas

Africa has become an important supplier of oil, in addition to its importance in providing hydroelectric energy and uranium. After years of search, oil has been found in Portuguese Angola (where an American company is active), Gabon, Nigeria, and the Sahara. Angola is apparently a small field and may produce around one million tons a year. In the Gabon, oil output has not reached a million tons a year and exploratory drilling is going on by a joint French-American effort. By 1961, Nigeria already produced oil at a rate of 2 million tons a year, and output is expected to rise fairly rapidly over the next few years. Further search for oil is underway.

All indications are that the Sahara field in Algeria and Libya is a major one—perhaps not as rich as the Middle East but ranking with the mid-continent field in the United States. One estimate put the reserves at around one billion tons of oil. In addition, large natural gas deposits have also been discovered. Saharan oil production and export is rising rapidly and had already reached 32 million tons in 1962. Active study is also being given to ways of exploiting the natural gas. The United Kingdom Gas Council is planning to import natural gas in tankers from Algeria. A rapid decision on the building of gas pipelines across the Mediterranean to Europe has, however, been held up as the result of new natural gas discoveries in Europe itself, notably in Holland and southern Italy.

The United States does not now have a vital need to import Saharan oil, though American oil companies are going into both the Algerian and Libyan Saharas and are actively looking for oil in Tunisia. The chief effect of North African oil on the United States will probably be its function as a source of marginal supplies, and through the impact it will have on the European market.

According to a Chase Manhattan study on the world oil situation, the position prior to the Saharan strike was that two-thirds of the oil reserves of the non-Communist world were in the Middle East. With coal output in Western Europe stationary, with practically all hydropower sources utilized, and with even a reasonably full development of nuclear power, the growth of Western Europe in the next generation would be primarily dependent on a growing consumption of oil. That is to say, European development is dependent on Middle East oil. The successful exploitation of Saharan oil thus greatly reduces the vulnerability of Western Europe to a shutdown of oil from the Middle East.

The United States can still get along without imports of oil, if necessary, by stepping up the drilling of more wells in known fields and by investing money in oil exploration to increase the rate of discovery. But the costs of finding and developing oil within the United States are steadily going up and, according to the Chase Manhattan study, it is becoming increasingly sound economically for us to import oil. We were still net exporters of oil in 1938, but in 1961 our net imports met one-fifth of our needs. Since the Saharan fields have become an important force in keeping down the price of oil abroad, they help hold down the cost of energy to us at home.

Uranium

Uranium was a significant export to the United States from the Belgian Congo since the war, when the Congo was our main source of supply. The Congo mine is now exhausted. In the last few years, uranium has become an important export of the Republic of South Africa, largely to the United States. South African exports in 1960 were over $150 million a year, and the Republic is the third largest producer in the Western world. An active search for uranium is now going on elsewhere, and the Gabon has already become a small producer.

Iron Ore

Iron ore is another item that is being exhausted; we are out-running our natural resources in a way that is pushing us toward reliance on imported supplies. From being self-sufficient before the war, we are now increasingly dependent on imports: In 1953, imports were 9 per cent of our total supplies and in 1961 they were about 25 per cent. We imported around 30 million tons of iron ore in 1961, at a cost of $250 million.

Liberia is now exporting over 3 million tons of iron ore a year to the United States and Europe, and by 1970 output may reach 15 to 20 million tons a year. Exports from Guinea and Sierra Leone to Europe each run 1 million tons a year. Algeria, Tunisia, and Morocco are also important producers and together export about 6 million tons of ore a year.

Currently, a new $140 million project is to come into produc-tion in mid-1963 to export 6 million tons of iron ore a year from near Fort Goraud, in Mauritania, by a company combining the French, English, German, Italian, and Dutch iron and steel industries. Bethlehem Steel is considering a project in the Gabon for production around 1970. A contract to mine and export 12 million tons of iron ore over a 10-year period from an iron moun-tain in Swaziland to Japan is to go into effect when a 137-mile railway to the coast from the mountain is completed in 1965.

AFRICAN DEVELOPMENT DEPENDS ON EXTERNAL FORCES

Dependent Economies

Africa is not only the least developed of the continents but also has the most dependent economy. The money economies in the African countries are primarily export-import economies; that is, they are dependent on international trade for their basic domestic requirements. Furthermore, they are able to sell abroad only one or two or at most three commodities in order to buy and import the whole range of needed modern commodities. (In Gambia, the classic case, peanuts comprise 97 per cent of total exports.) Rhodesia and the Congo each export well over one-half of the total of their gross national product; Ghana exports just under one half. The Republic of South Africa, where local development of industry has gone the farthest, exports more than a quarter of her gross national product.

The Vital Role of Overseas Trade

To Africa, her trade with Europe or the United States is vital, even though that trade is not very important to us in the United States. The bulk of African trade goes to Western Europe and North America; minor exceptions are Uganda, which exports cotton to the East, and recently Egypt. Since African economies are dependent upon export and import trade, economic conditions in Africa are shaped by the forces of the outside world. What happens in the West decides whether prosperity or depression will be the order of the day: The Africans have precious little to say about it themselves.

The importance of the American market for Africa is growing, but it is still far less important than the Western European market. Roughly two-thirds of Africa's trade is with Western Europe. Comparatively, the United States is much less significant: in 1938, 3½ per cent of African exports went to the United States, and in 1960, 8 per cent. The United States has only held its own as a source of supply for Africa—probably because of the continuance of import restrictions on dollar goods throughout most of the continent since World War II until quite recently, and the lack of American sales and distributing organizations in Africa. In 1938, Africa got 9½ per cent of her imports from the United States; in 1960, this had gone up very little and was still under 10 per cent. Liberia, which uses the American dollar as her currency, is an outstanding exception: More than half of Liberia's exports go to the United States, and more than half of her imports come from there.

General Dependence on Inflow of Capital

Africa's economic dependence on the West is even greater than the trade figures indicate. Whatever level of development the countries of Africa have reached has been due largely to the inflow of European capital, entrepreneurs, and skills. As de Kiewiet has pointed out, the economic development over most of Africa in modern times can best be understood as the result of two migrations: (1) the migration of European traders, officials, settlers, and entrepreneurs into Africa, carrying with them capital, equipment, skills, and governmental and economic organizations; and (2) the migration of the African tribesmen out of their subsistence economy into the new money economy created by the Europeans. The corollary of this statement is: Those parts of Africa which received the greatest migration of trained European people and capital have seen the highest economic development.

I have already mentioned the figure of approximately $6 billion as the amount of external capital invested in Africa south of the Sahara prior to World War II. This figure is roughly comparable to the total European investment in the United States prior to World War I. But whereas the United States thereafter needed no external capital to keep the economy growing, African economic growth has continued to be dependent on foreign capital. As early as Alexander Hamilton, enough of a capital market was built up in the United States to enable the government to finance most of its needs at home. But even now the governments of most African territories outside of the Republic of South Africa normally depend on getting from abroad most of the money they borrow.

Since World War II, there has been an enormous flow of investment capital and grant aid into Africa, totaling around $15 billion by the end of 1962. Most of this came from Europe, but about $2.5 billion came from the United States, about two-thirds government money and the rest private capital. The International Bank and its affiliates provided $900 million.

As in the past, the largest single amount of capital up to about 1958 went to the Republic of South Africa—a total of over $2

TABLE 2

United States Exports to and Imports from Africa, 1961

	Exports, Including Re-exports *(in millions of dollars)*	General Imports
Morocco	66	11
Algeria	42	*
Tunisia	36	1
Libya	30	*
Sudan	12	5
Somali Republic	1	*
French Somaliland	1	*
Ethiopia	11	31
Canary Islands	12	*
Other Spanish Africa	6	2
Cameroun	4	6
French-speaking Equatorial Africa	8	2
French-speaking West Africa	20	36
Liberia	50	32
Ghana	21	75
Nigeria	27	49
Other English-speaking West Africa	3	5
Seychelles, Mauritius	1	1
East Africa	19	52
Congo, Ruanda-Burundi	29	56
Malagasy Republic	2	13
Angola	10	28
Mozambique	10	5
Other Portuguese Africa	*	3
Rhodesia and Nyasaland	14	10
†South Africa	228	122
United Arab Republic (Egypt)	162	34
Total	827	583

* Less than $500,000.

† Includes the Republic of South Africa, South-West Africa, Bechuanaland, Basutoland, and Swaziland.

Source: U.S. Department of Commerce, *Trade Review, Economic Outlook for 20 Countries in Africa* (Washington, 1962).

billion. Most of this was British capital, with a large proportion from the continent of Europe. American private capital invested in the Republic since the war has increased by $240 million; the Export-Import Bank has loaned $150 million for the production of uranium from waste from the gold mines. The International Bank has loaned $220 million.

In the peak year, 1947, the net import of capital into South Africa was equal to 60 per cent of total gross domestic investment. For various reasons, this has tapered off and stopped. In the meantime, South African savings have increased so that even with

TABLE 3

American Investments in Africa
(in millions of dollars)

Private Direct Investments

	Republic of South Africa	Other Africa	Total Africa	Other Private	U.S. Govt. Net Credits	Total
1929	*	*	102	*	0	*
1936	*	*	93	*	0	*
1943	51	78	129	70	0	199
1950	140	213	353	100†	42	500†
1960	286	639	925	150†	314	1,400†

* No data available.
† Author's estimate. A. M. K.

Sources: U.S. Treasury, *Census of American-owned Assets in Foreign Countries* (Washington, 1947).
U.S. Department of Commerce, *Direct Private Foreign Investment of the United States, Census of 1950;* supplement to *Survey of Current Business,* August, 1953 (Washington, 1953).
U.S. Department of Commerce, *Survey of Current Business,* August, 1962.
U.S. National Advisory Council on International Monetary and Financial Problems, *Semi-Annual Report to the President and the Congress, January–June 1961* (Washington, 1962).

no capital inflow, gross investment is about 20 per cent of gross national product. This should be sufficient to keep the economy growing at a satisfactory pace. However, the real question is whether the people in South Africa who have accumulated these savings will be willing to invest in fields that are as productive as those in which outside investors placed their money, investors who were more enterprising and more willing to take risks.

The rest of Africa must still depend on outside capital if it is to develop economically at anything like a satisfactory rate. Rhodesia and the Congo in a normally good year used to have large savings—that is, savings of the European settlers and local corporations. Up to 1960, in addition, they were able to attract enough private capital directly or through the International Bank

TABLE 4

American Private Direct Investments in Africa, 1960
(in millions of dollars)

	Mining and Smelting	Petroleum	Manufacturing	Trade	Other	Total
Central and South Africa	119	114	110	34	17	394
South Africa						286
Rhodesia						82
Other						6
West Africa	125	80	1	9	75	290
Ghana						10
Liberia						139
Nigeria						24
Former French						103
Other						15
East Africa	1	42	—	4	—	46
North Africa	2	172	7	6	8	195
Algeria						21
Morocco						10
Egypt						58
Other						106
Total	247	407	118	53	99	925

Source: U.S. Department of Commerce, *Market Indicators for Africa,* World Trade Information Service, Statistical Reports, Part 3, 62-20 (1962).

TABLE 5

International Bank for Reconstruction and Development and Affiliates
Assistance to Africa as of December 31, 1962
(in millions of dollars)

Country	Number of Investments	Loans	Development Credits	Investments in Companies	Total
Algeria	2	60	—	—	60
Congo (Leopoldville)	5	120	—	—	120
East Africa	1	24	—	—	24
Ethiopia	6	28	—	—	28
West Africa (former French)	1	7	—	—	7
Gabon	1	35	—	—	35
Ghana	1	47	—	—	47
Kenya	2	14	—	—	14
Mauritania	1	66	—	—	66
Morocco	2	15	—	1.5	16.5
Nigeria	1	28	—	—	28
Rhodesia	5	147	—	—	147
Ruanda-Burundi	1	5	—	—	5
South Africa	10	222	—	—	222
Sudan	4	74	13	—	87
Swaziland	1	—	3	—	3
Tanganyika	1	—	—	3	3
Tunisia	1	—	5	—	5
Uganda	1	8	—	—	8
Total	46	900	21	4.5	925.5

to be able to achieve an economic growth that was more rapid than growth of their population without special governmental grants or other special help by European countries or the United States.

Special Problems in Other African Areas

Most of the rest of Africa has needed and continues to need special help from abroad to develop economically. Prior to World War II, the economic philosophy prevailed that colonies should stand on their own feet, and be financially self-sufficient. In contrast, after World War II both the French and British governments recognized the need to give sizeable special help to aid the development of their territories in Africa. The large-scale aid given was probably an important factor in speeding up the winning of independence by the African countries.

French Aid to French-Speaking Africa

It is almost completely certain that without special help the economies of the French-speaking African countries will not grow sufficiently fast to keep up with the growth in population. France has recognized this, and has continued her programs of aid to the French-speaking African countries, in most cases with very little change after independence. The very large magnitude and scope of France's normal aid to these countries, in relation to the amount of effort they themselves have been able to devote to their own development, is unmatched anywhere else in the world. In these countries, the French government is providing most of the investment for the basic services—railways, ports, roads, electric power, schools, hospitals—the "infrastructure" needed for growth. Under the postwar plans prepared for the territories, France undertook to pay one-half of the expenditure on economic development and two-thirds of the expenditure on social development. In practice, these proportions became bigger and bigger and by the time most of the French-speaking countries became independent in 1960, France was paying about 90 per cent of the total costs. The remainder was financed by loans at very favorable terms from the Caisse Centrale, a special part of the French Government. When the French-speaking countries of black Africa and Madagascar became independent in 1960, France had made available around $2.5 billion in grants and loans in capital investments. At least another $2.5 billion went into the three North African countries—Tunisia, Morocco, and Algeria—before they became independent.

French aid was not and is not restricted to help in financing investment alone. France subsidized the current budgets of the territories and is now providing assistance to the current budgets of most of the independent countries. Even in those few countries that nominally do not receive budgetary support, France pays for services that in other countries would come under the budget— this includes in most cases air, meteorological, and defense services, as well as a substantial part of the cost of the salaries of French personnel working for the countries.

The magnitude of French aid to the African countries after independence is difficult to calculate exactly because it consists of so many different elements. But, in any case, the burden on the French budget has been about $800 to $900 million a year.

The French effort has been very large in terms of providing trained personnel. Even Tunisia, which has proved able to staff the whole of her government administration with Tunisians, gets help from France in the form of teachers and some categories of engineers and technicians. With the exception of Algeria, where the French contribution needed in personnel is still unclear (except in the case of teachers, where France is providing 10,000), the total number of French personnel on technical assistance assignments in Africa in 1962 totaled over 20,000. These were French public servants on assignment to African governments for periods of more than one year. At the same time, there were around 5,000 others on assignments lasting less than one year.

In the light of the massive French aid to Africa that is indicated in the foregoing figures, it is not at all surprising that Guinea, the only independent French-speaking African country that has received no aid from France, is now engaged in negotiations to re-establish cordial relationships with France.

While no adequate figures are available on the amount of French private investment in Africa, it has unquestionably been in the $100 million range. In all, the investment financed by the French government has probably been more than two-thirds of the total investment in the French-speaking countries. Until very recently, American investment in these countries has been negligible. Now, American interests are in alumina production in Guinea, in the mining of manganese in the Gabon, and in possible investment in other mining ventures.

The only considerable U.S. Government aid, other than technical assistance in the French-speaking African countries, has been in Morocco and Tunisia. As a result of the Algerian war, aid available from France was limited, particularly in Tunisia. Partly because of the presence of American bases, total U.S. aid to Morocco to the end of 1960 was greater than to Tunisia, $156 million compared to $119 million. The U.S. has recently agreed to make available $180 million over the three years 1962–64 to Tunisia to help finance Tunisia's three-year plan if suitable projects can be found.

British Aid to British Territories

Less direct aid has been given by the British Government to its colonies and former colonies because private investment has been greater and also because the countries have been able to do more for themselves and have been allowed and helped to borrow in London and elsewhere—including the International Bank. The countries have used the London money market both as a source of capital and as a place to invest their liquid resources. Almost all the British capital invested in the colonies during the first part of the postwar period was offset by the short-term funds invested in London by colonies through the Crown Agents—the same function that Benjamin Franklin once performed for the colony of Pennsylvania. Since then, these countries have drawn down their balances.

Under the Colonial Development and Welfare Act (C.D. and W.), the United Kingdom had given the equivalent of some $425 million to the African countries by the end of March, 1962. This has been supplemented by $220 million of investments by the British Commonwealth Development Corporation (CDC) in various projects in Africa. The C.D. and W. grants totaled about a quarter of the public investment in the British African colonies —a not unimportant fraction. In the less developed colonies such as Gambia, British Somaliland, and the High Commission Territories in southern Africa, one can say (as in the French territories) that grants from the metropole were virtually the public investment program. From time to time, British Government grants even helped to meet some of the current expenditures. In these last areas, economic growth will for some years depend directly on the continuance of government grants to finance the necessary public investment.

When a former British colony becomes independent, it is no longer eligible for grant aid under the C.D. and W. Act, but can get Commonwealth assistance loans from the British Government. This policy created little difficulty initially, since the first English-speaking African countries that became independent (Sudan, Ghana, Nigeria) were able to get along with reliance on loans and using their accumulated reserves built up from the high prices of the early 1950's. Now, as the somewhat poorer countries of Africa (Tanganyika, Sierra Leone, Uganda, Kenya) become independent, the cutting off of grant aid creates greater problems. The British have attempted to give the newly independent countries a good financial start by endowing them with substantial amounts of grants and development loans on independence, to help them over the first few years at least. The Colonial Development Corporation, a British public corporation that was set up to make development investments in the colonies, was not allowed to make new investments in countries that had become independent. In 1962, however, this handicap was removed—the corporation was renamed the Commonwealth Development Corporation and permitted to continue to invest in the African countries after independence. The British Government also stands ready to help finance the extra cost of British civil servants kept on after independence and is, in addition, actively engaged in providing and helping finance personnel requested by the newly independent countries. The British also make strenuous efforts to help the new countries to secure needed aid from other sources: the U.S., Germany, other European countries, Japan, and the international organizations. In the negotiations with the European Common Market, the United Kingdom won the right for her former colonies to choose whether they wished the privileges of associated membership in the Common Market, including the right to receive funds from the Common Market institutions.

Other Countries

Somaliland, an Italian trusteeship under the United Nations, became independent in 1960. The Italian government had subsidized the territory directly, at a rate of from $5 to $7 million a year, and indirectly, by maintaining a protected market in Italy for Somaliland's principal export, bananas. After independence, Italy has continued to aid Somalia with grants on a smaller scale, personnel, and the purchase of bananas. Somalia has also secured about $5 million from the European Common Market Development Fund (FED) to which Italy contributes. Up to the end of 1961, the United States had made available $14 million, and the Communist bloc has promised $82 million, if suitable projects can be found.

Libya has been receiving an even greater amount of aid, principally from the British and American governments. The British Government subsidized Libya at a rate equivalent to $11 million a year. From the start of Libyan independence to the end of 1961, United States Government aid totaled $139 million. There is also a large program of U.N. technical assistance in Libya. With the discovery of large oil deposits in Libya, the need for outside help is rapidly diminishing.

The modern economic development of Liberia was largely based on the investments of two American companies, Firestone and the Liberia Mining Company (in which Republic Steel has an interest), and on United States Government assistance. Liberia's port of Monrovia was constructed by the American Government, at a cost of $19 million, from lend-lease funds during the war. In recent years, Liberia has received United States Government loans and grants of $59 million. With the large-scale development of new iron ore mines and plantations underway, Liberia's economy is beginning to grow rapidly.

Ethiopia received **very little** external assistance to help her economic development, inasmuch as she has had no continuing special relationship with any non-African power. Until recently, about the only equivalents of the enormous resources that France and the United Kingdom have made available to their African territories were the system of highways built during the Italian occupation and other assets which Italy left behind in Eritrea. French private capital constructed the only railway in the country, from Addis Ababa to Djibouti, and other European private capital is invested in various small enterprises. Altogether, foreign private investment probably does not exceed $100 million. Very little American private capital is invested in Ethiopia and Eritrea. The American government has given $40 million in grant aid, mostly in the last half-dozen years. The International Bank has made loans totaling $28.5 million to help put the highways back into shape, set up a telecommunications network, and establish a Development Bank. Ethiopia, surprisingly enough, is where the Communist bloc has granted the second largest amount of credits in Africa, next only to Ghana. Out of a total of almost $600 million in Communist credits to Africa to the end of 1961, Ethiopia had received $129 million; Ghana, $146 million; Guinea, $86 million; Somalia, $82 million; Mali, $55 million; Tunisia, $39 million; and Sudan, $22 million. But, as is true in most cases of credits, it takes many years before they take concrete form in specific projects. Very little of the credits to Ethiopia, Ghana, Somalia, and Mali has actually been used so far.

Much more important than the Communist bloc credits to Africa has been the aid given by the European Common Market itself. Up to the end of 1962, the Common Market had made available $581.25 million as grants to the 18 African countries associated with it (i.e., all the French-speaking black African countries except Guinea, Madagascar, the Congo, Ruanda, Burundi, Somalia, and French Somaliland). For the next five years, $730 million is to be made available to the independent countries in Africa, mostly in the form of grants.

THE WORLD MARKET AND AFRICAN DEVELOPMENT

The Situation in the Postwar Years

African countries had a special advantage for many years after the war. The prices for African export commodities were not only high, but relatively favorable in comparison to prices of the industrial products of which she is a consumer. This situation was brought about by the general failure to increase production capacity during the depression and through the war years. In the decade or more of subsequent prosperity and full employment, the supply of most primary products was inadequate to meet the greater world demand. Prices for such products rose more rapidly than did prices for industrial goods—for which production capacity could expand more rapidly.

Some African countries were able to siphon off or borrow some of the gains from these high prices and use them to help finance public development programs. This was particularly true of Ghana, Nigeria, Uganda, the Congo, and the Federation of Rhodesia and Nyasaland. For example, consider cocoa in Ghana. Cocoa is the principal export of Ghana and prices rose extremely high after World War II. The actual volume of cocoa exports increased by only 15 per cent; the money value increased more than seven-fold, while the real value, i.e., what it would buy in terms of imports, increased 2.5 times. As a result, Ghana was able to set aside about $350 million for her 1951/52–1956/57 development plan, of which less than 2 per cent came from British Government Colonial Development and Welfare grants. No borrowing or other external assistance was needed.

In the Federation of Rhodesia and Nyasaland, where copper is the principal export, the copper companies did so well, particularly with the booming prices in 1955 and 1956, that they were able to lend $56 million to help construct the Kariba project. They also agreed to pay a higher price on the power to be supplied to them until they have overpaid the equivalent of an additional grant of $28 million. One of the copper-mining groups, in which American Metal Climax has a majority interest, used some of its profits to finance a wide range of activities to help develop the area. It has financed technical and agricultural schools, given a building to an interracial society, sponsored a merchants' bank, and set up a major experimental agricultural project. The Federation Government itself adopted the policy of reinvesting in development projects all the revenues received from copper prices above the "normal" price of 30 cents a pound. The non-copper private companies and private citizens also prospered and could finance their own private investment out of profits. A large part of the investment in the former Belgian Congo was also financed in this way.

The Changing Price Situation and
Future African Development

Unfortunately for Africa, this phase appears to be over. First in agricultural commodities and then in minerals—where it took longer to bring new capacity into production—prices have eased off while the prices of the industrial commodities the African countries buy have continued to rise. Prices of African exports have dropped over 20 per cent on the average since 1955–57. Cocoa, which sold for 58 cents a pound in New York in 1954 and 37 cents in 1955, was selling around 20 cents in 1962; coffee has dropped from 78 cents in 1954 and 57 cents in 1955, to 35 cents in 1962; copper, from 42 cents a pound in 1956, was selling at 31 cents in 1962.

Africa's ability to meet her own capital needs has been decreased. During most of the postwar period, the profits from high prices and the external capital available kept most of Africa fairly well supplied with capital. While this varied greatly from territory to territory, most of the African countries received about as much capital as they could absorb. This may no longer be true.

The drop in funds available for investment is not the most important impact of the fall in commodity prices. The whole impetus to economic development is slowed. With the weakness in prices, the need to expand capacity is not so great. The fall in incomes of the Africans holds down the growth of the internal markets and makes it difficult to start new factories. The current income of the governments suffers and makes it difficult to increase the expenditures for education, health and research, which are needed for economic development to take place.

There are still other repercussions. Under the pressure of falling prices, the privilege the African countries associated with the Common Market have of selling their commodities in

Western Europe without paying tariffs becomes even more valuable. The United States objective of securing equality of treatment for the other primary producers of Africa and Latin America becomes more difficult to achieve. Furthermore, markets in the Communist bloc for African products become increasingly more attractive. The incomes of consumers in Communist bloc countries are high enough to permit them to purchase many African products such as coffee, chocolate, bananas, etc.; however, because of rigid state control of trade, the consumers so far have not been allowed to buy much of these products.

The United States is trying to help meet the problem of falling commodity prices. Probably the most important means of help is in accelerating the rate of growth of the American and European economies to provide more rapidly growing markets. In addition, U.S. policy is to work towards the reduction of restraints on consumption such as tariffs and specific excise taxes on coffee, cocoa, and tea. The Trade Expansion Act of 1962 authorizes the U.S. to remove duties on tropical products if the European Common Market will also do so. The international textile agreement provides for a gradual expansion of markets in Europe and the U.S. for the textile exports of developing countries. The U.S. is also taking a leading role in trying to work out international commodity agreements to stabilize prices of the major primary products of interest to Africa. Active study on an international basis is also going on of global compensatory financing schemes to offset, at least partially, cyclical fluctuations in export earnings, the idea being to provide short-term finance to countries whose exports temporarily drop in price to permit imports to remain fairly stable. The more important problem of long-term drops in price is being tackled by the device of commodity schemes, the first one being that for coffee. The idea here is that prices would be stabilized by a control of supply while the producing countries would take action to shift some of their producers and their land into other kinds of production.

It is quite obvious that this whole problem is a very difficult one, and that we are very far from sure that we have begun to solve it.

Conclusions

Summary of Major Points

In the discussion so far I have tried to bring out the following major points:

1. While Africa is more important to us than before World War II, she is still relatively unimportant economically.
2. Africa's main economic interest for us, aside from her great importance to Western Europe, is as a potential supplier of raw materials to help fill the growing gap between the needs of the American economy and our own domestic supplies.
3. In this respect, the African resources that appear to be of most interest to Western Europe and the United States in the immediate future are bauxite, hydroelectric power, oil, uranium, and iron ore.
4. Economic growth in most of Africa remains dependent on the inflow of capital and technical assistance from abroad. During the postwar period Africa received a large inflow, made up in large part of special government help from France and the United Kingdom. This inflow was supplemented by investment of part of the gains resulting from the very favorable world prices that African exports enjoyed.
5. As the African countries became independent, various arrangements have been made to maintain the flow of external capital, but the drop in the prices of their exports which coincided with their gaining independence is causing them great difficulties.

Greater Role for the United States

The United States has played only a minor part in the economic development of Africa. If the growth of the African economies is to continue as favorably as it has since World War II, we may have to play a greater role.

The British decided some years ago that by themselves they can no longer meet the needs of the Commonwealth for imports of capital, and they have therefore encouraged the independent countries and colonies of the Commonwealth to try to secure capital in the American market and from the International Bank. The French, Belgian, and Italian governments were instrumental initially in getting special provision for eighteen of the now independent countries of Africa in the European Common Market, and the African countries concerned have gotten an expansion and extension of these arrangements.

While Western Europe and the International Bank and its affiliates may continue to carry the greater part of the burden in Africa, the part played by the United States can be very important. In a few countries, for historical or other reasons, U.S. aid is preponderant and the U.S. is looked to for the lead in taking action to stop or reverse the fall in primary commodity prices.

The American private capital that has gone into Africa so far has gone largely into the Republic of South Africa and the English-speaking countries; the French-speaking countries are still largely unknown territory to Americans. In the new states, future economic growth will depend a great deal on how receptive these states are to European and American enterprise and capital and to the use of trained non-African personnel. In general, the African countries want to broaden the sources of foreign enterprise operating in their countries and welcome the thought of American investors coming in. On the American side, more consideration needs to be given to a greater variety of investments. In particular, American enterprise in manufacturing for local and export markets and in developing tourism would be of special help to Africa. The U.S. government is already carrying on a wide range of activities designed to assist American businessmen interested in Africa and to develop a climate favorable to private enterprise.

To conclude, the help that the United States can provide and the benefit that our economy will derive from the economic growth of Africa will depend a great deal on the degree of initiative and interest displayed by American enterprise in African investment possibilities.

SOCIETY

6. Culture and Changing Values in Africa

WALTER GOLDSCHMIDT

THE FABRIC OF SOCIAL LIFE

If we are to understand the future of a people, we must appreciate its past. For the way of life of a people in any time and place is built out of past customs adapted to present circumstances and needs. This way of life is what anthropologists call "culture."

Before we can look at the culture of Africa past, we must pause to consider what the term means—for it is central to the discussion of this chapter as it is to all anthropological inquiry and, I think, to any constructive attitude toward the continent of Africa. As anthropologists use the term, all peoples have culture; for culture is their customary way of doing things. It includes all aspects of life: the way they make things, the manner in which they wrest a livelihood from the soil, the way in which they organize their society, the way they look at the world about them; even the attitudes and sentiments and feelings they share. The important points about culture are that these things are shared by the group, that they are learned and are not biologically inherited modes of behavior, and that they are passed down from one generation to the next. There is a kind of internal consistency to culture; each part affects every other and all are tied into a whole which, under normal circumstances, makes an integrated and patterned way of life. Most important of all, each person is shaped by the culture in which he is raised, so that what he is, what he thinks and feels, what he does, are products of his culture. This is no mysterious process—though it is a subtle one —but takes place through gradual conditioning to the circumstances around him. Culture, then, is not merely a set of customs: It is a way of life. And each people has its own way of life.

If culture shapes the individual, what shapes culture? Many forces are at work. First, there is the accumulated knowledge and belief of the past, which comes down through tradition (and it has been said that the world is made up more of the dead than of the living). Next, there are the exigencies of survival—the special character of environment and terrain out of which, using traditional techniques, the people must satisfy their material wants. Again, there are the needs for social interaction, the demands made on every society to provide for the orderly conduct of its day-to-day business. Finally, there are the pressures of the neighboring cultures—cultures which may bring new ideas and knowledge (as Rome did to Gaul and Britain) and which may threaten with war and destruction. These and other forces result in the variety of past and present cultures; each different, yet none unique.

We must emphasize one element in culture that is particularly important to the subject before us: cultural values. In every culture, however primitive in technology or however crude its circumstances, there are certain qualities of persons, certain social situations, and (almost always) certain things that are considered especially desirable. Every people can distinguish between a proper and a crude person, between a superior and an inferior manner of acting and living. The criteria will vary from one culture to another, but will be more or less consistent within any one. A person characterized by these value attributes will gain the esteem and respect of his fellows, and will be accorded particular status. Usually there will be some way in which he can symbolize his special position—perhaps by possession of things, perhaps by holding a title, perhaps by no more than the deference shown him by his fellows.

The important point about cultural values is that they give direction to life. As we go from one culture to another we see different ideals and desires dominating the scene, but everywhere these ideals act as goals; everywhere parents direct their children down the path that their culture deems proper. Values serve as the lodestar to life.

This matter, as we shall see, is particularly germane to our concern with Africa. For the impact of civilization upon native people everywhere—and particularly in Africa—has been to undermine these value orientations. The superior power of Western civilization, coupled with the assumption of superiority by the white man himself, has forced the African to question his own values—the administrator and the missionary have purposively endeavored to change the values of the Africans, assuming the superiority of their own aims. But values are not simply replaceable parts of a machine; they are intricately woven into the fabric of life. Thus they truly change only when total life circumstances change so that new values come to have real meaning to the individual. To destroy a set of values is to leave a community without that sense of direction which is necessary not only to community life but to personal satisfaction.

DIVERSITY OF AFRICAN CULTURE

The great expanse that is Africa has seen a wide variety of cultures and diverse conditions among men. It was in this continent that Egyptian Pharaohs lived in decadent splendor when savages roamed through most of Europe. Writing, irrigated farming, and statecraft are among the key elements of civilization for which the African continent has a reasonable claim to priority. Yet today, Africa harbors two of the most primitive cultures of the modern world. The Bushmen of the Kalahari Desert eke out a livelihood wandering after game with crude bows and spears; the Pygmies in the dense forest of the Ituri are intrepid hunters but have a most modest cultural accoutrement. George

P. Murdock lists more than 5,000 separate tribes or ethnic groups in Africa, each with its own culture, and we can give but a scant summary of their variety.

Differences in Language

There are hundreds of distinct languages in Africa. Professor Joseph Greenberg, has grouped these into four great families—that is, language systems with remote genetic resemblances in which scholars can see an ancient historic unity, just as they can see a relation between Sanskrit and modern English.

One of these language families, the Khoisan, is limited to the Bushmen and Hottentots in southern Africa and a few scattered tribes in Tanganyika. At the northern end of the continent, north of the Sahara and running into Ethiopia, the people speak languages of the family that includes Semitic, Egyptian, Berber, and Cushitic, the last of which has penetrated as far south as Tanganyika. These languages tie Africa to Asia and include the languages of the developed civilizations of North Africa and the Near East.

The other two great language families are spoken exclusively by Negro peoples. The great family that Greenberg calls Congo-Kordofan, and which includes the Bantu family of languages as one general variant, is spoken from Senegal in West Africa in a band across the continent south of the Sahara and includes the whole southern half of the continent, except for the small population of the Khoisan speakers. The fourth great family, which Greenberg calls Nilo-Saharan, has a more limited distribution, chiefly in the central Sahara, the eastern Sudan, and extending through East Africa.

It seems clear that the first of these languages represents a very old stratum of population extending back to the Paleolithic, and the second represents a linguistic development of the centers of civilization that have spread—anthropologically speaking—in recent times. The other two language families represent the essential Negro population of Africa, and their dispersion must have beeen largely pre-Christian and possibly early Neolithic—an antiquity attested by the fact that they are divided into myriads of mutually exclusive tongues. This diversity of tongues has required the use of lingua franca in modern African states—usually the language of the metropolitan country from which independence has been gained.

Economic Differences

The Bushmen, the Pygmies, and a few other scattered tribes live exclusively by hunting and gathering wild products. North of the Sahara and in Ethiopia, the land is peopled with developed cultures that use the plow and draft animals. The rest of the continent sustains itself through a combination of two modes of production: keeping livestock and cultivating crops by means of short iron hoes. In some areas, forest and tsetse limit the distribution of stock; in others, aridity limits the area of cultivation. New techniques have, of course, been introduced in modern times, but most production of food remains essentially as it was before European penetration.

On the desert areas of the northern part of the continent, camels are the chief animals kept, but elsewhere throughout Africa, skirting the Congo Basin, cattle are favored, supplemented by goats, fat-tailed sheep, and donkeys. With rare exceptions just south of the Sahara the African has no horse; he neither rides nor harnesses animals to the plow or cart. Even the use of pack animals is rare.

The cultivation of plants is normally carried out by shifting agriculture; that is, bush is cleared and burnt, the land used for about three years and then fallowed until the bush has returned. The extensive fallowing, together with limited farm technology, tends to keep population density low. Normally the clearing is done by men, the cultivation by women, and harvesting by both. Millets and sorghums predominate in the uplands; roots, plantains, and edible fruits in the lowlands. Plantains and some other crops grow as permanent plantings and require no fallowing, which allows for higher population densities and greater stability. Casava (manioc) and maize are food plants that have been introduced to Africa from America, and often are of great importance.

Ox-drawn plows are now much used and tractors are beginning to appear on African-operated lands.

The occurrence of pure herding south of the Sahara is relatively rare, being found among a few tribes like the Masai and the Hottentots. More frequently, cattle are kept in association with hoe farming; usually the animals are the responsibility of the men and the crops of the women. Not infrequently, there is a local ethnic distinction between the stockmen and the farmers, and where this occurs it is usual that the cattle keepers are the overlords, political elite, or a higher caste dominating the peasants. Occasionally, however, the cattle keepers are merely ethnically separate and exchange products with their farming neighbors.

In terms of technical advancement, throughout Africa there was, in addition to those neolithic arts of pottery-making and basketry, a fully developed iron industry with smelting as well as iron-working. The development of bronze casting and gold work in West Africa is comparable to the best the world knows. Weaving is of limited distribution in Africa, skins and bark cloth having been the traditional materials for clothing. The African peoples south of the Sahara generally lacked certain very important features: the plow, draft animals, writing, the wheel, fertilization of crops, and irrigation.

Political Differences

In the organization of society, it is convenient to make a distinction between those peoples who have centralized political authority (states) and those without such unity. Politically organized peoples range from loose confederacies recognizing a paramount chief, to highly centralized, bureaucratically structured kingdoms, such as Buganda. In Africa, the king is widely thought to have divine power, though rule occasionally rests on clan, or caste, or "inherent" powers. Some states were highly autocratic (Buganda), others highly militaristic (Zulu), caste-ridden (Ruanda and Burundi), highly democratic (Ashanti), or loosely articulated (Shambalai). Centralized political authority was found in all parts of Africa; the states of West Africa and the lake area are best known. But kingdoms existed throughout the Congo and southern Africa, interspersed with people having no centralized political authority.

Those people without states organize their social life through ties of kinship, usually in the forms of clans or lineages reckoned either through the paternal or the maternal line, without any chiefs but with some means of maintaining orderly internal relationships. Such kin groupings, in fact, are found among practically all African peoples, whether or not there is also a political system. They often control both economic activity, through land-holding or stock ownership, and personal rights, through mutual protection. Other social groupings such as age grades (especially in East Africa) and secret societies (especially in West Africa) are elements in the structuring of human relationships. We must remember that the loyalties, the obligations, and the powers throughout Africa, whether in kingdoms or stateless societies, have rested largely on matters of kinship.

Religious Differences

It is more difficult to make a classification in the realm of religious beliefs and ideology. Leaving aside for the moment the influences of Islam and Christianity, the dominant features of African religion are a belief in ancestors as spiritual forces and intercessors, a belief in the pervading spiritual forces of nature, and a strong and pervasive belief in the reality of witchcraft and magic.

From the standpoint of our interest in modern Africa, perhaps the most important aspect of native African religious belief is the elaborate religious ideology supporting the systems of government, especially the notion of the divine right of kings. Closely associated with this is the veneration of the land, often elaborated in religious ritual and belief, which underlies the system of land tenure and the limitation on its use and sale. A third element that has particular significance for modern life is the veneration or worship of ancestors, which reinforces the bonds of kinship and the importance of clans and lineages. From this it can be seen that changes in economic structure and political organization often involve questions of religious beliefs.

Two Cultural Vignettes

It is as important, however, to understand the spirit and unity of cultures, and how they vary, as it is to know the basic features of African culture in general. For this reason, we present brief vignettes of two diverse African peoples.

Masai. Lying across the caravan routes between the east coast of Africa and the great kingdoms of the lake area are a nomadic, cattle-keeping people, the Masai. A century ago, it was Masai culture more than any physical barrier that prevented European explorers from penetrating inland and reaching the sources of the Nile. Still today, after a century of battles and of diseases of man and beast, and the even more insistent but insidious influences of civilization, the Masai cling to their old culture and their own values. To the annoyance of many modern Africans, one still sees the tall, straight bodies of Masai men, draped in blankets reddened by the red earth, spear in hand, among the closely herded cattle—men who perhaps in school have been as far as the Third Form. What is this Masai culture, which has given a peculiar and strangely ennobling meaning to the word Masai?

Masai culture centers about cattle. Cattle are literally its life blood. Not only do they supply milk and meat, but they are regularly bled to provide an important supplement to Masai diet. The Masai disdain other flesh, and hunt only to protect their cattle from predators; they disdain farming and consider vegetable food a poor substitute for nourishment. The only important supplement to the Masai diet derives from the sheep and goats, which they also herd, and which they milk, bleed, and eat.

From these facts we see that cattle have an important economic value. It is estimated that the 200,000 Masai, who occupy 80,000 square miles of the high plains extending through central Kenya to Tanganyika, have 2 million head of cattle and nearly as many goats and sheep—10 for every man, woman, and child. We may be sure that important as cattle are to the Masai for daily sustenance, they are not merely an economic good. Cattle are a gift of the Masai god, who gave cattle only to the Masai. Thus it is that all cattle are the rightful property of the Masai, and it is no more than justice when the Masai raid—retrieve—the cattle in other people's kraals. While it may be no more than right, it is still a task that requires both a militant attitude and a military organization. Next to the herding of cattle, raiding is —or was, for this is now largely abolished—the chief occupation of adult men, and the entire society revolves about these two activities. To understand this, we must examine the major institution of Masai life: initiation into age grades.

About the age of sixteen or seventeen, each boy is initiated into manhood in a rite that involves circumcision. Upon initiation he enters into a society of men with his fellow initiates, a group bracketing about ten years in age. As they are initiated, they move into a separate compound of initiates, accompanied by their mothers and sisters who look after their physical needs. Here as a group of men they form a *manyatta,* which is at once a small society, a community, and a military battalion. These men remain together for life, acting in concert under their own leader, maintaining a host of special obligations to their fellows, forming a fraternity. For a while they are junior warriors. When the oldest among them are in their late twenties, they become senior warriors (and a new younger age grade is formed). As they approach their mid-thirties they begin to marry, and soon the whole group become junior elders, then senior elders, and finally retired men past the time of leadership. Thus each age grade comes onto the scene with the ritual of circumcision and initiation and moves through a series of stages like an endless train.

The members of the warrior age grades form into a barracks, whose primary duties are to defend the country and, by raiding other tribes, to maintain and increase the herds. The men in these barracks abstain from tobacco and beer, but they are free to have their sweethearts visit them.

The initiation that brought a boy into manhood and into the class of warriors, cattle raiders, and protectors was also a test of stamina and restraint—for the youth must show no sign of fear or pain either during the circumcision or subsequently. Thus the values of fortitude and perseverance, which are to characterize the life of a warrior, are firmly enjoined from the outset. It is this quality that one sees expressed on the face of the lone herdsman on the sere plain. It is this quality that makes him able to spear a lion while protected only by a shield; it is this that makes possible the lightning raids on enemy cattle, and that made the Masai, at the height of their power in the mid-nineteenth century, the scourge of the East African highlands.

Cattle are the center of Masai life and of Masai values. A man's status is measured by the size of his herd, and he takes pride in the number and appearance of his beasts. Cattle enter into every major exchange. A man must have cattle to become a ranking citizen and to perform his proper social role. Among the Masai, the very privilege of marrying and rearing a family depends upon the herd, for to have a wife one must pay in cattle, and it is in the name of these livestock that a man endures the hardships of plains life. It is in their name that he learns those peculiar qualities of Masai demeanor that mark him as a proper Masai man.

Ashanti. In the central part of Ghana, there has long been a political state known as Ashanti. To understand that state and to appreciate the sentiments of its citizens, we must turn to three central elements of Ashanti culture—three elements that are closely interwoven, though in our own view they represent quite separate aspects of life.

The first of these is the agricultural mode of the people. The Ashanti are farmers; they plant small gardens by means of the hoe. To have use of land is a central consideration of all Ashanti. This, of course, we can readily appreciate. The earth is conceived as a female spirit born on Thursday; that day is sacred to her, and on it she must not be disturbed. It is important to be on good terms with her, to sacrifice to her for cultivation, and to thank her for a good harvest.

The second element in the social order of the Ashanti is the matrilineal bond. As Busia notes in opening his study of Ashanti political organization, the Ashanti theory of procreation holds that a human being is compounded of two principles, the "blood," inherited from the mother, and the "spirit," inherited from the father. Physical continuity is thought to derive through the mother; correspondingly, a person derives his rights and duties from his mother (the religious and educational ties are with the father), and therefore each man is identified with his maternal kinsmen. These kin form lineage groups, and membership in such groups determines succession to office, to property, and to all other obligations and rights in Ashanti law. The whole system of Ashanti government is an expression of this basic unit.

The third element in Ashanti life is the worship of ancestors. The Ashanti believe that the world where the spirits dwell is very much as it is upon earth. The dead man joins his kinsmen who have preceded him, but he does not sever his kinship ties with the living; the welfare of those who remain upon earth depends upon his good will, and failure to act in accordance with his instructions can only reap evil. As the body is covered, the mourners say:

> You are leaving us today; we have fired guns; we have given you a sheep; we have performed your funeral. Do not let any of us fall ill. Let us get money to pay the expenses of your funeral. Let the women bear children. Life to all of us. Life to the chief.

To the Ashanti, the world of the spirit is very close; the ancestors are believed always to be watching the behavior of their living relatives, giving aid to the deserving and punishing those who do not act properly.

The principle of kinship, reverence for ancestors, and the spiritual power of the earth combine to establish the basic patterns of Ashanti land ownership. While the earth is a powerful spirit, land belongs to the ancestors, who see that it is used properly and fairly by mortals. These mortals do not own the land; they have only the right to its use. Thus the land follows in the female line, and the Ashanti farmer is unwilling to sell that which is not his to sell, which is the sacred property of the ancestral spirits.

The head of the lineage is custodian of the lineage land; he sees that every member has a portion to farm. Sometimes the land is farmed jointly by the lineage, and often it has been cleared by their joint effort—a prodigious task for people with only hand tools. The lineage thus forms a work group sharing ancestral land and administered by its senior members. Men of the lineage act together and always remain in close association, and an individual cannot take any major action without involving his fellow lineage members.

These same principles of organization and belief inspired the political organization of the Ashanti kingdom. There is a hierarchy of chiefs, starting with the small, local lineage, proceeding through village, section, and division, until finally the chief of all Ashanti—the "Asantahene"—is reached. With each level there is a higher degree of authority, a greater responsibility, and more powerful spirits. Each leader is selected on a hereditary basis, but the chief is neither the oldest citizen nor the automatic heir. From among those who have a hereditary right to the post, and who are nominated by the "Queen Mother" of the particular group, the common people express their choice. Each unit—whether the lineage, the section, or the tribe—is free to determine its own internal affairs through its own highest-ranking official, but any dispute involving two coordinate units is taken to the authority that stands over both. The ultimate authority is the king, who maintains a kind of king's peace and has authority over major crimes.

The chief of any unit occupies a stool. Students of African history will remember the matter of the Golden Stool of Kumasi, the royal throne of the King of Ashanti, which led to the bloody Ashanti wars because unwise Europeans caused it to be defiled. This stool is a throne, but it is never sat upon. It has symbolic power. The ancestral spirits of the particular group over which the chief rules dwell in his stool. Indeed, it is the stool itself and the resident spirits that rule the group; the chief who occupies it is merely the spokesman and custodian of the deities, which are the true center of Ashanti power. Thus the belief in the living force of dead ancestors is the very substance of statecraft in Ashanti-land. And while we may not share Ashanti beliefs (though many comparable elements in Western society make them understandable), we can appreciate the whole philosophy in purely sociological terms. For whether or not the ancestral spirit does reside in it, the sacred stool is the manifest symbolic representation of the social order and the sacred and ancient traditions that support a continued prosperity and harmony.

The concept of the sacred duty of leadership suffuses Ashanti statecraft. The leader is not merely the selected head of his group; he is the spokesman for the ancestral spirits, and his obligations are clear. Those who acknowledge his leadership do so on the sworn oath of allegiance—an oath so holy that its breach becomes a cardinal sin. The legal spirit of the Ashanti is so dominated by religious sanction that the national law is a religious law. The king and the district chiefs have no jurisdiction over any private delict, but once a disputant speaks a sacred oath professing his innocence or the guilt of his adversary, the matter comes under official jurisdiction, and adjudication becomes the sacred duty of the chiefs; even the punishment itself is a sacred act. These awesome oaths—which are no more than the speaking of the day name sacred to the group—are the means of involving the whole machinery of government in private affairs. They demonstrate as well how the social actions of Ashanti society express the deep and tangible conviction that ancestral deities are involved in mundane affairs, and that the ties of kinship are not merely the practical means of getting the world's work done but are sacred entities within which life runs its course.

CULTURE CHANGE

Cultures are living things; they are constantly changing. Both internal and external pressures bring about alteration in the ways of life, and as far back as we can push our knowledge of Africa, there have been population movements, innovations, the growth and dissolution of states, and pressures from outside the continent.

We know practically nothing about such massive events as the spread of the Bantu-speaking peoples throughout southern

Africa, or the influence of the so-called Nilotics and Nilo-Hamitic peoples on the lake area of East Africa, except the evidence of their having taken place. Later external influences are better known.

External Cultural Influences

The east coast of Africa has been subject to external influence from the time of antiquity, and Arabic civilization flourished there long before the modern period of discovery, leaving a history of nations built and destroyed and influencing the coastal culture heavily and the interior indirectly.

The Islamic movement has, from its very inception, had a deep and penetrating influence on the whole of North Africa, which is essentially, though not purely, Moslem. This influence has penetrated south of the Sahara, and in much of the Sudan (the grassland zone extending along the southern edge of the Sahara) Mohammedanism is the dominant religion.

Finally, there has been a wave of influence out of Western Europe that started with the Portuguese travelers in the fifteenth century, followed by British, French, Belgian, and German penetration, and culminating in the partition of Africa and the establishment of colonialism in the second half of the nineteenth century.

These great movements have to varying degrees penetrated the deeper recesses of African culture, and transformed life-ways of the peasant and herdsman. We find evidence of Christian belief brought by the fifteenth century Portuguese in the Congolese religious cults, just as we find Moslem and Arabic influences on the political systems in western and eastern Africa.

The penetration of Africa by the European countries was in itself no greater than the Arabic and Moslem influences—indeed, because of European racial attitudes, it was in many ways less deep. But it has been accompanied by the great technological revolution and the emergence of a world community that, unlike the other movements, has had the ultimate effect of bringing Africa into the mainstream of civilization. It is useful to think of the Moslem influence as having been more considerable in the personal life in the villages that make up the bulk of African population, whereas European influence has been greater in altering society through the secondary effects of technological innovation. Even more significantly, the European colonies have maintained far closer ties with metropolitan centers than their North African and Asian counterparts, and have literally brought the Africans into Europe (and America) in a way much more significant than the Mohammedan pilgrimages to Mecca. In addition, the introduction of such simple but influential elements of culture as the plow, the grinding mill, guns, and, more recently, the Land Rover have literally changed the face of Africa. It is useful to consider the changes taking place under three somewhat technical terms: acculturation, urbanization, and detribalization.

Acculturation

By acculturation, we mean the actual transforming of a culture through the introduction of new elements, whether they be new tools or techniques, new religious ideas, or new systems of authority and control. Acculturation is always an amalgam between the old elements and a new introduction, but we must remember that the introduction of a single item such as a maize mill may have repercussions, for instance, in the role of women, the pattern of family life, and the division of labor. We may simplify the term by saying that acculturation is a process of changing tribal life through the impact of outside civilization. Predominantly, it is a change that takes place in the villages.

We may exemplify the acculturation process with the Sebei, a people of Uganda among whom I lived a few years ago. They are not unlike the Masai in their basic culture, except that, some centuries prior to European infiltration, they took up hoe agriculture and are therefore more settled and less warlike. The Sebei have been relatively remote from the forces of civilization, having had contact with Europeans for little more than half a century and close involvement for but a generation. In this time they have learned a great deal about the trappings of modern life; clothes, bicycles, cars, literacy, the plough, sugar, tea are part of the inventory of new acquisitions. Some of these elements have influenced life generally, some have affected only the avantgarde of Sebei. Yet an initiated Rip van Winkle who went to sleep when Major Austin came to Sebei-land in 1897 would have found life greatly altered had he awakened during my stay in 1954, even though many of his age mates were still alive.

For instance, a combination of British law and that of the powerful Buganda nation (the old kingdom from which Uganda gets its name) has supplanted old legal forms. Old Sebei, like peoples everywhere, had their problems with lawbreakers. In earlier days, justice might be brought about in several ways. The clan or the lineage of the wronged man might retaliate against the culprit. Or he might be brought to trial before the elders of the village and, when judgment went against him, the villagers would kill his stock or plunder his garden in a retaliation calculated against the nature of his wrong. But in particularly knotty cases, where the guilt of the victim was in doubt, the ancient practices of oath and ordeal would be brought to play. The oath is a powerful instrument—we practice it still when we take the witness stand—especially when the parties are convinced of its sacred character. When a Sebei, before his fellow men and in front of the sacred and magically potent altar, vowed publicly that the earth might swallow him if he were guilty of a crime, he would not readily forswear himself. But such oaths were repugnant to the British and have been banned in Sebei. (They are probably still resorted to in private ceremony, but psychologically and sociologically their effectiveness is curtailed by being deprived of a public.) Some modern Sebei men, highly adjusted to the present ways of life in other matters, openly question the effectiveness of signed testimony of witnesses, whose powers of perception they consider to be less than those of the unseen spirits, and whose motives, they feel, are perhaps less pure. Yet with the doubt cast upon the native religious beliefs through contact with Christianity and Islam, the effectiveness of the oath is also impaired. The whole jural system is thus altered. If it appears less repugnant to Western eyes, it appears less just to the Sebei.

Another Western influence is brought about by an enforced

Pax Britannica. Formerly, the Sebei, like the Masai, engaged in raids, but being a landed people they were less well-organized for militant action and were largely the losers in this game of raid and warfare. Warfare constantly checked their numbers and reduced their wealth, so that in old Sebei there were no pressures on land resources. As with the Masai, land was not valued and wealth was measured in cattle. With a half-century of peace, the population has increased. Overgrazing is a problem and new farming methods have resulted in greater dependence on agriculture. Only now, in part of Sebei, are they beginning to adjust their land laws, beginning to draw up boundaries, beginning to place as high a premium on land as on stock.

This is not to say that livestock have ceased to be of value. Today, as in ancient times, a Sebei man measures his wealth in terms of his herds. Cattle are his source not only of status, but also of well-being, and he endeavors to increase their numbers rather than their quality. All serious legal matters, even a man's life, may ultimately be measured in stock. So, too, is the very character of his household measured; for, as is so widespread in Africa, wives are purchased with cattle and a man cannot take a wife unless cattle are available to him. Since a man of importance must have many wives, it follows that he must accumulate cattle to acquire them. The desire for many wives is tantamount to the desire to be esteemed in native cultural values, and this is true even of persons highly influenced by Western culture. One chief explained that he gave up teaching in the Anglican mission because he took a second wife.

Cattle and wives, the two major symbols of success for Sebei men, are interchangeable. But now a new value intervenes. It was another young official, an educated Sebei and a self-made man, who placed the dilemma in values before me. A handsome girl was throwing herself at him—not to his displeasure—and I asked if he were planning to take her to be his fourth wife. There was no doubt about his ambivalence, for he was truly in a quandary. His sons were growing up and he wanted them to have an education. He wanted the girl, but perhaps he should keep his cows to provide money for the boys' schooling. I do not know how he resolved his dilemma, but certainly a new set of values was competing with the old—and a man was faced with a new choice as a result of normal acculturation processes.

Urbanization

We are so imbued with the urban environment that we take it to be the natural condition of man. It has not always been so. Wherever industrial cities have come into being, they have transformed the character of social life. If we examine the paintings of Hogarth in the eighteenth century, or the novels of Dickens in the nineteenth, we see evidence of cultural turmoil. In Africa, urbanism is a twentieth-century occurrence.

Urbanization has been called the culture of cities. It is the organization of cultural features made necessary by the constraining force of city life. Essentially, the fact that cities are large, dense aggregates of heterogeneous people means that the intimate ties of interpersonal relationship are replaced by transitory, impersonal and largely pecuniary relationships. The diversity of background means that assumptions of common norms and morals cannot be sustained, so that rules must be formalized and sustained by a police force. It is this situation which makes for such phenomena as prostitution, delinquency, and crime, but these are not the essence of urbanism, only side effects. The true essence of urban life is the depersonalization, the shift of social forces from the kin group to the market place. Let us follow an imaginary Ashanti, going to some urban center like Accra, and see how these forces work.

In leaving his native village, our Ashanti leaves behind him the sacred earth he knows. He comes out from under the rule of his ancestors and the hierarchy of chiefs who speak for them. He is no longer surrounded by the relatives who make up his lineage and his social environment. He no longer takes up the familiar rounds to which he was accustomed since youth. He comes to a city of unfamiliar sights and sounds, filled with strange objects. He might well share the impressions of the Mende youth to whom Kenneth Little spoke.

> I knew nothing of the world, and I did not think that there were any more people beyond the town limits of Largo and Kenema. I

only knew of one tribe, Mende, to which I belong and all my people and the inhabitants of the towns around. . . .

I became a sort of idiot as we moved along, for I stood to gaze at whatever English-made articles I have never seen before, for example, cycles, motorcycles, and cars. I took a very keen interest in gazing at the two-storey buildings, I admired people moving in them, and I often asked my brother whether they would not fall from there. . . .

At the start of the engine [of the train] I could not even open my eyes to see what beautiful things may be of interest to me. I was in that restless condition until we got to a station. The engine piped again, but this time I was encouraged by a friend to brave it out. On looking out I was stupefied at seeing, and at once assumed that everything else moved with us as we rode on.

Arriving in the city among strangers, our Ashanti will seek out the area in the town where people of his tribe, clan, or village reside. For the cities of Africa tend to be mosaics of small communities made up of people of common tribal background; the newcomer seems impelled by some unseen force to gravitate to the area where his friends and kinsmen are. Doubtless he will seek out some classificatory brother, some person whom he recognizes as close kin according to his native system of reckoning family ties, who will take him in and help him through his most difficult period of initial adjustment. Here he will learn how to find a job, where the chances are good, how he must behave in an urban surrounding. In short, he will have a brief introductory course in how to live an urban life and, needless to say, not all that he learns will be good. Ultimately he will find some job suited to his limited capacities —perhaps a minor clerkship if he happens to be literate, but more likely something involving the use of his muscles.

Life with his "brother" is not entirely serene. The "brother" and his family seem to have lost some of their proper Ashanti manners, for the newcomer no longer seems quite welcome in the home. In all fairness, however, the burden of the visitor is great. The crowded house in a compound or native quarter, or even in a residential section, cannot easily be enlarged by use of native materials. Food has to be purchased on the local market, and an extra mouth to feed is that much more expense. The visitor cannot help in the fields to meet the burden he creates, as he would have when visiting a relative in the country. His relative's job carries a fixed wage which does not expand with new obligations. The visitor must either contribute a regular sum to the menage or establish his own; ultimately, strains will appear that lead him to the latter course. When this happens, he becomes the typical urbanite, living on his own.

He will still be surrounded by tribesmen and kinsmen, but as he walks the streets or rides in the lorries that serve as buses, or as he works on the docks or in the office, he is surrounded by strangers from foreign lands, who express strange ideas in strange tongues, and who demonstrate very different ideas of right and wrong, very different cultural orientations. The whites hold few surprises for him, for he has known the district officers and Lebanese traders since infancy. The array of Africans— so like himself and yet so different—is what gives him an awareness of the true diversity of cultures. In the cities of Uganda— Kampala and Jinja—more than eighty different tribes are represented, and the figure is probably not much different in the cities on the west coast.

As our Ashanti feels himself increasingly alone in this strange sea of humanity, he will begin to seek out those associations which might supplant the loss of kinsmen. There are two reasons why he will do this: first, because he is lonely, and second, because he needs the mutual aid that unity offers. In response to this felt need, innumerable special associations have grown up throughout West Africa. Kenneth Little says:

> These include a host of new political, religious, recreational and occupational associations as well as the more traditional mutual aid groups and secret societies out of which some of the more recent organizations have developed. What generally distinguished the latter kind of association is its more formal constitution and the fact that it has been formed to meet certain needs arising specifically out of the urban environment of its members.

Little points out that there are fundamentally four types of voluntary associations in West Africa: tribal unions, friendly societies, occupational associations, and entertainment and recreational associations. Similar types of associations have also been reported from Rhodesia. The tribal unions range from small ones consisting of a few members of some extended family or clan to much larger bodies such as the Ibo state union, which is a collection of village and clan unions. Their main aim is to provide members with mutual aid while out of work, sympathy and financial assistance in case of illness, and funeral expenses and aid to the survivors in the case of death. Another purpose is to keep alive an interest in the tribal song, history, language, and moral belief, and thus to maintain the person's attachment to his native village, lineage, or tribe. The tribal unions are also becoming a factor in modern political organization, sometimes forming the basis for a political party or a pressure group. Some of these unions exist in the rural areas, where they are a means of coordinating local tribal activities.

The objectives of the friendly societies are limited to mutual aid and benefit. They are savings associations; each person contributes a sum of money each week and receives the total week's sum when his turn comes around. Even when they are directed to the practical purpose of saving or similar aid, they have some purely social function and constitute a group of people who maintain intimate and friendly contact in the alien environment.

In Accra, our young Ashanti might join the *Nanamei Akpee*, which provides funeral benefits, charity, and savings in one association. Its headquarters are in Accra, but there are branches in several coast towns and literally thousands of members. The monthly subscription is a shilling. When a member dies, the surviving relatives are given at least ten pounds toward the cost of funeral expenses. Money for loans is raised at weekly collections, which begin with a community sing. Each person gives the amount of money he feels he can afford, but it is carefully recorded. The money collected is given to the member whose name takes first place on the list, and on each succeeding week the next person on the list receives the money. In this way, each person ultimately gets a sum of money to meet larger expenditures. (The Tontine and Friendly Societies of the seventeenth and eighteenth centuries in Europe served a similar purpose.)

The occupational associations bring together people of like economic interests. Women who sell special goods such as yams or fish, craftsmen such as goldsmiths, tinkers, tailors, and barbers, and laborers such as the motor drivers, have banded together to form guilds resembling those of medieval Europe or unions on more modern lines. They require registration, maintain reasonable standards of work, rules of apprenticeship, and prices, and often settle disputes either between master and apprentice or between craftsman and customer. Some unions are also concerned with the character and deportment of their members.

The fourth type of association is concerned with dancing and music. Many of these, such as the drumming companies found in Ewe villages of Ghana, still retain much of their traditional character, but many of them in the city operate to provide social functions and entertainment for their members, and pattern themselves as best they can on the model of European social clubs.

Through these new ties and new occupations, our young Ashanti becomes an Accra man. He will not have lost all of his old Ashanti ties, but these will take on new forms and new meanings. More and more his associations will be divided into explicit contacts—here a work group, there a social club, and elsewhere a neighborhood—just as his daily life involves different orientations. Gone is the deep and involved personal contact with a group of kin with whom he spent his life, and in its stead is the very special relationship operating fundamentally in monetary terms instead of on the basis of kinship.

Detribalization

Detribalization is the process of removing the individual from tribal life, so that he is not living in the context of his traditional culture at all and no longer owes special allegiance to it. It is characteristic of those situations where the African works in European cities, mines, and the like, deprived of his normal social institutions and provided for by an alien economic and social system. It involves removal from the cultural milieu physically and alienation from it spiritually. The difference between urbanization and detribalization depends upon the conditions under which the shift from the native homeland to the urban or industrial center has taken place. Under urbanization, the migrant to the city seeks his own social life; under detribalization, either he is not free to seek such a pattern of existence, or he does not have the economic and social opportunities to find it.

Perhaps the most dismal portrayal of detribalized Africans is that given by Ellen Hellman of a compound called Rooiyard in Johannesburg. Here, in 105 rooms—most of them put together out of old lumber and beaten tins—lived 376 people from 11 different tribes, served by 6 latrines and 1 operating water tap. The time is 1932 and the conditions are particularly deplorable, but the situation described by Hellman is far from unique. However, we are not concerned with the squalor and indignity of a situation that derives from cupidity and unenlightened policies, deplorable as this is. Rather, we are concerned with what happens to the culture itself. Let us see what Miss Hellman has to say, selecting statements from different portions of her classic report.

> There is very little evidence of the survival of Bantu material culture. . . . The persistent endeavors of the native to absorb European material culture are limited only by his poverty. He aspires to possess the amenities which the invading culture has to offer him and a great part of his labor is conditioned by this desire. . . .
>
> There is no greater cohesion between families belonging to the same tribe than between families coming from far distant parts of the Union . . . [Indeed], analysis of the families reveals that the breaking up of the family is one of the first results of urban residence. Parents are well aware of the harmful effects of rearing children in the yard environment. They realize that the European school . . . is no substitute for the complete and harmonious system of tribal education. And hence many children are left to grow up in the country [among the tribesmen, but without the parents], so that they are not "cheeky like town children."
>
> Whereas the older people dwell with loving reminiscence on the joys of their former rural life, this attitude of contempt for their backward rural kinspeople is commonly encountered among the

younger urban Natives and especially among those who have spent their early years in an urban area.

Only two institutions built upon native life exist in this setting. One is the use of native medicines and of a medicine man (incidentally, the man who was the protagonist for the psychiatric novel *Black Hamlet*). The other is the brewing of native beer. While the illicit making and selling of beer became the center of Rooiyard life, it was in no sense the old beer-drinking custom. Thus Hellman says:

> The traditional offering to the ancestors before the living partake of the beer has been discarded by the majority. . . . As a sacrificial offering beer, too, has lost practically all of its original importance. . . . When they offer beer to the ancestors, [they] do so in the hope that [languishing business] may quicken and prosper. . . .
>
> The whole context and meaning of beer brewing has changed in an urban center. . . . The economic function of beer brewing has . . . far outstripped its social significance and recreational function.

There is still movement between the city and the tribal areas, but the next generation does not find it easy, for

> when families left Rooiyard to return to their rural homes, the parents went gladly but the more mature children were greatly disappointed. To the parents it meant return to the environment from which they had sprung. To the children it meant an uprooting from a familiar environment to alien surroundings.

Studies show that throughout Africa the natives who have lived for long in the city never fully readjust to the rural area. They say that once you become accustomed to the ways of Europeans, you cannot accommodate to the "uncivilized" way of rural people. Further, the villagers are distrustful of those who have "followed the Europeans." One put it this way: "The village people like you to come back for a few months, but if you stay for good they will poison you."

More recently, Clyde Mitchell has been studying urban workers in Northern Rhodesia. In his analysis of the Kalela dance, he shows how in the changed setting of industrial labor, the meaning of tribal origins has been transformed so that the worker no longer identifies with the specific community from which he comes, but with the larger social entity of which that community is a part. The Kalela dance has evolved out of older tribal dances, but it is now a town dance in which companies of young men, dressed to the nines in modern European clothes, form teams representing their tribe and contest with one another for supremacy in dancing and appearance. Mitchell finds the significance of this dance is that it displays the sense of the tribal origins, much as the Scottish and Welsh retain their ethnic identities, but without any real sense of personal involvement with tribal affairs and customs. The so-called "coloured" population in the Union of South Africa is a social element which, in generations past, has undergone this process of detribalization.

Acculturation, urbanization, and detribalization are type situations. They can vary in degree, and there can be mixture among them. Each contains some element of continuity and some element of change. It can easily be shown that even the least acculturated people of Africa have been subjected to some of the influences of Western civilization, while even the most severe detribalization does not entirely remove the cultural background of the individual subjected to the process.

CULTURAL BACKGROUND AND THE NEW STATES

To what extent are the old ways of culture to be incorporated into the new societies that are being formed in Africa? Can ancient patterns be built upon in the formulation of institutions designed to meet the exigencies of modern, increasingly industralized life? And if so, what are the problems that the African leaders must face? Such questions are as significant as they are difficult.

In Economics

First of all, we must appreciate the fact that many more Africans are living in the bush, cultivating land and herding stock, with but minor modifications of their ancient methods, than are living in the cities engaged in industrial pursuits. These latter are the visible part of Africa; it is their voice that is heard in distant lands. The Africans in the villages are acculturating to western society much more slowly, and they maintain the aboriginal patterns, with modification and improvement of their techniques. Thus far, efforts to make radical changes in rural life-ways have rarely met with success, the Gezira scheme in the Sudan, which was carefully planned, being a notable exception. On the other hand, such plans as the land consolidation among the Kikuyu of Kenya and the creation of the *paysannat indigène* in the former Belgian Congo, while rationalizing old methods of farming but not destroying old practices, appear to be successful changes that make for improved production and reduced labor costs, without disrupting the life-ways of the people.

The foods grown by African peasants remain important to the urban population. Indeed, a study of urban food consumption patterns in Ghana has shown that the city dwellers of all income groups eat much the same foods as the rural people. The whole food industry in Ghana, and elsewhere in Africa, operates on a system that has grown out of ancient customary uses. The foods are still raised by peasant farmers on small plots cultivated with the hoe. These foods are brought to the local market by the peasant himself—or, more accurately, herself. These markets are an age-old tradition. They dot the countryside, so that every piece of farmland is within an easy walk of several markets, and these markets are so coordinated that they fall on different days. In ancient times, they provided a means by which commodities moved from areas of plenty to areas of scarcity. Now, they are means of moving commodities from the food-producing areas of the hinterland into cities such as Accra. The only significant change has been the introduction of lorries, which enable the foodstuffs to move (once they leave the orbit of the local market) directly to the cities; significantly, these lorries are largely in the hands of women. Though commodities frequently change hands a dozen times between producer and consumer, the system appears not only to be effective as a means of distribution, but is responsive to the fluctuations of supply, demand, and price.

A similar redirecting of products to urban centers appears in the cattle markets of East Africa. Though traditionally people like the Masai and Sebei have considered their cattle to be wealth that should be hoarded, rather than exchanged for other goods, nowadays they are sending their surplus stock to the towns of Kenya and Uganda, where they form a significant part of the African diet. To be sure, this is done with stimulus from government officials who want to reduce overgrazing of the range and from Asians who dominate the trading. Although tribesmen may market their stock with reluctance, the new pattern is contributing to the modern economy without significantly disrupting the ongoing patterns of life.

African peasants have, in some places, shifted from subsistence farming to commercial production—notably in the growing of cocoa in Ghana and coffee and cotton in East Africa. These commodities are produced by peasant farmers; their introduction has brought cash to the villagers and has been a major source of revenue for the countries involved. But, as the social aspects of the production of such commodities are not very different from those of subsistence farming, they can be produced within the same general cultural environment. The contrast between the Chaga coffee-growing area in Tanganyika and the nearby sisal estates is apparent to the casual observer: In the former, the families live on the land and their social life continues in modification of age-old patterns; in the latter, the families—or, more often, single men—live in company housing away from ties of kin and neighborhood.

The important point of these illustrations is to show that the African rural economies can be transformed to meet the needs of modern life without wholesale destruction of the established order. This does not mean that they remain unchanged, nor that they should remain unchanged. Through technological innovation, the agricultural production of Africa can evolve slowly and transform the countryside gradually without a major disruption in the life-ways of the people. A good Ashanti cocoa-grower or a good Sebei cattleman can live a prosperous life, gradually improving his mode of existence, without destroying the pattern of his social relations.

In Society

Institutions adapted to village life may not easily meet the exigencies of modern industrial society. Land ownership patterns illustrate this better than anything else. Land in Africa is often owned by the kin group. The situation is actually more complex than this implies, for a single tribe may have many different types of landholdings, with special rights held by various kin and other groups, often under special religious sanction.

A detailed study of the Nigerian cocoa farmer by Galletti, Baldwin, and Dina treats the problem of landholding. The Yoruba cocoa farmers have clear ideas of property in personal possessions and the distinction between right of occupancy and of alienation, but they do not at any time seem to have thought of the land as belonging to a single individual or authority, nor to have considered the holder and user of land to have an unrestricted proprietary right. The authors describe some of these complications as follows (though this is far from the total complexity):

> It would seem that the essential rights in Yoruba thinking are those of use and not those of final disposal. . . . As the principal rights of use have been hitherto those of farming the land and harvesting the trees standing on it, and these rights have with few exceptions been exercised by individuals or families, not by larger groups, the main elements of the system of land rights can be stated fairly simply.
>
> It is much more difficult to elucidate the customary but changing "law" governing transfer and alienation. For the rights to dispose of land, unlike the rights to use, are for the most part held by groups rather than by individuals. . . . For the present purpose [these groups] can be listed in rising order of amplitude as the elementary family, the joint or extended family, the compound or sublineage, the lineage and the kindred, as kinship groups; and the quarter, the village, or town, and the "community" or "tribe" headed by the chief as groups of increasing local extent.
>
> An individual may hold land as a member of any of these groups: but that group may in turn hold land as a member of a larger group or a group of a different kind. For instance, the individual may be allowed to cultivate certain land held by the extended family to which he belongs, the extended family may have been allotted this land by the head of the *idile* or *ebi* of which it is a part, and the *ebi* may de-

rive its rights from a grant made by the *Oba* as representing the whole tribe.

The "community" is not always the same thing, cannot easily be defined and exercises its rights in ways which vary. . . . In practice rights over land are not claimed by any authority representing the Yoruba people as a whole: but they may be claimed by the tribal group headed by a Native Authority or by the town or village represented by its chiefs and council. . . .

But in all areas there still persists, sometimes as a faint survival, sometimes in great strength, the concept of "village" control over the land of a settlement.

The complexity of land rights deprives it of use as security on loans. This hampers development by farmers and small entrepreneurs, who find it difficult to get adequate development capital. The report notes that:

where, as in the Yoruba country, the title to land is held by groups and the encumbrance of land or buildings by individuals is hedged around with conditions, the very basis for mortgage lending—clear and transferable title—is lacking.

To this day in most parts of the Yoruba country there is no right allowed to the individual farmer to pledge land held by his lineage or kindred as a group. If such land is offered to a lender as security he must make difficult and lengthy inquiries to make sure that all the parties entitled to be consulted have given their consent. Even moneylenders in the home town of the lineage may find it hard to assure themselves that they will be able to secure possession or enforce the sale of the security if the borrower fails to keep up his payments. . . .

There is a limit to what even the most benevolent lender will lend on personal security. The farmers' personal goods and chattels do not constitute a satisfactory security for large loans. Even co-operative primary credit societies in which all the members are known to each other and linked by mutual goodwill cannot afford to lend freely when other forms of security are not available. The mortgage of land and buildings is necessary if the capital of the farmer "sunk" in these assets is to be mobilized again for working capital and emergent needs.

Whether the problem thus created can be compromised, or must simply be legislated away, is not clear. A gradual transformation appears to be emanating from the urban centers where Europeanized land rights are more frequent.

In many parts of Africa, clans and lineages are adopting modern institutional techniques to preserve and utilize their old kin loyalties. Thus one finds the development of clan chairmen and treasurers, and the establishment of treasuries for the aid of indigent members, for the purpose of providing funds for schooling and the like. Clan organizations can formulate themselves into modern corporate entities for the purposes of holding and handling estates. This would not, in itself, permit of the alienation of land, but it would permit the rationalization of land-holdings and ease the accumulation of development capital.

The question of cultural continuity is an insistent one for those who are trying to forge legal systems for the newly emergent governments. Colonial jurisprudence had left most local matters to customary rules and native practices, applying European law chiefly to major crimes and urban and European affairs. In Ghana, for instance, an effort has been made to recognize customary procedures in the formulation of modern laws, and the same is true for the newly drafted Ethiopian code. The process is extremely difficult for several reasons: (1) native law varies from one ethnic group to another and frequently has not been recorded (though efforts are currently being made to record tribal law); (2) Africans have had variant experiences with Western law, and not all of them want to return to old rules and procedures; (3) most important, native law is often imprecise, justice being administered by persons who know the full background and context of local disputes and hence render judgments in the light of such considerations rather than merely by application of formal regulations. Nevertheless, in matters pertaining to inheritance, succession, and family law in general, the law must take into account established customs.

In Statecraft

For the most part, even where old kingdoms exist, modern states have built their institutions of government along the lines of their metropolitan tutors rather than in accord with their native social institutions, just as they have thus far accepted (with minor modifications) the definition of their state boundaries in terms of colonial partition. At the same time, there is a desire to maintain old political ties and loyalties, particularly where strongly articulated kingdoms existed. A notable example is Uganda, home of the centrally organized state of Buganda. There were other lesser states within modern Uganda boundaries as well as tribal societies without political organization. The Baganda are a proud and progressive people and, partly because of their old political superiority, they have come to dominate Uganda. Their social institutions were adopted by the British for administering the country, so that tribes of the hinterland (such as Sebei) now have a modified form of Buganda institutions. Further, the Buganda Kingdom still exists as a state within a state, its people owing loyalty to their Kabaka (king), and meeting in their Lukiiko (council). Lloyd A. Fallers, in a recent essay, sets forth the degree to which, despite modernization, the Buganda Kingdom has maintained itself intact. If the modern country of Uganda was coterminous with the old kingdom (or nearly so), there would be no difficulty in re-establishing it and maintaining a modern parliamentary monarchy. Unfortunately for this simple solution, the spread of Buganda administrative techniques did not make Baganda of the outlying people, and politics in newly independent Uganda centers on the conflict between Buganda and her neighbors.

Similarly, the Ashanti kingdom once controlled a large part of the territory of Ghana, and pre-independence politics involved the conflict between Ashanti and others. But here the Ashanti have become the minority and Nkrumah is opposed to the political power of the Ashanti and of all tribal chiefs, who gained authority during the period of "indirect rule." Significantly, Ashanti-land remains a center of opposition to the Nkrumah government. Yet even so, some observers consider the basic orientation of modern Ghana government to derive from the generic pattern of indigenous political institutions.

An intermediate course is possible: a central government operating on modern constitutional lines, which allows for a high degree of regional autonomy. This has been the solution in Nigeria, where three major cultural divisions—the north, the east, and the west—are highly autonomous. In Kenya, on the eve of her independence, political parties are divided on precisely this issue. There were no kingdoms in Kenya, but certain tribes—notably the Kikuyu and the Luo—were large and strong and had grown in importance. Many political leaders, following the line of Jomo Kenyatta, desire a strongly centralized government—one which would override tribal loyalties. The smaller ethnic units, which fear the unified strength of the larger tribes, are concerned with the loss of their lands to them, and believe a centralized authority would deprive them of the privilege of maintaining their old customs. They favor a high degree of regional autonomy. In this context, it is interesting that the leaders of the several so-called Nilo-Hamitic peoples in East Africa—Nandi, Kipsigis, Pokot, and Masai (and the Sebei of Uganda)—have created a new unity they call Kalingen, based upon remote cultural and linguistic ties, despite the fact that they had formerly been enemies. This is the emergence at the political level of that tendency toward wider tribal loyalties that Mitchell found expressed by the Kalela dance in the Rhodesian copper belt. As of this writing, the two major parties in Kenya seem to be arriving at a compromise in degree of regional autonomy.

In Sentiments

The conflict between old customs and new demands expresses itself in the realm of cultural sentiments and ideology. The new leadership is recruited from among that element of the African population which is most highly acculturated, most thoroughly urbanized, and alienated from their tribal backgrounds. The very fight for independence required such persons who are impatient with old ideas. Nkrumah, Mboya, and Nyerere have all expressed in one way or another their distaste for tribal orientations and old customs, and have acted to destroy or diminish the powers of traditional leaders.

But contrary sentiments also exist. No people likes to deny its cultural ancestry, and there is a strong reassertion of old cultural values. We find the public expression of such attitudes in names like Ghana and Mali, which refer to ancient kingdoms, in the use of old symbols of state—such as the Ashanti sword and drums—in modern African parliaments, and in the return of African leaders to old forms of dress, at least for public occasions. African musicians and artists often seek to build upon old forms—though here it must be admitted that Africans prefer sociological novels to the African-based works of Tutuola, whose *Palm Wine Drinkard* is much admired outside Africa.

The psychological need to assert cultural roots finds expression in the development of an African-oriented history. In the hands of European historians, African history has been concerned exclusively with the conquest of the continent, leaving to the anthropologist any discussion of events purely African. As Immanuel Wallerstein points out, the Europeans had used the teaching of history as a means of justifying notions of European cultural superiority, and African efforts to rewrite their histories may best be seen as a natural reaction against this. They have thus extolled the Africans who resisted European invasion as heroic, and have created a past which gains intellectual justification for modern national aspirations. Indeed, they have projected histories that not only link modern African states to ancient Sudanic kingdoms but even back to cultural origins in Egypt. This is not only the manifestation of the intellectuals; I have myself seen it happen on the tribal level. Young Sebei political leaders tell a mythical story of their origin which links them and all Kalingen peoples, thus giving a kind of historic justification for the new political grouping of these tribes in Kenya (and, naturally, placing the Sebei in a most favorable position)— stories which are not known to their elders from Sebei.

Thomas Hodgkin summarizes this ennoblement of the African past in his *Nationalism in Colonial Africa* as follows:

Perhaps the most important, and deeply felt, aspect of the nationalist answer to the myth of African barbarism is the new stress placed on the qualities of pre-European African societies: their achievements in such fields as the plastic arts, work in gold and bronze and ivory, music and dancing, folk story and folk poetry; the complexity and depth of their religious beliefs and metaphysics; their conception of the community—as "consisting of the dead, the living and the un-born"; their rational attitude to sexual relations and to the place of women in society—their delight in children and reverence for the aged; their view of education, as a process continuing through life; their dislike of autocracy, and their delicate political mechanisms for securing the expression and adjustment of different interests and wills.

In this period of African nationalism, these histories tend to be nationalistic, but Pan-African sentiments are also put forth. The most highly elaborated ideological expression of this is in the concept of Negritude, developed by French West African intellectuals over the past thirty years. In this concept, they assert the essential virtues inherent in the Negro personality, stressing in positive terms many of the very characteristics that have been made the subject of prejudice by outsiders, such as warmth of personality, capacity for love, and sense of rhythm. There is a natural appeal to the African in this conception when expressed in the poetic form of the creators of this senti-ment, Leopold Senghor and Alioune Diop. It is doubtful whether the essential racism of these sentiments can be sustained among a people who have themselves been subject to the prejudice of racial thinking. This certainly is the response of the South African author, Ezekiel Mphahlele, in his recent work, *The African Image*.

SUMMARY

Now that the era of colonial rule is drawing to a close, the Africans are themselves masters of their destinies and once again in charge of their social systems. History has treated them badly; it has taken from them the security of past ways of life and put them on the road to modernization. Yet this process is, so to speak, contracted for but hardly begun.

The period of colonial rule has been condemned for the brutalities inflicted and the injuries done. We have come to be aware that this colonial rule was no unmitigated evil; that the legacy in economic infrastructure and technical education has given some advantage to ex-colonial territories not shared by areas like Liberia and Ethiopia, which had no European masters. But the real hardship of colonialism lies less in these brutalities and injustices than in the undermining of native institutions, the destruction of cultural values, and the demoralization of the population.

The establishment of homogeneous societies out of atomistic tribal communities would have been difficult under any circumstances. To the disparity of cultures and languages must now be added the diversity in degree of Westernization and acculturation, in value orientations extending from the tribalistic to the modern and including a considerable sector lacking commitment to any coherent set of values.

It is the task of African leadership to forge integrated societies out of such hetrogeneous populations. They will have to seek means of formulating institutions for modern, increasingly industrialized societies out of the social systems of the past. They will have to revitalize old values and make them meaningful to peoples engaged in new tasks. They will have to reintegrate the conservatives of the hinterland with the progressives of the city and give the disaffected a sense of commitment to the new societies.

Americans, like all those who stand at the side but wish the best for the Africans, must appreciate the magnitude of the task. We cannot expect that the institutions, the values, and the sentiments will be replicas of our own, nor should we wish it. Rather, we should direct our actions to the end that the Africans can develop their own societies in conformity with their culturally derived needs; societies in which all sectors share the same values and obtain satisfactions through the achievement of their own cultural aims.

7. Social Change and Social Problems in Contemporary Africa

ST. CLAIR DRAKE

Between Two Worlds

Kobla and his Family

When I first met him in 1954, Kobla was a cook for a British professor at the University College of the Gold Coast, near the capital city of Accra—proud of his skill and his job. Like many of his Ewe fellow tribesmen, he had crossed the border from the neighboring French territory of Togoland, to the more prosperous Gold Coast. Ewe cooks and stewards were in demand, as local tribesmen (Fante, Ga, Ashanti) had higher ambitions than being house servants. Nowadays Ewes are moving up into better jobs, and members of the Ijaw tribe from Nigeria have been doing this kind of work. (Tribes from "backward" northern Ghana do the very dirty work in Accra.)

Kobla was then in his forties, vigorous and healthy, riding his bicycle two miles to work every day and performing as leader of the strenuous Ewe dances on Saturday nights and Sunday afternoons. He was a polygamist, living with his three wives and eleven children in a large mud house which his brothers and cousins had helped him build in a predominantly Ewe village near the college.

Kobla earned thirty dollars a month. His wives cultivated cassava, condiments, and vegetables on a patch of land which he and his "brothers" had cleared for planting. They also collected firewood in a forest preserve nearby, carrying it home in large bundles on their heads (the small children bring cans of water on their heads from a standpipe), and took turns keeping house and selling some of their produce and other articles in a nearby market. Income from wages and marketing was pooled, each wife drawing a small allowance. The bulk of the meager joint income was spent for clothes, books, and school fees for the older children. Kobla had the reputation of being a just and fair husband, and a skilled and patient arbiter between occasionally angry and disputatious wives.

Kobla had a well-thought-out orientation toward the modern world. Once he said to me, "I send the children to school and to the Roman church. I tell them when they be big they cannot be like me. I pray to the *trowo* [Ewe lesser gods] but they need to know the Christian gods. My women work and they help me. The educated women my sons will marry will not help them this way. They will ask the husband for radiograms and clothes from the store and maybe even for motor cars. I tell these sons, 'You marry only one woman.' "

Kobla had no apologies to make for his own way of life. He was proud of his reputation as a good manager of a polygamous household. He was also a *bokor*—a healer using herbs and magic, and therefore respected in the village by chiefs and elders as well as by ordinary men and women. But Kobla was a realist. He knew that his children were confronting a rapidly modernizing world. He was trying to help them to get the most out of it.

When I returned to the college in 1958, I saw much of Kobla. His "master" was preparing to return to England and Kobla was seeking help in finding a new one who would respect his sense of personal dignity as the old one had. (Despite his use of the term "master," Kobla's bearing and his tone always revealed that it meant no more to him than our word "mister.") Above all, he wanted a new employer who would help him to educate his children, the professor having already agreed to sending his eldest son to a technical school. I received Kobla's sincere thanks for having helped a sister's son (for whom he was responsible) get a job, and before I left for America, Kobla had maneuvered me into paying high school fees for a young cousin who had been placed in his care. By now, Kobla had taken a fourth wife (all three of his wives had been pregnant, and by custom he could not have sexual relations with any of them until they had borne and weaned the babies) and had fifteen children.

During the summer of 1961 I was in Ghana as a consultant for the Peace Corps, and Kobla paid me a courtesy call. Never before, living as he was in an alien land, had he been willing to discuss politics with me. This time he volunteered a political observation, smiling broadly: "I have a country now. We have 'big man,' too, now—Mr. Olympio." Kobla had become a proud citizen of a new nation, but he was not planning to return home. Economic opportunities were still better in Ghana, and the "socialist" politicians there were talking of free schooling and free textbooks—not of balancing the budget as in Togo.

Just before he left, Kobla unwrapped a package he had brought. It turned out to be a large book with yellowed leaves. He had a favor to ask. The book was a mail order catalog from a now defunct Chicago company that dealt in occult goods. Would I send him a set of the beads with the cross and one of the Egyptian rings made like a coiled snake and with "diamonds" in the eye? My mind flashed back immediately to the time his nephew had asked for money to consult an *afa* for medicine to protect him against the jealousy of villagers whose sons and nephews had no patron; he was preparing to sit an exam. I wondered whether Kobla was now seeking some even heavier magic —from Chicago—to strengthen the protective shield which he was trying to throw around the kinsmen upon whom he was expending so much thought, hard work, and money. Or did he simply want to enhance his prestige in the village?

Just before I left Ghana, I returned Kobla's visit. We sat in his shabby room with its bunk bed and two battered chairs, cluttered with his few treasured personal possessions. His old mother from Togo happened to be visiting, as well as two literate friends. The old lady's breasts were bare and hanging low. When her son explained that I was the professor-friend from America who was helping "the family," she made a dignified half-curtsy as she would have for a chief, and then withdrew to become a silent spectator. No one felt embarrassed. Her son and I went on to discuss wages and the high cost of living. As I was leaving I noticed on the wall a picture of Kwame Nkrumah—not Olympio, the President of Togo—and I remembered that somewhere in northern Ghana was Kobla's younger brother who had been born in Ghana and was now a "big man"—a civil servant. Kobla had sent him through school.

Traditional Ties in Transformation

There are thousands of families like Kobla's throughout Africa, polygamous, and maintaining close ties with relatives, but with some members of the family bound into and participating in a structure of modern occupations, voluntary associations, schools, churches, and a governmental apparatus which has been expanding with almost explosive force since the beginning of World War II. Kobla stands between two worlds, enjoying a modestly successful and apparently satisfying life-way. Through him we can look forward and glimpse the outlines of an emerging new society, just as through him we can look backward to the ancient system of social relationships and culturally defined attitudes which still have a hold upon Africa.

Despite their desire for money and the products of European and American factories that it can buy, and a widespread demand throughout the continent for more schools and hospitals, electricity and better housing, and more and more comforts and conveniences, most Africans still live their lives deeply enmeshed within the web of traditional society.

At least seven out of every ten inhabitants of Africa have their roots down deep in villages or cattle camps, and are engaged in some combination of agriculture, pastoralism, fishing, and hunting. No more than one African in five works for wages, and most of these are employed in some type of agricultural labor or in forestry. The great forces of urbanization and industrialization have barely touched the majority of the people on the continent, and even those involved have not all been alienated from the traditional way of life. Furthermore, over 80 per cent of Africa's people are illiterate, so that human and verbal symbols learned as children, reinforced by ritual, have more influence upon them than the cold type of printed pages. Again, wide areas of life are regulated by sacred customs, not to be questioned; a sense of the supernatural is a vivid reality, and belief in the rewarding and punishing power of gods and ancestors reinforces adherence to custom. Myth and ritual related to creation, fertility, birth, puberty, marriage, and death help to give cohesion to society and meaning to life. These are basic reasons why traditional society has survived and is still amazingly viable.

THE FORCES OF TRADITION

The Network of Kinship

As with us, it is to members of his immediate family that the African feels *really* close—not to his co-nationals or members of the same race or ancestry group, nor to residents of town or city. This family (which sociologists call a primary group to distinguish it from less intimate secondary groups) is universal. It is the critical link between the individual and his society. To a far greater degree than in Europe and America, the African family is closely tied into a broader web of kinship that extends outward the bonds of intimate social expectancies.

When an African says "my family," he may very well mean a group quite different from the one that includes his mother and father, his wife and children; he may be speaking of what anthropologists call his "lineage"—that is, a group of his relatives who trace their descent from a known common ancestor, perhaps a great-grandfather or great-grandmother (depending upon whether descent is traced in the male or female line). For most Africans, the lineage is the group that really matters, although in some areas a person may also belong to a clan, a larger group of people who claim descent from an even more remote ancestor, and to which he has very real and meaningful obligations.

Traditionally, lineages have worked upon the active principle of "We brothers and sisters are each others' keepers" (and in lineages, even distant cousins are "brothers" and "sisters"). A man and wife and their children may work together to maintain a home or a compound, and have profound respect and affection for each other, but both husband and wife are still tightly bound to their own respective lineages (rules of exogamy require that they be of different lineages) and have obligations to them: to aid financially in the celebration of marriages and funerals and to participate in them, if possible; to extend mutual aid to one another in cash or kind; to put pressure upon each other for correct behavior; and, today, to help in educating one another's children. Members of a lineage who have the most in terms of money, housing space, or strategic contacts are expected to contribute the most. To evade obligations or to disgrace the group may bring down retribution from ancestors, as well as social pressure.

A French social scientist studying Leopoldville just a few years before Congo independence, attacked what he called "family parasitism . . . the plague of the urban proletariat." He was referring no doubt both to the conjugal family and the lineage, decrying the fact that urban members still seemed to be tightly bound to rural society. I suspect, however, that most Africans would see something laudable—not reprehensible—about Leopoldville's city folks sending over 200,000 francs every month by postal money orders from meager wages to relatives in the back country, and taking another 200,000 francs worth of food and other gifts each month to the villages by bus, bicycle, train, and truck. They would feel it to be good that urban houses always have a sleeping place and food for relatives who come to town, keep children who are sent to them so they may attend a city school, or give assistance to indigent family members. Christian Congolese would probably combine sentiments of idealism and practicality in the quotation: "Cast thy bread upon the waters. . . ." It may, indeed, have come back during

the Congo crisis, when Leopoldville citizens sometimes sought
refuge and food in the villages.

Lineage Obligations and Problems of Social Change

Some Africans are coming to share the French scholar's ap-
praisal of lineage obligations, particularly those who hope to
accumulate capital or want to enjoy their own conspicuous
consumption, and among literates who find lineage ties preventing them from detaching themselves from tribal society as
completely as they would wish. Only 45 per cent of a group of
African students studying in the United States felt that "ful-
fillment of one's 'family' obligations is the proper thing," according to Alvin Zalinger of Boston University. A few years
ago, the widely read African magazine *Drum* ran an illustrated
interview-with-the-man-in-the-street feature on "Are Our Families Bleeding Us Dry?" A surprisingly large number of people
said "Yes," echoing sentiments of a Nigerian college student in
America who had told Zalinger that "our family obligations
place too much of a strain on successful individuals. It isn't
the close ties that I object to but the dependency." Literate
wives who have learned to treasure privacy and to value the
small close-knit conjugal family can be particularly sharp in
their criticisms of the lineage system. They *do* object to the
close ties as well as to the dependency.

Whether or not the lineage system can survive under modern
conditions is a matter for frequent discussion. Zalinger quotes
one student as saying: "I feel sorry to see the old way go. The
bond of family love has weakened. The family is getting further
apart. But I know that we cannot have both this and progress."
Another student had no ambivalence about the matter: "If the
price of industrialization and Westernization is the breakup of
the traditional family, it is a good price to pay. We cannot let
the family system stand in the way of these developments."

Some of the leaders of new African states, among them Nkrumah, Kenyatta, Nyerere, Sekou Touré, and Senghor, are committed to the building of what they refer to as "African socialism," and there is a tendency for some of them to emphasize the

lineage system, along with communal land tenure, as the two cornerstones of traditional society upon which a new, slowly industrializing, decentralized, modern society should be based. Leopold Senghor, poet-President of Senegal, incorporates this idea into his hope for a *"humanistic* African socialism," in contrast to what he feels is an undesirable type of socialism for Africa—the modified Marxism of Sekou Touré and Kwame Nkrumah. Yet these latter ideologists, too, sometimes speak of preserving "the good features of our family system." When they say this, one thing they have in mind is the fact that the lineage system helps to keep down the rates of destitution within urban areas by providing a vehicle through which the aged, the temporarily unemployed, and the sick can receive some care.

Those interested in extending free enterprise find some comfort in the fact that in at least one area in West Africa competent businessmen within a lineage have been known to invest the family funds in real estate or in securities, to manage the collective property and to make annual reports. As an African college student observed in Ghana, "There is neither any legal or logical reason why an *abusua* [matrilineal lineages of the Ashanti and Fanti] couldn't be turned into a joint-stock company or limited liability corporation or be set up as a cooperative."

While ideologically-oriented West African leaders may fantasy about the place of the lineage in some future socialist society, they have plenty of worries about its actual effect upon their new mixed-economy states involved in rapid economic growth and bureaucratic expansion. The strategically placed politician is usually under pressure to give jobs to his "brothers." Also, since the "big men" in the lineage are expected to be generous in helping others with school fees, doctor bills, contributions toward funeral and wedding ceremonies, and "bride-price" (where that is the custom), and are expected to extend hospitality to relatives, carefully garnered capital is sometimes drained away by a series of family crises. There is thus a temptation to accept bribes or to "borrow" from public funds. One West African state tried to stimulate small business by making loans to entrepreneurs, but had to stop because of the high number of bankruptcies and defaulting on loans. Using the money for lineage obligations was cited as one, though not the only, factor in these failures. "We should go in on a mass scale for co-ops," one young party militant said. "Then a man who works for the co-op can say, 'The money isn't mine. If I let *you* 'chop' it, they send *me* to jail.' Our socialist enterprises will protect you from your brothers' pressure."

Ethnic Groups or Tribes

People who speak the same language and share a common set of customs and values constitute an ethnic group, of which there are over 5,000 in Africa. Most of these are tribes (educated Africans usually dislike the term) that were not organized as political states, and the basic solidarities within them are those of kinship. African ethnic groups vary in size from the Yoruba of Nigeria, with 3 million members, to the Kung Bushmen in the Kalihari Desert, with only 4,000 members. Most African nations are composed of more than one tribe, while frequently a tribe has been split between two or more states. As a sense of belonging to a tribe is a living reality throughout Africa, the transfer of loyalty from ethnic group to nation forms a fundamental problem. Ethnic groups with powerful traditional rulers often give cunning and stubborn opposition to the innovations of modern Western leaders.

Ethnic identity does not necessarily dissolve when Africans move to cities, as Goldschmidt suggests elsewhere in this book by the distinction between urbanization and detribalization. In fact, ethnic identity and solidarity may operate as stabilizing forces in cities that are absorbing large groups of migrants. For instance, in some West African cities, police do not book a man arrested for minor infractions of the law, but refer such cases to the tribal headman, letting him either arbitrate or, with his council, try the case and assign blame and punishment—or, perchance, effect some kind of restitution or reconciliation.

Many young people will no longer accept the authority of

tribal headmen and chiefs who speak with the wisdom of the headman of a Rhodesian mining town:

> A good person is not quarrelsome, but peaceful; he does not use abusive words; he shares his food with others and is hospitable; he keeps secrets told to him, and tries to reconcile families who hate each other; if he sees a person developing bad habits like stealing, he stops him and talks to him—but not in front of others.

Nor do they any longer carry out tribal customs, but this does not mean that their sense of ethnic identity has been lost. "Ethnicity," in the sense of identification with an ethnic group, may eventually replace tribalism. An Ibo of Nigeria will then think of himself primarily as a Nigerian citizen, in the same way that a Scotsman is loyal to the United Kingdom without ever losing his pride in being Scottish.

The Transformation of Cultural Conflict into Social Problems

The most important forces affecting the transformation of traditional society in Africa have been the introduction of education under the auspices of Christian missions, the wide extension of a money economy, and the development of modern commercial and industrial activity, including the growth of cities. Until recently, these processes have taken place within a political framework of European colonial administration; now, throughout most of the continent, they are proceeding within newly independent states whose leaders are intent upon modernizing them as soon as possible.

African societies are involved in a process of profound *social* change, one important aspect of the broader process of cultural change. Individuals are forced to adjust to a constantly shifting constellation of social groups; old types of relationships are increasingly difficult to maintain, and shifting values and varying rates of change are confusing to the individual and disorganizing to the society. Social change is a two-way process involving the adaptation of traditional forms of social organi-

zation to new goals as well as the elaboration of new institutions
to cope with novel situations.

The modern Africans are everywhere involved in continuous
discussion of social change and its effects upon themselves. They
seem to be in constant dialogue about right behavior and wrong
in their complex new situation. (Some of this fascinating dialogue is presented verbatim in Aidan Southall and Peter
Gutkind's study of the slums of Kampala, Uganda, *Townsmen
in the Making* and in Hortense Powdermaker's *Copper Town*.)
Sociological investigations in all parts of the continent, as well
as editorials, feature articles, and letters-to-the-editor in African
newspapers and magazines reveal an amazing amount of intellectual ferment and critical awareness, among illiterates as
well as literates. As C. Wright Mills observed in *The Sociological
Imagination,* people are in the process of turning personal
troubles into social issues—that is, they are defining social problems. Much of the popular comment and discussion, and some
of the demands for social action, center upon the moral order
in its relation to various aspects of family and kinship relations, upon marriage customs and the place of women in the
society. There is an increasing tendency to extend criticism to
include the whole context of social change. We can only give
examples.

The Changing Status of Women

So crucial are family and kinship relations to the stability
of society that the changing status of women, and of their own
conceptions of what that status should be, is of constant concern to some segments of African opinion. Among illiterate
males, for example, there is an uneasy feeling that "women are
out of control," or that "woman palaver" is increasing. Illiterates
are not trained in analyzing social forces, and therefore it is not
surprising that some African males everywhere have attitudes
approximating those that have arisen among the Fang tribe in
Gabon, and which the eminent French sociologist, G. Balandier,
characterizes as "the development of a veritable anti-feminism
which attributes to the fact that women have become 'wrong-

headed' all the alleged disorders and especially the decline in fertility of men and the soil." (Women seem to have served as scapegoats for society's ills from the time of Pandora and Eve to the American, as well as the African, present.)

Women were never so subordinated in traditional African society as Western critics assume, nor so "free and equal" as some of the more romantic nationalists and anthropologists imply, but in traditional African society, as in all folk societies, there was a balance of rights and duties and a division of labor that was not deemed unfair. Economic forces have destroyed this equilibrium, and familiarity with other ways of life has caused some women in Africa to question their position even in those isolated areas of the continent where society and economy are still in balance.

African women are becoming "liberated" psychologically, and the frequent travel of even illiterate women on visits with various delegations to Europe, America, China, and the U.S.S.R. is speeding up the process. Women are translating new wishes into action and are demanding that some of the new freedoms with which they are now experimenting be institutionalized. Many men—both literate and illiterate—deplore and resent Africa's "new woman." A few accept and admire. The problem for more sophisticated African males who have acquired some education is of a different order—how to find an "educated" wife, since the education of girls has not kept pace with that for boys.

The status of women is closely bound up with customs of betrothal and marriage, and of the sharing of duties and responsibilities within family and kinship units. "Bride-price" and polygamy are widely discussed as two traditional institutions around which problems are arising. We shall consider one of these as an example of how social problems are defined.

Polygamy as a Social Issue

Kobla does not question either the ethics or utility of polygamy for himself, though he thinks it may not be expedient for his sons. But the rights and wrongs of polygamy come in

for considerable discussion among people interested in modernizing African societies, though most African families are actually
monogamous. It is perhaps ironic that some Africans are asking
for vigorous action to outlaw polygamy at the very time that
many missionaries have come to accept the position of anthropologists that polygamy has functional utility in African agricultural societies under certain conditions (the Mende have a
proverb, "It takes four wives to make a rice farm"), and are
inclined to wait for education, Christianity, and economic
pressures to force it gradually out of existence.

The original definition of polygamy as undesirable was made
by missionaries, who considered the practice immoral, and
often made monogamy a condition for church membership or
the taking of communion. Other non-Africans also tried to discourage polygamy in attempts to mold an emerging working
class into a Western image, to prevent disputes between women
over their husband's wages, and to reduce housing costs. Thus
the mining companies of the Northern Rhodesian copper-belt
instituted a rule that no worker with more than one wife could
occupy a house in the company towns. The Belgian administration devised a similar regulation for municipally-owned housing in the African sections of Congo cities. Such attempts by
white industrialists and colonial powers to alter established
custom were really not effective. It is reported that one result
was an increase in the number of women who were registered
as "sisters" by male household heads, and in the number of
women who became "concubines." From time to time, the
administrations in French Equatorial Africa, the Congo, and
Portuguese territories have held up the prize of special civil
rights for Africans who would abandon polygamy. They had
few takers.

The significant development in contemporary Africa is that
Africans themselves are questioning both the utility and morality of the custom. African Christians, quite understandably, are
concerned with the issue. For instance, the Lumpa Church
(60,000 claimed members, predominantly illiterate) founded in
Northern Rhodesia by the prophetess Alice Lenshina, has an
article in its constitution which reads: "A Christian may not

be a polygamist." On the other hand, the head of a very flourishing West African church which had seceded from the Methodists made this cynical comment: "I say marry the women and take responsibility for them and the children. That's better and more Christian than having concubines." Other African separatist church leaders defend the right of their members to be polygamous by quoting Biblical texts.

Some sensitive and sophisticated Africans, with a political orientation, feel that the existence of polygamy exposes their continent to the charge of being "primitive" by both the Communist world and the West. A growing number, too, argue that under modern conditions, the potential for the exploitation of women that was always latent in the system is apt to be accentuated, that "custom becomes corrupted."

Another situation forcing critical reappraisal of polygamy is the coexistence in some African countries of marriage by customary law with civil and church marriage. Some men marry the one woman allowed "under the ordinance," or by the church, and then several others by customary law, often evading responsibilities to the children of the latter, and bringing dismay to the educated first wife who expected her husband to remain monogamous.

The main opposition to polygamy comes from literate women. Kobla suspects that the spread of education will weaken the system because it will prove too expensive for men with educated wives who will refuse either to work or to put their money in a common pool. What is much more likely, however, is that as more and more women are educated, they will simply refuse to accept the status of being a wife in a polygamous household. A study of secondary school students in Ghana by Dr. Peter Omari of Ghana University's sociology department, revealed that while more than 50 per cent of the boys approved of polygamy, not one girl did. Studies by the *Institut Français d'Afrique Noire* (IFAN) show that in Dakar the percentage of polygamous families drops sharply as one moves upward from the illiterate segment of society through ordinary white-collar workers, to people doing professional work.

Eventually, social problem definition creates a demand for

governmental action, but African political leaders may be no more successful than colonial governments were in trying to legislate against entrenched customs. Ghana had been experimenting with a law preventing men from marrying under two systems, providing that they may be tried for bigamy if they take wives under customary law after they have contracted a marriage under civil or church law. The Convention Peoples Party, in 1962, under pressure from female members, wrote a plank into its seven-year "Work and Happiness Program" promising to find a way to make polygamous marriages illegal in the future without injury to those now so married. However, when the bill came before the Legislative Assembly, at least half of the male CPP legislators were opposed to any such action. It was not passed. The debate goes on, inside parliament and out.

Problems of Induced Change

Some attempts to shake off the onus of "primitive" or "savage," which the outer world has hung on Africa, lead to unusual types of problem definition. Such is the case of "nudity" in Ghana, which throws light on problems of induced change.

The women in southern Ghana take great pride in wearing colorful dress, but in some parts of the less developed north women wear very scanty clothing. Popular feeling has grown over the last five years in the more sophisticated south that this "nudity" is a "disgrace to modern Ghana," and a legislator from the north, reacting to southern citicism, proposed to introduce a bill "abolishing nudity" (as well as clitoridectomy and scarification). The Department of Social Welfare and Community Development persuaded the government to have the sociology department of the University make a thorough study of "factors in the wearing and non-wearing of clothing in northern Ghana" before embarking upon hasty legislation.

The survey revealed that neither men nor women in the "nude" tribes, except those in school or with some education, defined the scantily-clad state as a problem, although they showed some bemused understanding of why others thought so.

(Others were uncomprehending, as in the case of an old lady who said, "Look at me. I need 'cloth'; but for the young unmarried girl there—who wants to buy a goat in a bag?" They were not uncooperative to the study, but welcomed the opportunity to thrust back, "Go tell the white man who sent you [i.e., the government] that when they pay more money to our boys who work in the south they will have money to buy cloth for their wives." It was clear to the sociologists and anthropologists that in some areas the lack of clothing was related to the excessively heavy bride-price men paid, which made them feel that the woman's family should provide her clothing; in an area of scarce water, women preferred not to soil their clothes in general wear but to keep them for festive occasions; elsewhere, the great value placed upon men being well-dressed left little money from meager wages for women's clothes; in one tribe, makers of leather waistbands would be thrown out of work if women shifted to wearing cloth; in another instance, the wearing of leaves around the waist—the only clothing—was a matter of ethnic pride and a symbol of ethnic identity (this tribe had previously been hounded out of the Ivory Coast for "nudity" and for insisting upon wearing lip plugs).

Proposals for legislation were dropped, and an educational campaign was launched that included the distribution of free clothing by an energetic women's leader, who began to appeal for clothing among Negro organizations in America. She was persuaded to drop this approach when it was realized that the image of "the naked African" was simply being reinforced. Meanwhile, regulations were posted in northern Ghana rest houses warning visitors not to take pictures of nude women. Finally, the whole campaign was turned over to the Department of Social Welfare and Community Development, with instructions for it to use its own judgment about what to do. Enforcing a compulsory school law will eventually "solve" the "problem," of course. A new government had learned a lesson about the complexity of changing entrenched custom: that the various parts of the social structure are interrelated and interwoven with the economy, the geographical setting, and the cultural values; that unintended consequences of change are as inevitable as those intended.

Urban Social Disorganization

There is growing awareness among Africans that the urban setting in which increasing numbers of individuals and families now live their lives is a significant factor in social disorganization. Less than 5 per cent of Africa's sub-Saharan population lives in cities, but the contrast between the urban way of life and that in rural areas is so sharp that it generates wide reflection and comment. A Ghanaian sociologist, Dr. K. A. Busia, in a study of the port city of Sekondi-Takoradi, portrays a town in which people are continuously complaining that there is too much illegitimacy, divorce, prostitution, juvenile delinquency, and family conflict, and where it is felt that these conditions are getting worse. Illiterate Nyakyusa men in Tanganyika, who migrate great distances to South African cities to seek work, say they leave their wives at home because, in the cities, "wives learn bad habits, become lazy, and demand continual supplies of money."

In Sekondi-Takoradi, as in other cities of rapid growth since the war (Dakar doubled in size and Lagos tripled), there is no doubt about the increase in forms of delinquency. Given the heterogeneity of city populations, the excess of men over women in most cities, and the loosening of traditional social controls, some social disorganization is to be expected.

The social scientist sees these disorderly and disturbing phenomena as an inevitable concomitant of rapid social change, as part of the price that is paid whenever urban communities grow up in an unplanned and uncontrolled manner. The contrasting orderliness in the pre-independent African areas of Elizabethville, Leopoldville, and Stanleyville was paid for by strictly imposed rules providing that no one could have more than one wife and that no unemployed could live there. South African cities use pass-laws and the curfew in attempts to "protect" more stable neighborhoods. Africans may not wish to pay such a price for orderliness.

The Quest for "Wholeness"

Social change in Africa has been traumatic and sometimes tragic, but there has been nothing anywhere to compare with the massive dissolution of social bonds and its consequences that Europe suffered during the Industrial Revolution, leading to such outbreaks of alienated peoples as in the French and the Russian Revolutions. Nor, perhaps, at the worst, are conditions in any African cities so bad as they were in England during the early days of the Industrial Revolution. But every urban community, and many villages, have suffered disturbances of the social bonds that unite people into cohesive groups, and which tie such groups together harmoniously.

Dr. Emory Ross, elder statesman among American missionaries, and a thoughtful student of Africa and its problems, has often stressed what he calls the "wholeness" of traditional African society—the fact that each ethnic group presented its people with a satisfying pattern of life, customs that fitted together, and beliefs that provided explanations of the meaning of life and of why people do as they do. The world made sense to individuals brought up in any specific culture. That wholeness has been shattered by the forces of social change and the conflicts due to culture contact. Some Africans began the quest for its restoration even before the voters gave a mandate to the new African political leadership to plan for the future. For example, almost two decades before Nigerian political leaders invited the Israelis to help them organize farm settlements, a small group of Yoruba fishermen, "influenced by Bible reading and under the guidance of three outstanding local men," chose a site on the coast a hundred miles east of Lagos, and proceeded to build a community called Aiyetoro—"The World is at Peace." Dr. G. H. T. Kimble described it in 1961 as

a progressive, well-run, thriving town of some 3,000 people . . . a well-planned town complete with shade trees, playgrounds and all modern conveniences. . . . No money is credited to individuals. Instead they get free rent and excellent housing, clothes in great variety, free food in abundance and recently even free electric lights.

But utopian communities based upon apostolic communism and the tabooing of alcohol and smoking are no more likely to have a wide appeal to modern Nigerians than New Harmony in Indiana did to nineteenth century Americans, or Hutterite communities do today. Aiyetoro is, however, an index to the creative potential within the semiliterate sector of African societies. The more sophisticated "African socialists" who lead some of the new nations profess to be trying to achieve this quality of wholeness within a secular frame of reference and on a national scale.

REGIONS OF SOCIAL CHANGE

The problems resulting from social change vary in accordance with (1) the character of the pre-existing culture, (2) the behavior and attitude of those outside people who conquered the region, and (3) the kinds of economic activities which came to dominate the area. Though there is almost infinite local variation in the problems created by these forces, it is possible to define five broad regions according to the manner in which they have been operating to transform traditional society.

North Africa

Tribal societies disappeared thousands of years ago in the Nile valley, being replaced by a semifeudal system which eventually evolved into an oppressive system of absentee landlordism with its effendis and fellahin. Throughout the rest of the region, tribal societies were eliminated from the coast by a series of invading settlers but they continue to exist in the mountains and desert oases. European settlement in the nineteenth century introduced modern farming and a small amount of industrialization in the coastal areas of Morocco, Tunisia, and Algeria, along with considerable alienation of land and a substantial measure of racial and cultural discrimination against the indigenous peoples. Urban overcrowding and unemployment, as well as rural poverty, exist on a scale not present in

SOCIO-ECONOMIC REGIONS OF AFRICA

1. NORTH AFRICA
2. WEST AFRICA
3. SOUTHERN AFRICA
4. LATIN CENTRAL AFRICA
5. EAST AFRICA

Dept. of Geog., U.C.L.A., J. Carlton

FIGURE 1

other parts of Africa, but now, with independence, large-scale development plans are under way.

For over a thousand years, Islamic-Arabic institutions and beliefs have been permeating the fabric of traditional society, and have also exerted a profound influence, through warfare, trade, and missionary zeal upon the peoples in the savannah lands south of the desert, along the northern rim of what is sometimes called "Negro Africa," the primary focus of this discussion.

West Africa

The 80 million inhabitants of this region belong to over 200 ethnic groups which have been only lightly penetrated by Islamic and Christian influences, despite centuries of contact. European conquest during the past century did not bring permanent white settlement on the land, and Africans are still rooted upon ancestral soil. There are few foreign-owned plantations; rather, hundreds of thousands of families grow cash crops for export, such as coffee, peanuts, cocoa, and palm products, while ethnic groups on the savannah raise cattle for the West African market. In Nigeria and Ghana, the level of prosperity is high by African standards.

The volume of industrialization is low, but a small proportion of the population has been drawn into the labor market to work for wages in gold, diamond, bauxite, manganese, and coal mines. There is some migration from the less developed northern areas southward for employment, but the movement does not have a disorganizing effect. African traders move freely from country to country over long distances, in accordance with ancient custom.

Indigenous cities in the savannah and forest areas have existed for centuries as centers of trade and government, and new coastal cities grew up later in response to trade with Europe and the Americas, but little detribalization has occurred in either type of city. Prolonged contact with the West resulted in a small but energetic group of moderately well-educated men in all territories by World War II. Women play an important part in trade in coastal areas.

In the absence of white settlers, race prejudice has not been a serious problem, and with the rise of African-controlled nations, racial discrimination and segregation have virtually disappeared. France and Britain, the dominant colonial powers in the region, offered little resistance to demands for independence, and now virtually all of the people in the area are citizens of African nations.

Southern Africa

Southern Africa contrasts sharply with West Africa. Permanent white settlement on the land was firmly established over a period of three hundred years in the Union of South Africa, and the pattern was extended to Northern and Southern Rhodesia and Nyasaland during the nineteenth and twentieth centuries. Throughout southern Africa, the land has been divided between Africans and European settlers—to the advantage of the latter. Large enclaves exist where the traditional way of life has been preserved (including the authority of traditional rulers), such as in the relatively independent territories of Bechuanaland, Basutoland, and Swaziland; Barotseland in Northern Rhodesia; and Zululand and other "reserves" in the Republic of South Africa. In general, the best land has been pre-empted by Europeans, and the reserves are generally on poorer land or too small to support growing populations.

White settlement has attracted capital and managerial skill, and the highest degree of industrialization and urbanization on the continent is to be found in this region. So great is the demand for labor, and so widespread the need for money to pay taxes and the desire to acquire imported goods, that extensive migratory movements have arisen, the volume and extent of which are portrayed in Figure 2. Each year, more than 300,000 Africans from Portuguese Mozambique cross the border for work in the Republic mines (and incidentally bring revenue to their home country). Normally, 30,000 men from Basutoland are employed in the mines around Johannesburg, and a total

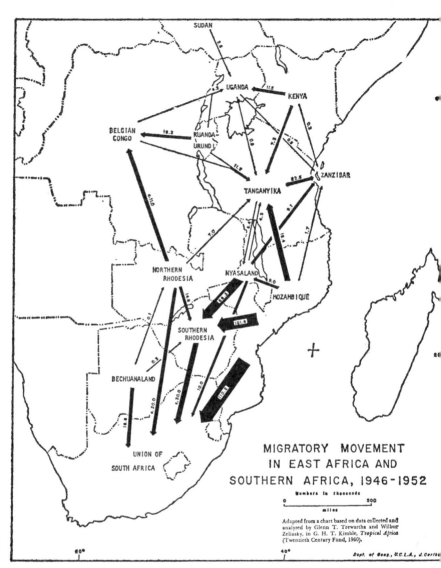

MIGRATORY MOVEMENT
IN EAST AFRICA AND
SOUTHERN AFRICA, 1946-1952

Numbers in thousands

0 ———————— 500
miles

Adapted from a chart based on data collected and
analyzed by Glenn T. Trewartha and Wilbur
Zelinsky, in G. H. T. Kimble, *Tropical Africa*
(Twentieth Century Fund, 1960).

Dept. of Geog., U.C.L.A., J. Corbet

FIGURE 2

of 100,000 are away from home. The number of workers employed outside of Nyasaland is larger than the number working inside the country—160,000 to 100,000. Traditional society in villages throughout the region has been seriously disrupted by these massive population movements, but the basic patterns of village life remain intact since most men are not permanent migrants.

Throughout southern Africa, some people who live near the cities take up permanent or semipermanent residence in town, but migrants from far away usually return home. In the Republic, parts of families and lineages tend to move first from overcrowded native reserves to work on white men's farms; then to the mines, where wages are higher but still very low; and finally to the town, where wages are highest. But they keep their rights to clan or lineage land and sometimes have their relatives build up cattle herds for them. Thus, they keep open a line of retreat for periods of unemployment and have a source of supplementary food when living in town. A more or less permanent urban population estimated at over 2 million persons has come into being in the Republic, and a similar pattern has been arising in Rhodesian cities. Some Africans have learned to prefer city life.

Most migrants, however, want to work for short periods to earn money for specific purposes and then return to their villages. Everywhere in the cities of southern Africa they find white men in control, not only giving them orders as well as low wages, but also restricting their movement and telling them where in the cities they may live. They find it difficult to carry out the customs associated with birth, puberty, marriage, and death. They find crowded slums instead of open spaces, and miss the security provided by the extended family. So they come and go, watch and wait, spending a part of their lives in the city and sending on their sons to do so, but keeping their permanent residence in the rural area.

The cities of southern Africa are "white men's cities," not indigenous creations as in West Africa. A voluminous literature exists—composed of fiction as well as sociological studies—dealing with the impact of social change upon southern Africa and especially with social conditions in those great terminal points of the movement of men: the seven cities on the North Rhodesian copper-belt: Ndola, Luanshya, Kitwe, Mufulira, Kalulushi, Chingola, and Bancroft where 120,000 Africans live; the nine African locations and slum areas of Johannesburg with a half million men and women; Capetown, and Durban. Among the detribalized masses of these cities, new types of African social systems and new values are in the making.

The most distinctive thing about southern Africa is the form which race relations have taken. The use of Africans in the gold, copper, and diamond mines involves a division of labor in which white men monopolize the skilled jobs and Africans are confined to unskilled occupations by custom and law. This pattern has had a tendency to carry over into all other types of industry. The color bar in mining and industry is paralleled by insistence upon residential and social segregation, and a determined effort to prevent Africans from exercising political power. Racial ideologies developed by Afrikaner farmers in their struggle with the Bantu for the land have been used to reinforce the struggle of white labor to prevent black competition. The doctrine of apartheid which, if carried to its logical conclusion, would remove all Africans from participation in business and industry with white people, dominates politics in the Republic. Portuguese Mozambique does not have an official policy of racial segregation nor foster an ideology of racial superiority, but supplies a very large proportion of the workers for the mines of the Republic.

Discontent with segregation and discrimination has been widespread in recent years, and African pressures have resulted in a commitment by the British government to allow Northern Rhodesia and Nyasaland to develop as African nations. This action has increased tension in Southern Rhodesia, the Republic, and Portuguese Mozambique, and makes a future violent clash between Europeans and non-Europeans seem inevitable. The presence of a large Asian population in the Republic, as well as the Coloureds, further complicates racial and ethnic relations.

Latin Central Africa

In this vast area between western and southern Africa, European penetration during the late nineteenth century involved large grants of land to private concessionnaires, who used compulsion and violence to force workers from the land to labor on plantations and for portering and construction work. The exposure of labor abuses in the Belgian Congo led to reforms early in the twentieth century and eventually to a policy under which the government and the mining companies exhibited a degree of concern for worker welfare unmatched elsewhere in colonial Africa. A very high level of urbanization and industrialization has been reached in the Congo, and Africans have been permitted to acquire technical skills and a moderate level of formal education. By 1960, literacy rates in the Congo were among the highest in Africa, but independence found only 16 college graduates among over 13 million Africans! Higher education and top posts were reserved for Europeans.

The level of industrialization, urbanization, and education remained very low in the less well-endowed and less efficiently administered French Equatorial Africa; forced labor was not abolished until after World War II. In the even less prosperous Portuguese Angola, forms of compulsion are still utilized to secure labor for white settlers and public works, and the literacy rate is among the lowest in Africa.

Despite forced labor and widespread segregation and discrimination against Africans, the Latin-Catholic culture of the colonizers mitigated the asperities of racial prejudice except in small areas of the Congo and Angola where white settlers lived. Following political independence of the French and Belgian colonies, a violent struggle for independence in Angola is being supported by leaders in the other areas.

Eastern Africa

This whole region is an arena in which a centuries-old contest for land between agricultural and pastoral tribes was being fought out until European administration was consolidated in the early twentieth century. This historic opposition still influences the politics of the region. Arab cities and states have existed along the coast for centuries, and invaders from Arabia established a semi-feudal society in the Ethiopian highlands which, except for brief periods, has remained free of European political control. Indigenous states in what is now Uganda, however, eventually came under the control of Britain, and that country also established administration over three-quarters of eastern Africa, creating a framework in which Western institutions took root.

Economic and social development in Uganda took place along lines similar to West Africa, while Kenya developed patterns of white domination similar to southern Africa. The Somali people, divided between Britain, France, and Italy, and with limited natural resources, sustained very little economic and social development. A small volume of interterritorial migration exists, and some of the population movements have involved the area in economic relations with the Congo and southern Africa. (See Figure 2.)

Except for Uganda, the level of literacy in the area has remained extremely low, and nowhere has the volume of industrialization been high, although white-settler farming in Kenya and plantation agriculture in Tanganyika have resulted in high levels of production for export. With the impending accession to independence of Kenya, colonial control will have ended, and African leaders are already discussing the organization of a federation which will make rational planning for the whole region possible.

EDUCATION, SOCIAL MOBILITY, AND NATIONAL DEVELOPMENT

The son of the King of Kongo who studied for the priesthood in Portugal in the early sixteenth century was only the first among a trickle of children of chiefs, emirs, and kings in western and Latin Central Africa who studied theology, law, and medicine abroad. The spread of mission schools during the nineteenth century widened the availability of elementary education, although literacy levels in no country in Africa are yet above 30 per cent. There is today an insistent demand for more schools throughout the continent.

In colonial Africa between the two world wars, finishing primary school and getting a job as a messenger or clerk was probably the quickest way of making a short upward move toward greater prestige and financial security. This was the most that all but a few Africans could aspire to. Government bureaucracies and commercial activity had created a modest demand, and mission schools and local native authority schools scattered throughout the British and French colonies supplied a pool of candidates to vie with each other for such jobs.

After World War II, the extensive development plans in all the colonial territories responded to the African demand for education with many free or low-fee primary schools. By 1960, finding employment for thousands of "school leavers" had become a widespread problem. The large cadre of potential secondary and technical school pupils had neither adequate facilities nor teachers to accommodate them—the great bottleneck in African education.

Getting ahead once meant acquiring just enough education to secure a white-collar job, even though it might be a meager and lowly paid one. A modest amount of education beyond the primary level gives elite status in villages and small towns. The school teacher, the medical technician, and the postal or governmental clerk are usually respected and influential, and sometimes the only literate persons in the community. Ten or twelve years of moderately capable application to studies can usually qualify a person for such a post.

A modicum of schooling not only supplied a skill, but also allowed one to escape from the ethnic appraisals made of one's capabilities; for traditions, myths, and perhaps culturally induced temperament created preference for certain tribesmen as "good boys" for domestic service, as laborers, or for other types of occupation. World War II, however, began to alter both the conceptions of what a good job is and who could do it, as well as the opportunities for employment. Cities grew rapidly in size, some young people were drawn into the armed forces, and soldiers from several nations were stationed in Africa. Attitudes toward work were changed, new skills developed. In southern Africa and the Congo, the increased demand for minerals and manufactured goods during the war not only stepped up the flow of labor toward mines and industries but also produced such labor shortages that Africans were employed in light manufacturing.

Technical training acquired a popularity it had not had before. In Ghana, for instance, recent studies by Dr. Philip Foster of the University of Chicago of the aspiration levels of school boys reveal that technical pursuits now outrank white-collar jobs when students are asked "What do you want to be?" Yet nowhere are the highest pay and prestige associated with manual work.

The College Tradition

The professions and the best jobs in the civil service require a college education. While it is not impossible for boys from illiterate families to go to college, the attrition rate is very high, and the risk of failure in countries where entrance examinations are rigorous and scholarships rare makes the investment in effort and money dubious.

The tiny minority of Africans who had finished colleges by the early postwar years had usually studied overseas (except in South Africa and Sierra Leone, where degree-granting institutions were open to Africans). Three types of students had graduated: those whose families had been able to accumulate enough money to send them overseas; those who had won scholarships; and those who had "worked their way through." Most of this last group had found their opportunity in the United States.

A few college students from the Congo and the Union of South Africa studied in the United States around the turn of the century, but the flow was shut off by governments which felt that an American education bred "subversives." Between the two wars, a considerable number of students from British colonies and Liberia found their way to America, and an unusually successful group of political leaders eventually emerged among these graduates, including Nnamdi Azikiwe, the Governor-General of Nigeria; Kwame Nkrumah, President of Ghana; Ako Adjei, for many years the Minister of External Affairs of Ghana; Hastings Banda, Prime Minister of Nyasaland; and many members of West African parliaments. By 1945, the belief was widespread among Africans that "American style" education produced leaders, while education in Britain and Europe only trained scholars and civil servants. Africans generally approved of American education, while colonial administrators disapproved.

The flow of students from West Africa continued after the war, and to it was added a stream of students from East Africa and Northern Rhodesia, culminating in the dramatic "student airlift" organized by Tom Mboya and his American friends, which brought nearly a thousand students to the United States. The American contribution to the small college-educated group of East African leaders includes Julius Kiano, Kenya's first African Minister of Commerce and Industry (and, incidentally, that country's first African Ph.D.); Joshua Luyimbazi Zake, the Minister of Education in Uganda; Mbiyu Koinange, Executive Secretary of the Pan-African Freedom Movement of Eastern, Central and Southern Africa; as well as a few doctors, lawyers, college professors, and senior civil servants.

Few French-speaking Africans came to the United States, but a small group secured higher education in France, among them the distinguished poet-President of Senegal, Leopold Senghor. Belgium allowed no Congolese to go abroad for an education until almost a decade after World War II, except for a few who went to Rome to study for the priesthood, and the settler-dominated areas of eastern and central Africa did not encourage overseas study.

The leaders of new African nations, plagued by a shortage of highly trained technical personnel, have been critical of the existing universities. The system established throughout Africa was, naturally enough, patterned after the universities in the metropolitan countries and having close connection with partic-ular institutions (e.g., Uganda, Ghana, Southern Rhodesia, and Nigeria affiliated with the University of London; Belgian Congo with Louvain). Educational policies designed to prepare a highly sophisticated elite in broad intellectual matters did not meet the need for technicians and administrators and, according to African leaders, also "educated the elite away from the people." Curricula are being reorganized and relations are being estab-lished with a wide variety of institutions in other countries, and new institutions are coming into being such as the University of Addis Ababa (assisted by the University of Utah) and the University of Nigeria (with close ties to Michigan State University). The trend in Africa is toward using the power of awarding scholarships and control of passports to have Africans pursue their undergraduate work at home, going overseas to both the East and the West for graduate and professional training. But the shortage of personnel is so great that for a decade to come non-Africans will be required both to man university posts and to supply technical services. Scarcity gives university-trained Africans very high status.

STATUS AND SOCIAL CLASSES IN MODERN AFRICAN SOCIETY

Some traditional African societies were egalitarian; others had high degrees of differentiation. In general, the former were tribally-organized societies without any political head, whereas the latter were the politically-organized states. In the former, the social standing frequently rested upon cattle, wives, military prowess, or personal attributes; chiefs were no more than *primus inter pares,* their ways of life no different from anyone else in the community. Among the latter, status differentiation was often as wide as any place in the world. Africa was extensive and their life highly elaborated with slaves, wives, concubines, and personal trappings. In some societies, notably Ruanda and Burundi, there was a strict caste system based upon ethnic differentiation.

Modern political development has undermined much of the force and effect of these old systems of status—though it has not destroyed them—and set up a new system of status based upon education, occupation, wealth, and style of life. George R. Horner, in Kimble's *Tropical Africa,* describes the emerging social status system in French Equatorial Africa which, in general, can be applied to most of Africa. Based upon the criteria enumerated above, he finds that there are three social strata, as follows:

1. The elite class, consisting of government officials, rich, educated planters and store owners, directors of schools, pastors, priests, professionals, etc.

2. The *evolué* class, including lesser school and government functionaries, clerks in commercial employ, small planters, carpenters, masons, truck drivers, domestic workers, specialists in ivory and ebony handicrafts, tailors, and educated women.

3. The great mass of uneducated, illiterate, or preliterate villagers.

Although Horner's status distinctions are real and the social hierarchy is a dynamic element in the new African society, the important question is: Are these social classes in the Marxian sense of cohesive social groups, standing in economic conflict? To answer this question, we must examine the patterns of social relationships as they are emerging in Africa.

In the cities and larger towns of Africa, there are enough Africans of higher status to permit the selection of friends based upon similarity of education and occupation and to provide the basis for the formation of voluntary associations within status levels. In the Congo, for instance, formal *cercles d'evolués* arose in the cities. Outside of the Congo and southern Africa, the "fashionable upper class set" usually included Europeans along with high-status Africans. It is now composed of new African leaders and their families and the *nouveaux riches* who have acquired wealth either through business or by virtue of their connections. There is an increasing demand made upon members of this set to live according to standards commensurate with such positions when held in the West. Much of this "pressure" emanates from their wives.

To some extent, there appears to be syncretism between the old and the new—that is, the traditional statuses of kings, obas, emirs, sultans, and chiefs, can be held by members of the modern elite who still retain their old functions; occasionally one finds an individual who is a chief, a college graduate, and the holder of a knighthood, or the Order of Merit, at the same time. Though in most of the new nations there is clearly a community of persons who form an elite, it is too small and heterogeneous a group, and also too mobile, to constitute a true social class.

The *evolué* class is less cohesive than the elite groups. Nevertheless, there is a large and growing body of educated and urban Africans who do not form a part of the elite but who have a status higher than the ordinary farmer and unlettered workman. They are not, however, to be regarded as a true middle class because they do not have the independence of operation that characterizes middle-class existence. Indeed, it has been pointed out frequently that the development of African political systems suffers from the absence of a middle class, economically independent of government and having sufficient wealth and standing to exert a force in the community. The lineage system, already discussed, is a cultural deterrent to the development of sharply defined social classes. It is difficult for people to coalesce into social classes based upon small homogeneous families living in one-class neighborhoods as Westerners do, and most members of the African higher status groups have not yet manifested a strong desire to do so. At all social levels, some cultural traits from traditional society are retained and blended with Western practices. A distinctively African system of social stratification is emerging, and resident Europeans find it difficult to adjust to this new African society-in-the-making.

The Racial Factor in Social Class Development

Prior to 1950, patterns of residential and social segregation on the basis of race were customary throughout sub-Saharan Africa. In the Congo, the Rhodesias, and Kenya, custom was reinforced by law until the late 1950's, when an attempt was made to stem the nationalist tide by a relaxation of barriers, and segregation is still enforced by law in the Republic of South Africa.

Except in southern Africa, there has been a tendency to justify the segregation of the illiterate masses not on the argument that they were innately inferior, but rather on the grounds that cultural differences in standards of sanitation, public behavior, and conceptions of sexual morality demanded it for the protection of resident Europeans. The question of how to treat educated and "assimilated" Africans posed a problem. In French and Portuguese areas, the practice arose of according special status to elites, *evolués,* and *assimilados,* ranging from complete social acceptance to the mere enjoyment of certain legal privileges. The Belgian Congo developed a similar policy which, by 1952, professed to grant full equality to assimilated Africans. Even in South Africa, until after World War II, the Coloureds, who had a European way of life and spoke Afrikaans, enjoyed privileges denied to the Bantu, and a large segment of the white population was committed, in theory at least, to Rhodes' dictum of "equal rights for all civilized men." This policy is sometimes referred to as the substitution of a "culture bar" for the color bar.

Few Africans, however, have been willing to accept the proposition that political and civil rights should be made contingent upon the adoption of a European way of life. Even Africans who by education and occupation ranked as elites and *evolués* often did not value social acceptance by Europeans so highly as to be willing to abandon all African customs or to break their ties with kinsmen. In any event, the proportion of assimilated individuals in Angola, the Congo, and southern Africa was never large, for adequate educational facilities were not available to produce them. The aspects of the color bar which have seriously concerned Africans have not been refusal of social acceptance by Europeans but rather the inequities of segregation in public places, the limits imposed in government and industry, and the implication of inferiority—cultural and racial—always present. They came increasingly to interpret the concept of a culture bar as a device for maintaining continued white domination. In all of the continent except southern Africa, however, the controversy is now a dead issue, for Africans are in control of the political machinery and are using it to root out the last vestiges of the color bar. It is likely that they will erect their own version of a culture bar as their own social class systems take shape.

Social Mobility and the New Elite

At the close of World War II, virtually all the higher posts in commerce, politics, education, and church affairs were held by Europeans. Kimble states in *Tropical Africa* that even as late as 1955, "no African was employed in the central government of Uganda above the level of district officer," and that in 1954 fewer than a thousand Africans were in the senior posts in the Gold Coast civil service. In British-controlled areas, however, a sizable group of Africans had risen to positions just below the top in all territories except those with strong white-settler influence—Kenya, Tanganyika, the Central African Federation, and, of course, the Republic of South Africa. A similar though smaller group existed in French West Africa. In the Congo, on the other hand, although primary education had been widely extended, the Belgian administration had prevented Africans from occupying top posts in government, and it was not the policy to advance them to the highest posts in church and business. Nationalist movements set as one of their primary goals the "Africanization" of these posts in all institutions. They have "broken through to the top" throughout the continent (except in southern Africa) in all the pyramids of power and prestige except commerce and industry.

African businessmen are present in all regions, but nowhere do they own the largest commercial and industrial enterprises in either town or country, or even have any significant proportion of middle level enterprises. Thomas Hodgkin, in his *Nationalism in Colonial Africa,* has called attention to the role businessmen were playing in the 1950's as a part of what he called the "new middle class":

> With the growth of a market economy, increasing differentiation is taking place throughout colonial Africa, illustrated by the situation in the cocoa-producing areas of Western Nigeria and the Gold Coast, where there is now an influential class of large farmers, substantial employers of labor, with their motor cars, town houses and comfortable standards of living. It is this new middle-class—traders, contractors, transport owners, professional and administrative workers, as well as farmers—which has so far tended to dominate the emerging national movements.

In Ghana, French West Africa, Nigeria, Uganda, and the Congo, it was the hope of ambitious businessmen that they would someday take the place of the great European commercial houses that dominated the business scene in colonial Africa, and would be given loans to help them out-compete the Asians, Syrians, Greeks, and Lebanese in middle levels of commerce. They hoped, too, eventually to become owners and shareholders in new industries to be built, and they expected lucrative contracts from their own African governments.

Contracts have been forthcoming (and not always in accord with the highest ideals of public probity), but African business-men lack the capital and experience necessary to compete with Western commerce and industry in the early stages of rapid devel-opment. In many of the new nations, too, the political parties are encouraging the development of cooperative and state-owned en-terprises in sectors where businessmen expected to expand. The political leaders, rather than businessmen, dominate the new African states. One source of tension and conflict in some of the new nations arises from the frustrated expectations of business-men who desire a more decisive role than the new politicians have been willing or able to accord them, and from discontent over "corruption" where special groups of businessmen have been favored.

Regional variations in social mobility exist, and these are dis-cussed with refreshing candor and gentle humor in Ezekiel Mphahlele's *The African Image,* particularly in his chapter on "Those Cheeky Kaffirs, Those Impertinent Natives." In one respect, what he said of his native South Africa is true of the whole continent:

> While guest speakers continue each year on school speech days to tell you that the African must make the best use of his opportunities so as "to uplift" his fellow men, you know nothing could be farther from your intentions. You want to get a better job and earn a living and support your parents and their other children.

In the Republic, there can be no opportunities such as those in the independent states where the game can be played for high political status, and where Mphahlele feels that "the purpose of politics is for personal prestige and supremacy, or for that of a clique or clan." This South African writer lived in West Africa as a refugee and held a post at a university there. He found the lad-der the colonial powers had erected still available for social climbing, and he speaks scornfully of its use:

> The main concern of the average educated African in Nigeria is to get into Government service, which affords him civil servants' quar-ters, a car, at least two servants and a comfortable living. There is a mad rush to pass examinations as a gateway to this Eldorado.

He does not mention that one goal of the young African nationalists in the Republic is to climb on a similar ladder from which white men now bar them.

Like intellectuals everywhere, Mphahlele wants a society in which the true elite consist of the intellectuals and artists who have rejected the "Philistine" values associated with wealth and bureaucratic status, as well as preoccupation with folk culture as expressed in the concept of Negritude.

The Growth of an African Working Class

The vast expansion of mining and industry during World War II, the increased plantation production, and the servicing of troops, caused a dramatic growth in urban populations and in the number of Africans working for wages. Postwar development sustained this growth, and today between five and six million Africans, at any given time, are working for wages. (Compared with Europe and America, however, the number and proportion are low—the whole of Africa has a labor force no greater than the Chicago metropolitan region.) The most extensive and rapid industrial development occurred in the Congo and southern Africa.

In western Africa, where the industrial take-off is just beginning, between one and two million people are working for wages and the majority of these are employed by national or municipal governments, including the railroads. In other regions of sub-Saharan Africa, however, the major employers are European-owned plantations and white-settler farms. Even in Southern Rhodesia, where the largest proportion of Africans between the desert and the Limpopo are working for wages (over half a million) and where the number employed in manufacturing rose from 15,000 in 1938 to more than 100,000 by 1960, 3 Africans are employed in commercial agriculture to every 1 in industry. In the Congo, on the other hand, where by 1955 4 out of every 10 adult males were more or less permanent wage workers, only a third were in agriculture. In Northern Rhodesia, the proportion in mining and industry now slightly exceeds that in agriculture. In both industry and agriculture, the bulk of African labor is unskilled, but an increasing number are being employed in semi-skilled and skilled pursuits. Other parts of Africa are about to embark upon an industrial revolution which will certainly lead to an increase in the number of African wage earners.

It has been estimated that there are at least 40 million adults in Africa, of whom some 30 million must be continuously engaged in growing food to support the population, given present methods of cultivation. Between 5 and 6 million wage workers are required for commercial agriculture, mining, and industry at present levels of production. This labor demand is now largely though not entirely met by migratory labor.

There has for some time been a feeling in the Congo and parts of southern Africa that "stabilization" of the labor force would be desirable, and beginning in the 1920's the government of the Belgian Congo encouraged the mining companies to erect good housing for their workers and to provide for the accommodation of their families. Later, minimum wage laws and a labor welfare code were passed. During World War II, government and industry began to implement plans of stabilization in Leopoldville, Stanleyville, and other cities, as well as in the Katanga mining area. Racially segregated neighborhoods were established. On Union Minière properties in Katanga an office was opened with authority to construct houses for either lease or sale, and to make loans to Africans for building. Under the leadership of a well-known administrator, Grevisse, some 8,000 houses had been built and sold to Africans by 1953. The company itself paid high wages by African standards and provided social services and medical treatment. It also paid a bonus to every mother confined in a maternity ward and provided two special nutritious meals a day for young children in an attractive dining room. A compulsory school law was enforced for children from five to twelve years old. Special training classes for women in home economics and hygiene were given by a professional staff. In the city of Elizabethville itself, the financing of the building of homes was carried out jointly by the Belgian administration, the Elizabethville municipality, and the mining company. There is no reason to assume that these policies (except for the racial segregation) will not continue under the new African government.

Similar housing projects and welfare activities have been provided by the mining companies on the Northern Rhodesian copper-belt, although many workers object to the strict controls of company towns, and satellite towns to these have grown up to which unemployed Africans are drifting. But permanent urban populations are taking root.

The development of an African working class is conditioned by the fact that labor relations usually involve race relations, and in some areas, they *are* race relations. Very few Africans are working for other African employers (except relatives), even in western and eastern Africa. The African working class, insofar as it is employed in privately-owned commerce, industry, and agriculture works for white men, or for Asians and Levantines. The race relations aspect of labor relations is reinforced by the fact that black workers in southern Africa face constant hostility and discrimination from white workers protecting their monopoly of skilled jobs and managerial posts. Equally significant, however, is the fact that in Ethiopia, Liberia, and the new nations, a very high proportion of the wage-earning population is employed by government agencies and although the paymaster is African, management is still often white. Workers in the new nations not only expect their governments to give them better working conditions and higher wages, but also to support them in disputes with foreign firms and with white or Asian government personnel.

Less than 10 per cent of Africa's small working class is unionized. Unskilled, illiterate, split by tribalism, and often migratory, the masses of workers are difficult to organize. The strongest unions in the independent states are in former French and British territories among skilled workers on government-owned railways and harbor installations, employees of all levels in public works departments, and lower civil servants and school teachers. (Nigeria and the Republic of Sudan each have over 100,000 union members, and there are almost as many in former French West Africa. In no case, however, do they make up as much as 5 per cent of the labor force.) In these strategic sectors strikes can be both embarrassing and effective, especially if unions are allied with opposition political parties, and irresponsible trade union action in the private sector can frighten away much-needed foreign investment. So, parties in power try to handle this delicate situation by fostering "loyal" trade unions which stress high productivity as well as higher wages, by limiting the right to strike, and by devising elaborate grievance machinery. However, it is hard to sell the idea of the quiescent trade union to either leaders or rank and file.

Even in the more highly industrialized areas of southern Africa and the Congo, wages for Africans are low by Western standards, but wages in industry and mining are so much higher than those available elsewhere and the fringe benefits so much greater that wage disputes have not been the major source of conflict in these areas. The major grievances are against practices which earmark the best jobs as "white" and which sometimes pay white men more than Africans for doing the same work. Northern Rhodesia has allowed Africans to express their grievances through unions, and the African Mine Workers Union, with its 30,000 members, has used strike action with success in opening up new job opportunities. After 1946, the Congo allowed unions but limited their right to strike, but in Southern Rhodesia African unions are still illegal. In the Republic of South Africa, African unions are legal, but any kind of militant action is defined as "subversive." Organized labor is a threat to the color bar.

From this it would appear that nowhere between North Africa and the Limpopo is there either a rootless proletariat or an organized working class. Whether either will appear depends upon the rate of industrialization and urbanization and the extent to which these processes are controlled and planned by government. The persistence of lineage and ethnic ties and the operation of independent churches and mutual aid societies have prevented the atomization, poverty, and sense of futility out of which labor class movements are generated. Modern societies are utilizing these traditional practices to drain off urban unemployed into such voluntary agencies as the Workers' Brigade in Ghana, and to force them into agricultural camps, as in Brazzaville. These factors and others previously mentioned have also kept trade unions weak. Though occasional strikes occur (the strikes by railway workers in Ghana, in 1961, and civil servants in Kenya, in 1962, were crippling), they do not seriously threaten the stability of new African governments. There is, in all this, no seedbed for either socialism or Communism in the Western sense or in the Indian or Chinese model.

South Africa, and perhaps the Rhodesias and the Katanga, present another story. Although controlled migrant labor mans the mines, several million Africans are now more or less permanent urban dwellers, poorly paid and badly housed, detribalized, sophisticated, and to a high degree literate. Neither frantic efforts by government to rehouse Africans nor the tightening up of pass-laws can cope with the drift to town from overcrowded reserves and white-settler farms. Here, a rootless proletariat has emerged. Within this frustrated, unstable, urban mass there are, on one hand, *tsotsis* and gangsters organized for antisocial ends and, on the other hand, close-knit, well-led, nationalist organizations. Although trade unions are weak, there is a 40-year-old history of disciplined protest by a variety of organizations, a story told in fascinating detail in Edward Roux's *Time Longer Than Rope*. European and Indian Communists, though active since World War I, have not been discouraged by those failures to attract Africans which George Padmore analyzes with insight in *Pan-Africanism or Communism?* Movements on the Mau Mau model have arisen in the reserves and African terrorists in the cities have already begun to use dynamite. Against these forces is arrayed the power of a government pledged to preserve white domination and a highly organized white trade-union movement. No one can estimate the consequences when the forces of discontent have coalesced and the inevitable clash occurs.

Prospects and Problems

Traditional society has been undergoing change for several centuries, arising from contact with bearers of Western values and institutions, and from the spread of a money economy. New values and styles of life are becoming part of an emerging system of social stratification in which higher and lower status levels are defined by type of job, public behavior, and consumption patterns, and in which acquiring additional education is the primary factor in social mobility. The lineage structure is still operative, and people at all status levels retain some values and customary behavior from traditional society in combination with new elements. Rapid social change has generated anxiety and tension—particularly in urban areas—and this is reflected in widespread discussion about the morality and utility of values and customs, old and new, as people of all social levels continue to define "social problems."

World War II greatly accelerated the speed of social change throughout the continent, stepped up the process of industrialization in the Congo and southern Africa, and stimulated more modest industrial development elsewhere. New vistas of opportunity and achievement were opened up. In the postwar years, African political leaders took over and expanded development plans which had been initiated by the colonial powers to increase production and trade for the mutual benefit of metropole and colony, and to meet African demands for a rising standard of living, more extensive medical facilities and educational opportunities, and a higher level of purchasing power. The leaders of the new nations are now held accountable by their people for continued economic and social development.

In southern Africa, racial discrimination and segregation by white settlers who monopolize economic and political power has slowed up the movement toward greater participation by Africans in government and denied them access to the higher paid skilled and managerial posts in industry. They have, however, shared in the general material prosperity of the area and the Republic literacy rate is among the highest on the continent. Economic and political relations thus take on the form of race conflict during a period when race relations are becoming increasingly harmonious elsewhere in Africa. It is in the Republic, alone in sub-Saharan Africa, that a large, rootless, self-conscious, politically disfranchised, and socially disaffected urban working-class population exists, displaying all of the potentials for violent conflict which characterize such strata.

All of the newly emergent nations are experiencing tensions between new elites and traditional rulers, and between African businessmen and political leaders who espouse African socialism, to which must be added the stresses and strains generated by development programs, conflict, wide gaps in income levels, rapid urbanization, unemployment, increased taxes and the inability to deliver a quick "payoff" on party promises. Leaders tend to control the situation through authoritarian governments, by imposing "labor discipline" upon trade unions, and (as a last resort) by the use of force—the same techniques used by colonial powers faced with similar situations.

Although there has been much grumbling and occasional disturbances within the independent states during the past five years, there has been no popular support for attempted coups in any state, nor any threatened mass revolts. Nor will there likely be, in the next few years, crises of the kind that periodically shake the Middle East, Asia, and parts of Latin America. Some of the stabilizing factors lie in the following situations:

1. New leaders are able to blame "backwardness" and inefficiency upon the "imperialist oppressors" of the past and the "neo-colonialism" and indifference of "white nations" in the present. With power having so recently passed from the hands of white men to black, citizens of the new nations are inclined to give the new leadership a chance to show what it can do.

2. The great expansion of local economies which began with World War II has continued during the postwar years with investment and technical assistance from the former colonial powers and the United States (and more recently from the Soviet bloc and China). This has made possible continuous expansion of educational facilities and occupational opportunities and kept the channel for rapid mobility open. There has been enough visible evidence of progress in the form of new schools and clinics, expanded scholarship programs, Africans occupying posts once held by white men, and similar gains to offset moods of disillusionment or doubt about the value of independence.

3. The viability of traditional society operates as a stabilizing factor. The very tribalism that makes the achievement of national unity difficult also hampers the organization of unified opposition; the emotion of respect and habits of loyalty to

traditional rulers carries over in some measure to the new educated African heads of state; and the persistence of a traditional family structure and a system of communal land tenure, both sometimes considered a "drag" on development, also spread poverty through sharing and act as a shock absorber for unemployment.

4. Social change is impinging directly upon tribal-type societies in which land has never come into possession of a landed aristocracy (except in isolated spots in Uganda, Nigeria, and Ethiopia). There is no poverty-stricken landless peasantry waiting to revolt.

5. The level of urbanization and industrialization has not been great enough to produce either a rootless urban proletariat or a disciplined organized working class manipulable by demagogues of the Right or Left. Insofar as the new states do not suffer sharp economic reverses, serious dislocations are unlikely in the foreseeable future. In southern Africa, however, where African political and economic development is controlled by Portugal, an unyielding colonial power, and by white-settler domination, future violence is very likely to occur. Detribalization in urban areas has gone far and will condition the nature of the conflict.

American Action and African Democracies

Despite lingering racism in America and occasional African overtures toward the Communist world, there is a deep and abiding common interest between our nation and the new countries of the African continent. Americans naturally and quite legitimately are concerned with the preservation of the "inalienable right" of all peoples to "life, liberty, and the pursuit of happiness," and to the extension of the promises embodied in the Universal Charter of Human Rights of the United Nations. A society that does not provide for these rights is, in our eyes, an unjust society. African leaders share these aspirations and most of them recognize the fact that the United States is trying to realize such a society, though slowly, painfully, and not without conflict. They recognize, too, that traditional African societies also occasionally fail to fulfill these demands, and in general seek to rectify injustice and to expand opportunity. They ask for patient understanding of their problems, just as Americans ask others to understand their own. They react negatively to preachments about democracy, but respond positively to assistance proffered for moving toward a free and open society devoted to common welfare and the protection of civil liberties and minority rights. They rightly see that the key to progress in this direction depends upon rising standards of living and increased education.

The average American citizen can do little to assist the African nations financially, except to support public programs of assistance. There is much, however, that they can do to help individual Africans acquire the insight and training needed to cope with their problems. Before World War II, the most significant impact America had on Africa (except in Liberia) was through the Christian missionary movement; the importance of this effort cannot be overestimated. Nearly all schools were mission schools and the few students graduated from them have had an influence on Africa far out of proportion to their numbers. The missions have injected into African society a change in values that has been revolutionary. Today, however, Africans are no longer willing to think of themselves as "heathens" nor to have outsiders endeavor to "civilize" or "Christianize" them. They pursue an open-door policy toward all religions, including their own traditional beliefs, and insist upon their own freedom to decide among available spiritual alternatives (expressing surprise that any human beings can be atheists). Missionary effort continues and is not opposed by Africans insofar as it is increasingly transformed into a relationship between equals, is not subversive, and does not demand the right to dominate the field of education. Similarly, political leaders defend their right to know what is going on in the Communist world as well as in the West and to incorporate values from all parts of the globe in their transitional societies.

The postwar American impact has been largely secular and instrumental. America is now primarily furnishing financial and technical assistance, both governmental and private. There has been little pressure by Americans for conformity to political and economic ideals, and Africans are grateful for "aid without strings attached."

There are also wide areas in which the American public can foster the growth and development of democratic ideals to which both the United States and Africa are committed:

1. The role of African intellectuals—novelists, poets, essayists, journalists, artists, scholars, and religious leaders—is critically important in this period of rapid social change. It is vital that Americans in all walks of life engage in a dialogue with these Africans through cultural exchanges. This means not only communicating our own values but endeavoring to understand those of the emergent "African personality."

2. A small group of African social scientists and social welfare workers are currently endeavoring to evaluate the social problems of modern Africa. There have been conferences and symposia on unemployment, welfare, women and children, juvenile delinquency, and the consequences of industrialization and urbanization. American nonprofit foundations have generously supported research on such problems, but research institutes and universities have a chronic shortage of high-level personnel and there is a demand for consultants and resource persons in these areas. Young scholars, professors on sabbatical, and others willing and able to invest a year or two can still fill critical needs in this area.

3. Perhaps nothing is more important to African development than the rapid growth of secondary and higher education. To this purpose, modest scholarship aid programs for Africans studying in America have been implemented through the cooperation of universities, foundations, and government, though these are not so extensive as they should be. Voluntary associations can play a crucial role in increasing the number of scholarships available, especially to women, and in sponsoring training in the United States. Cooperation with such agencies as the Institute of International Education in the arrangement of hospitality during holidays and vacations, the provision of part-time employment, and perhaps most importantly, the development of warm personal relations between visiting

African students and American families are direct means by which individuals can further African ambitions.

4. The critical need for high school teachers and vocational education has been met in part by both government and private agencies. Hundreds of teachers have been supplied through the Peace Corps, at the request of African governments, and have been received everywhere with enthusiasm. Columbia University sponsored a very successful Teachers for East Africa Project. The success of such programs recommends their expansion, but this requires both public support and a pool of volunteers. Retired teachers could usefully supplement their pensions and contribute to African development.

There has been an encouraging growth of interest in Africa, as witnessed by improved reporting in newspapers and magazines; by a wealth of new books dealing with modern African problems at all levels, from the very popular to the highly scholarly; by increased interest in African problems among foundations and American universities (there are now centers for African studies in many colleges throughout the United States); and in various conferences such as that held in Boston in 1961 under the sponsorship of the United States Commission for UNESCO. There are a number of interested organizations specializing in African affairs, such as the African-American Institute, the American Society for African Culture, the American Committee on Africa, the American Negro Leadership Conference on Africa, the African Scholarship Program of American Universities, and, particularly, the Women's Africa Committee of the African-American Institute. Through such organizations and their publications, Americans can and are becoming informed on African affairs and can contribute to this important dialogue.

But there are many voluntary associations concerned with national welfare and American churches, all with international outreach, which can and should take responsibility for furthering our relations with Africa. Members of all such organizations should see that Africa is included in their programs, that information from national centers is available at the local level, and that local units initiate activities in accordance with the objectives of their national programs. It is characteristic of American social organization and culture for individuals to reach out directly to others through such associations, and it is at this grass-roots level that the American impact on Africa can have its maximum effect. It is in the character of the African to respond positively and with warmth to such extensions of friendship and aid.

APPENDIX

The African Operations of United States Government Agencies

VERNON McKAY

When the new states of Africa began to play an important role in world affairs after 1957, the machinery of the United States Government for handling African affairs was, of necessity, greatly expanded. The structure and operations of this machinery are treated below.

THE STATE DEPARTMENT AND FOREIGN SERVICE

Since World War II, and especially in the last five years, there have been a number of encouraging improvements in the machinery and quality of the work of the Department of State and Foreign Service in African affairs: (1) in general, the Foreign Service sends better officers to senior posts in Africa than it did fifteen, or even five, years ago; (2) promising young diplomats are beginning to ask for African posts; (3) the quantity and quality of political and economic reporting from African posts have much improved; (4) our African posts have increased enormously, almost doubling from 1957, with 248 posts, to 1962, with 494; (5) within the Department's administrative machinery, the status of African affairs was raised on September 10, 1956, by the establishment of a semiautonomous Africa unit of 34 officers headed

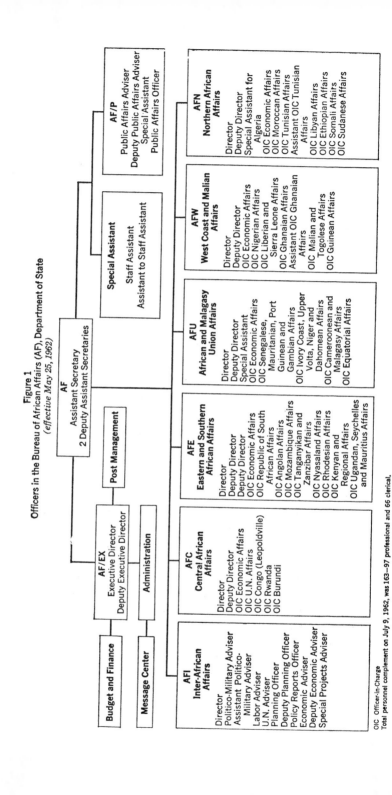

Figure 1
Officers in the Bureau of African Affairs (AF), Department of State
(effective May 25, 1962)

AF
Assistant Secretary
2 Deputy Assistant Secretaries

Special Assistant
Staff Assistant
Assistant to Staff Assistant

Post Management

AF/EX
Executive Director
Deputy Executive Director

Administration

Budget and Finance

Message Center

AF/P
Public Affairs
Public Affairs Adviser
Deputy Public Affairs Adviser
Special Assistant
Public Affairs Officer

AFI
Inter-African Affairs
Director
Politico-Military Adviser
Assistant Politico-Military Adviser
Labor Adviser
U.N. Adviser
Planning Officer
Deputy Planning Officer
Policy Reports Officer
Economic Adviser
Deputy Economic Adviser
Special Projects Adviser

AFC
Central African Affairs
Director
Deputy Director
OIC Economic Affairs
OIC U.N. Affairs
OIC Congo (Leopoldville)
OIC Rwanda
OIC Burundi

AFE
Eastern and Southern African Affairs
Director
Deputy Director
Deputy Director
OIC Economic Affairs
OIC Republic of South African Affairs
OIC Angolan Affairs
OIC Mozambique Affairs
OIC Tanganyikan and Zanzibar Affairs
OIC Nyasaland Affairs
OIC Rhodesian Affairs
OIC Kenyan and Regional Affairs
OIC Ugandan, Seychelles and Mauritius Affairs

AFU
African and Malagasy Union Affairs
Director
Deputy Director
Special Assistant
OIC Economic Affairs
OIC Senegalese, Mauritanian, Port Guinean and Gambian Affairs
OIC Ivory Coast, Upper Volta, Niger and Dahomean Affairs
OIC Cameroonean and Malagasy Affairs
OIC Equatorial Affairs

AFW
West Coast and Malian Affairs
Director
Deputy Director
OIC Economic Affairs
OIC Nigerian Affairs
OIC Liberian and Sierra Leone Affairs
OIC Ghanaian Affairs
Assistant OIC Ghanaian Affairs
OIC Malian and Togolese Affairs
OIC Guinean Affairs

AFN
Northern African Affairs
Director
Deputy Director
Special Assistant for Algeria
OIC Economic Affairs
OIC Moroccan Affairs
OIC Tunisian Affairs
Assistant OIC Tunisian Affairs
OIC Libyan Affairs
OIC Ethiopian Affairs
OIC Somali Affairs
OIC Sudanese Affairs

OIC Officer-in-Charge
Total personnel complement on July 9, 1962, was 163—97 professional and 66 clerical.

by a Deputy Assistant Secretary of State. Divided into an Office of Northern African Affairs and an Office of Southern African Affairs (the latter was renamed the Office of Middle and Southern African Affairs in 1958), the new Africa unit remained structurally under the Bureau of Near Eastern, South Asian, and African Affairs for nearly two years. On July 10, 1958, an act of Congress authorized a separate Bureau of African Affairs with its own Assistant Secretary. The number of officers in the Bureau rose to 44 in 1960, to more than 70 in 1961, and to 97 in 1962, when it was further reorganized.

Basic Organization

The organization of the Bureau of African Affairs as of May 25, 1962, is shown in Figure 1. Although there was a Special Assistant for Algeria in the Bureau, it is only since the independence of Algeria in July, 1962, that responsibility for Algerian affairs was transferred from the Bureau of European Affairs to that of African Affairs. Egypt remains under the Bureau of Near East and South Asian Affairs. It was not until January, 1956, that the South African desk was transferred from European Affairs to Near East, South Asian and African Affairs, and until the end of World War II, all of Africa (except Egypt, Ethiopia, and Liberia) was handled in offices dealing with European Affairs.

If it seems strange that the State Department did not have a separate Bureau of African Affairs until 1958, it should be noted that the United States Foreign Service had 256 officers in the single country of West Germany in 1957, in contrast to only 248 officers in the whole of Africa. Since German affairs were combined with those of all other European countries in a single bureau, it was sometimes asked why a separate bureaucratic structure was needed to handle our small African operations. The main reason was clear. When African affairs were handled in the same bureau that dealt with Near Eastern and South Asian problems, they could not be given sufficient attention because top officials were too busy with other crises.

In 1939, the United States had 3 legations, 3 consulates general, 8 consulates, and 1 consular agency in Africa. In October, 1957, there were 9 embassies, 1 embassy branch office, 13 consulates general, and 10 consulates in 22 African countries; by August, 1961, there were 31 embassies, 1 embassy branch office, 11 consulates general, 13 consulates, and 3 consular agencies in 38 African countries (see Table 1). The number of Foreign Service and other officers manning African posts rose from 644 in October, 1957, to 1,411 in August, 1961.

Centers of Responsibility

Within the Department of State, the responsibility for initiating action on most African problems rests with the Bureau of African Affairs, where the country "desk officer" is the main point of contact with the African country or countries of his office. He also maintains close relations with their embassies in Washington. He is primarily an operations officer who makes decisions on routine matters. He also participates in policymaking by drafting proposals for approval by the office director and the Assistant Secretary.

Officers in the Africa Bureau must clear important decisions with officers in other interested bureaus. Africa policy is thus seasoned by many cooks, some of whom have conflicting tastes. These may be geographical bureaus, like the European Affairs Bureau, or functional bureaus, like the Economic Affairs Bureau or the Legal Adviser's Office, all of which have officers who keep an eye on Africa. In the 1950's, particularly, if an African issue was sufficiently controversial to arouse the British, French, or Belgian ambassador to call on the Secretary of State, the Bureau of European Affairs was likely to have a powerful voice in the final decision.

On matters of greatest importance, policy recommendations go to the National Security Council. Created in 1947 to advise the President on the integration of domestic, foreign, and military policies involving national security, the National Security Council is composed of the President, Vice-President, Secretary of State, Secretary of Defense, and Director of the Office of Defense Mobilization. Others may participate by invitation of the President. The NSC has a Planning Board which prepares papers that

TABLE 1

United States Diplomatic and Consular Posts in Africa

Offices	Foreign Service	ICA Officers	USIA Officers	Army, Naval and Air Attaches	Foreign Agricultural Service
Embassies					
Abidjan, Ivory Coast	8	7	1	2	
Accra, Ghana	24	34	6	1	
Addis Ababa, Ethiopia	18	121	3	6	
Bamako, Mali	8	5	2		
Bangui, Central African Republic	4		1		
Brazzaville, Congo	7		1		
Cairo, Egypt	45	34	17	13	2
Conakry, Guinea	12	2	1		
Cotonou, Dahomey	4		1		
Dakar, Senegal	12	6	2		
Dar-Es-Salaam, Tanganyika	7	2	3		
Fort Lamy, Chad	3		1		
Freetown, Sierra Leone	8	5	1		
Khartoum, Sudan	20	69	5	5	1
Kigali, Rwanda	2				
Lagos, Nigeria	20	49	7	1	1
Leopoldville, Congo	17	7	5	4	
Libreville, Gabon	4		1		
Lomé, Togo	6	3	1		
Mogadiscio, Somali Republic	14	52	3		
Monrovia, Liberia	13	86	5		
Naimey, Niger	5		1		
Nouakchott, Mauritania	4				
Ouagadougou, Upper Volta	4	2	1		
Pretoria, South Africa	16		2		
Rabat, Morocco	27	30	4	4	1
Tananarive, Malagasy	7	5	1		
Tripoli, Libya	18	102	11		
Benghazi Office	6		2		
Tunis, Tunisia	17	54	8		
Usumbura, Burundi*	5		2		
Yaounde, Cameroon	10	3	2	1	

TABLE 1 (cont.)
United States Diplomatic and Consular Posts in Africa

Offices	Foreign Service	ICA Officers	USIA Officers	Army, Naval and Air Attaches	Foreign Agricultural Service
Consulates General					
Alexandria, Egypt	5		1		
Algiers, Algeria*	9		2		
Cape Town, South Africa	4		2		
Casablanca, Morocco	9		1		
Johannesburg, South Africa	7		1		
Kampala, Uganda*	5		2		
Lourenço Marques, Mozambique	3				
Luanda, Angola	5				
Nairobi, Kenya	11	14	4		1
Salisbury, Rhodesia-Nyasaland	13	9	5		1
Tangier, Morocco	9		14		
Consulates					
Asmara, Eritrea	5		1		
Constantine, Algeria	2				
Douala, Cameroon	4		1		
Durban, South Africa	3				
Elizabethville, Congo	3				
Enugu, Nigeria	3	6	1		
Ibadan, Nigeria	3	15	1		
Kaduna, Nigeria	4	1	2		
Oran, Algeria	1		1		
Port Elizabeth, South Africa	2				
Port Said, Egypt	2				
Stanleyville, Congo	2				
Zanzibar, Zanzibar	2				
Consular Agency (Beira) and Resident Consuls					
Beira, Mozambique	1				
Blantyre, Nyasaland	1				
Lusaka, North Rhodesia	1				
Total	*494*	*723*	*140*	*45*	*9*

* Since these data were assembled, Kampala and Algiers have been raised to Embassy status; Usumbura has been demoted to a Legation.

ordinarily serve as the basis for its policy recommendations to the President, who makes the final decision. Since 1947, the Department of State has also had a Policy Planning Staff to formulate long-term programs for the achievement of U.S. foreign policy objectives.

Still another bureau has initial action responsibility for the difficult African issues which arise in the United Nations. This is the Bureau of International Organization Affairs, which prepares the "position papers" that guide United States Delegations at United Nations meetings. Within this Bureau is an Office of Dependent Area Affairs which deals with problems of trust and non-self-governing territories. Because of the great decline in the number of dependencies, it went out of existence as a separate office on June 1, 1962, when it became a unit of the Office of U.N. Political, Security and Dependent Area Affairs.

A third Department of State office handling African matters is the Office of Research and Analysis on Africa in the Bureau of Intelligence and Research. In principle, research officers in this Bureau refrain from making policy recommendations, but their research is oriented to consider the possible consequences of various policy alternatives. In addition, the Africa Office receives many requests from policy-making officers for spot comments on current crises. In its early years, the Bureau of Intelligence and Research operated on the principle that it should include only trained research workers. The amalgamation of the Department of State and the Foreign Service in the mid-1950's strained this rule by bringing in analysts who lacked research training, although many had had first-hand field experience in Africa. In 1961, the professional staff of the Africa Office declined from twenty-three to fifteen, when certain long-term African research activities of the Department of State were transferred to the Central Intelligence Agency.

A major United States operation in Africa is the educational exchange program, which is the responsibility of the State Department's new Bureau of Educational and Cultural Affairs, established in April, 1960. It deserves higher priority in foreign policy. Public and private educational exchange projects which bring Africans to the United States and send Americans to

Africa are a broadening and deepening experience of immeasurable value. However, from the end of World War II to June, 1961, the United States invested $84 billion in economic and military assistance to other nations, while spending less than 0.5 per cent of this amount on the educational and cultural exchange programs of the Department of State. The Fulbright Act, Smith-Mundt Act, and important new Fulbright-Hays (Mutual Educational and Cultural Exchange) Act of 1961 all further the expansion of exchange activities.* Unfortunately, this wider foundation for expanded exchange operations was not supported with a commensurate increase in funds at the very time African developments were offering a unique opportunity to make use of the broader authority granted by the Fulbright-Hays Act. Exchange initiative, therefore, has been moving to agencies like AID and the Peace Corps, whose larger budgets are making it possible to increase American exchange operations significantly at virtually all levels.

Exchange grants for Africa were slow in getting under way. In the nine years from 1949 through 1957, only 224 government grants were given to Africans for study or consultation in the United States, while only 107 grants were made to Americans for study in Africa (not including 384 Egyptians who came to the United States and 161 Americans who went to Egypt). In 1958 a change occurred, and a general expansion of America's African activities began. This is evident in the State Department's 1958 budget for educational exchange, which provided for 299 exchanges with Africa at a cost of $1,679,517. Even with this increase, however, the cost of exchanges with Africa was still only 8 per cent of the total exchange budget. Meanwhile, our diplomatic and consular posts in Africa began making more and more specific requests for exchanges, and it soon became clear that the Department of State could easily have spent in 1958 twice the funds it was able to allocate to Africa.

As a result of these and other pressures, the budget for African educational exchanges doubled between 1958 and 1961.

* For details of nature and impact of these acts, see Vernon McKay, *Africa in World Politics* (New York: Harper and Row, 1963).

In 1960, the State Department financed 362 African and 62 American visits, the International Cooperation Administration supported 456 visits by Africans and 585 by Americans, and the Defense Department financed the visits of 65 Africans and 6 Americans—all at a total cost of $15.5 million. For the fiscal year ending June 30, 1961, the allocation for the State Department's educational exchange program amounted to $3.3 million. The State Department has also given two grants totaling $125,000 to the Council for Educational Cooperation, formed in July, 1961, by six private agencies, which attempts to coordinate the private educational aid given to Africans and to mitigate some of the problems of African students in the U.S.

AGENCY FOR INTERNATIONAL DEVELOPMENT

Basic Organization

The Agency for International Development (AID) was established in the autumn of 1961 to revamp, rejuvenate, and expand the foreign aid program. It is thus the latest in the line of postwar aid agencies which includes the Economic Cooperation Administration, the Mutual Security Administration, and the Technical Cooperation Administration. The new Agency also took over the operation of the Development Loan Fund and certain local currency dealings of the Export-Import Bank.

The Administrator of AID is responsible, subject to the approval of the Secretary of State, for the formulation and execution of foreign assistance policies and programs. His instructions go through our ambassadors in AID countries to the directors of AID missions. In the 1961 reorganization, many officers were shifted from functional offices to four new regional bureaus, each headed by an assistant administrator. The Assistant Administrator for the Bureau of Africa and Europe has a legal adviser, a Development Planning Office, a Technical Support Office, a Management Operations Office, and Geographic Area

Offices which include East-South African Affairs, Central African Affairs, West African Affairs, and Mediterranean Affairs.

Foreign Aid

During the 16 fiscal years from 1946 through 1961, the United States Government made available a worldwide total of $90.5 billion in foreign aid, a figure that includes $29 billion for military assistance. The continent of Africa, including Egypt and South Africa, received only $1.8 billion, or 2 per cent of the total aid. More than 95 per cent of the aid to foreign countries was economic assistance, however, only $81.5 million being for military assistance. Of the grand total for Africa, $993.4 million was in the form of grants and $873 million in loans. It came from the following sources:

	(in millons of dollars)
International Cooperation Administration	652.0
Public Law 480 (agricultural surplus disposals)	528.0
Export-Import Bank Loans	320.1
Development Loan Fund	155.8
Military assistance administered by the Defense Department	81.5
Other economic programs	71.9

This $1.8 billion does not include that portion of the aid to France used for the postwar reconstruction of French North Africa, which has been estimated at about $365 million. Nor does it take into account the fact that the United States contributed about 35 per cent, approximately $335 million of the $968.8 million, of aid to Africa from the United Nations and the specialized agencies by June 30, 1961. If these two contributions are added to the total, the United States made $2.5 billion available for aid to Africa during these 16 years. The $1.8 billion that can be accurately identified is distributed among more than 33 African countries, as shown in Table 2.

To carry out its program, AID had 1,310 U.S. nationals in Africa on May 30, 1962. At the same time, about 750 Africans were training in the United States or third countries. The Afri-

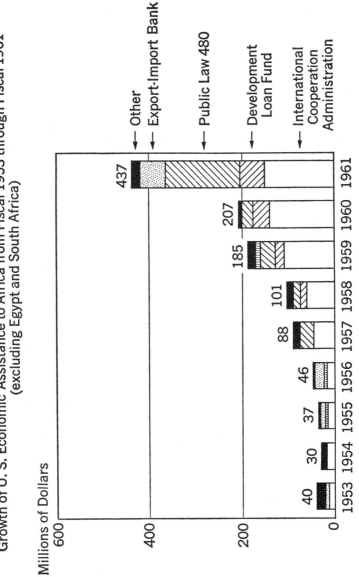

Figure 2

Growth of U. S. Economic Assistance to Africa from Fiscal 1953 through Fiscal 1961 (excluding Egypt and South Africa)

can countries with the largest complements of American aid personnel were:

Nigeria	190
Ethiopia	182
Liberia	172
Sudan	117
Libya	106
Tunis	59
Somalia	59
Morocco	59
Egypt	47

Mention should be made of one other general point, namely, the growth pattern of grants and loans to Africa. This is illustrated in Figure 2 by a chart from the 1962 AID publication on *U.S. Foreign Assistance.* Since the total aid to Africa in the seven years from 1946 through 1952 was so small, the chart does not begin until 1953.

THE UNITED STATES INFORMATION AGENCY

The United States Information Agency has become an essential part of our Africa policy machinery. In the use of propaganda as an instrument of foreign policy, the Department of State in 1945 inherited the staff of the Office of War Information. In the effort to make the information program more effective, it was expanded and reorganized five times between 1945 and 1953, when the USIA became autonomous. Its Africa operations were slow in gaining momentum. In 1953, only one USIA officer in Washington was assigned exclusively to the African area, although there were already seventeen USIA posts in twelve African countries, including Cairo and Alexandria under the Middle East section and Algeria under the European Division.

The wind of change hit the USIA in 1957, however. Despite a budget cut that forced a retrenchment of its operations in other areas, USIA decided to expand in Africa. By the end of September, there were 4 officers in the Africa section handling 19 posts in 14 African countries. In 1960, the Africa section

TABLE 2

United States Foreign Assistance to Africa
Obligations and Loan Authorizations from Fiscal 1953
Through Fiscal 1961

(in millions of dollars)

Country	Economic Aid Grants	Economic Aid Loans	Military Aid Grants	Military Aid Loans	Total Aid
United Arab Republic (Egypt)	157.4	227.0			384.4
Morocco	109.3	192.9	*	*	302.2
Tunisia	202.7	51.9	*		254.7
Ethiopia	57.2	67.4	55.8		180.4
Libya	166.8	8.5	3.7	*	179.0
South Africa		155.7			155.7
Liberia	28.1	85.0	1.0	1.4	115.5
Sudan	41.2	10.0			51.2
Rhodesia-Nyasaland	0.9	32.4			33.3
Ghana	6.4	20.0			26.4
Nigeria	15.4	3.9			19.3
Congo (Leopoldville)	13.3				13.3
Somalia	11.1	2.0			13.1
Mozambique		12.5			12.5
Kenya	7.3				7.3
Tanganyika	2.5	1.9			4.4
Guinea	4.0				4.0
Senegal	3.6				3.6
Dahomey	3.1				3.1
Mali	2.5		0.6		3.1
Cameroon	2.2				2.2
Ivory Coast	2.1				2.1
Upper Volta	2.0				2.0
Niger	2.0				2.0
Togo	1.9				1.9
Mauritania	0.2	1.4			1.6
Uganda	1.0				1.0
Sierra Leone	1.0				1.0
Malagasy	0.5				0.5
Chad	0.1				0.1
Gabon	0.1				0.1
Congo (Brazzaville)	0.1				0.1
Central African Republic	0.046				0.046
Sterling Areas	0.7				0.7
Portuguese possessions	0.3				0.3
French Community	6.0				6.0
Regional	3.3		15.4	3.6	22.3

* Classified information.

achieved the status of a separate division with 14 officers. In addition, it had a research branch for Africa composed of 4 officers. The United States Information Service, the foreign service of USIA, hoped to have 133 American officers assisted by 476 local employees in 43 information centers in 31 African countries by the end of fiscal 1962. To ensure coordination with other U.S. agencies, all major USIA programs are implemented by these officers only after review by either the State Department or the "country team" on the spot, or both. The country team is headed by the American ambassador and composed of the senior members of other U.S. agencies in the host country. By fiscal 1962, USIA's planned obligations for Africa, including obligations under Title I of PL 480 but not including reimbursements from other agencies, had risen to a total of $11.2 million out of total USIA obligations of $122.7 million.

The USIA tells the American story in Africa through four principal media—radio, libraries, films, and the press. The introduction of television offers a new opportunity. Radio is perhaps the most important communications medium in Africa, both present and potential. At the end of 1961, there were an estimated 5,385,300 radios in all of Africa excluding Egypt. To reach this audience, special English and French programs for Africa are now being broadcast regularly, and Swahili and Hausa occasionally. A Voice of America relay station being constructed near Monrovia, Liberia, is scheduled to go on the air by the end of 1963. This should resolve the problem presented by frequent complaints of poor VOA reception in Africa. Supplemental coverage of West Africa has been provided by a powerful relay station recently constructed at Greenville, North Carolina.

The impact of USIA libraries in Africa is particularly notable. Their influence is difficult to evaluate because the effect of reading miscellaneous American books and magazines is more intangible than radio, press, and film programs specially tailored for Africans. It is nonetheless significant that 1.7 million persons attended USIA libraries in 30 African cities during the last six months of 1960 and the first six months of 1961. These libraries are small, normally containing from 1,000 to 5,000 volumes, but in many towns the USIA library is the only free library, and in some it is the only library, and in every case, including South Africa, it is open to all races.

The film program of USIA includes documentaries on American life, newsreel coverage of significant events, and special films on such subjects as President Nkrumah's 1958 visit to the United States. The USIA's most popular film product, the monthly newsreel *Today,* is produced in English, French, and Arabic. By the end of 1961, it was being shown in some 710 theaters in 20 African countries to an estimated annual audience of 33 million.

In its press and publications program, its fourth principal activity, the USIA publishes its own materials, and radio-teletypes daily news in English, and sometimes in French, to Africa for the use of American officials and for release to local editors and others. Several African posts publish newspapers and magazines in the host countries. Outstanding among them is the *American Outlook,* published in Accra, a monthly journal of 16 pages which had a circulation of 114,000 in 1961.

In January, 1960, the Press Division of the USIA stepped up its Africa output by inaugurating a daily radio-teletyped report especially prepared for about fifteen monitoring posts in Africa. It planned to reach twenty-nine country posts by the end of June, 1962. This USIA "Wireless File" to some extent supplements such commercial agencies as the Associated Press and United Press International, and provides among other things a daily account of important policy statements in Washington. It also endeavors to counter the effect of some of the news releases of the British agency, Reuters, which is conspicuous for disseminating throughout Africa stories of racial incidents in the United States. The USIA does not deny such incidents, but stresses the progress made in the United States in improving race relations.

In addition to these radio, library, film, and press activities, USIS officers operate the State Department's exchange of persons program in the field and foster a number of other activities, including a promising program of teaching English to selected groups of adults in nineteen countries of non-English-speaking Africa. Under a special President's Fund Program, outstanding

American athletes and artists are brought to Africa. As Africans take control of their own affairs, they show considerable interest in the American experience in government, and USIA has responded to many requests about it.

The Peace Corps

The Peace Corps is a unique combination of aid, information, and exchange, with the accent on youth. Unlike members of the Foreign Service, USIS, or AID, the Peace Corps volunteer is not an official of the United States government. Instead, he is a private citizen who is expected to perform valuable aid service and to help dispel misunderstanding.

The Peace Corps was created and given temporary status as an agency within the Department of State by an executive order of March 1, 1961. It selects projects proposed by host countries and trains its own volunteers. In January, 1963, of a total of 4,369 members of the Peace Corps (including those still in training), 1,448 (213 of whom were still in training) were serving in Africa. Seventeen African countries had received or were soon to receive Peace Corps members, including Cameroon, Ethiopia, Gabon, Ghana, Ivory Coast, Guinea, Sierra Leone, Senegal, Nyasaland, Nigeria, Niger, Morocco, Liberia, Tunisia, Togo, Tanganyika, and Somalia.

AFRICA MACHINERY IN OTHER AGENCIES

Outside the Department of State and its related autonomous agencies, the major departments that have officers working on Africa are the Departments of the Army, the Navy, the Air Force, and Defense; the Departments of Agriculture, Commerce, and Labor; and the Department of Health, Education, and Welfare. A brief catalogue of their African activities will complete this analysis of the African policy machine. Comparable information is unavailable on the Central Intelligence Agency, which collects and analyzes information and conducts operations in the field to support American policy. In theory, all these offices serve in an advisory and supporting capacity to the Secretary of State insofar as they deal with foreign policy matters. In practice, they sometimes take steps which have the effect of policy decisions.

The Department of Defense

Many officers in the Department of Defense and the Departments of the Army, the Navy, and the Air Force deal with African problems as a part of their general duties. These include both military and civilian specialists on such matters as military intelligence, military operations, military assistance, and technical services for transport and communications.

The responsibilities of the Department of Defense include the development and coordination of policies, plans, and procedures in international political-military affairs. The principal adviser and assistant to the Secretary of Defense on these matters is an Assistant Secretary for International Security Affairs, whose office established a Middle East–Africa unit in 1955 and a Regional Directorate for Near East, South Asia, and Africa in 1957. Since October, 1960, the number of officers in the Africa section of this Directorate has risen from one to four.

The Africa section has responsibilities for the two major bases of the United States in Africa, the Navy and Air Force base at Port Lyautey in Morocco and Wheelus Air Base in Libya. The United States Air Force is also permitted to use Moroccan bases at Nouasseur and Sidi Slimene, but has withdrawn from bases at Ben Guerir and Ben Slimene. It has agreed to withdraw all other military personnel, including those at Port Lyautey, by the end of 1963.

In addition to these bases in Libya and Morocco, the Defense Department supports two Military Assistance Advisory Groups of American military personnel in Africa, one in Ethiopia and the other in Libya, and four military missions in Liberia, Mali, Morocco, and Tunisia. It also has an important Army and Navy communications facility at Asmara in the Eritrean province of Ethiopia. Furthermore, the National Aeronautics and Space Administration maintains satellite tracking and space exploration facilities at Kano, Nigeria, near Johannesburg, South Africa, and in Zanzibar.

The Department of Labor

In the Bureau of International Labor Affairs, headed by an Assistant Secretary of Labor, one of the Bureau's five area specialists follows labor developments in Africa with the help of an assistant Africa area specialist. In the Bureau of Labor Statistics there is also a specialist on Africa in the Division of Foreign Labor Conditions who analyzes embassy reports and other sources of information and prepares research memoranda and country monographs on labor in Africa.

In 1962, seven Foreign Service officers were stationed in Africa as labor attachés in Ghana, Guinea, Kenya, Morocco, Nigeria, Senegal, and Tunisia. Other Foreign Service officers supplement the work of the labor attachés by occasional reporting on labor matters. In addition to reporting to Washington on African labor affairs, the labor attachés attempt to promote in Africa a better understanding of American labor policies and practices.

U.S. labor programs involving training and technical assistance projects in Africa are carried out by the Agency for International Development. When AID or the State Department brings African labor leaders to this country, their programs are arranged by the Department of Labor. The Department of Labor does special research and publishes training material tailored to the needs of the AID missions. It recruits or provides labor experts to give technical assistance to ministries of labor, trade unions, and other organizations and agencies. It also provides programming and training for exchange program visitors to the United States whose primary interests are in the labor field. In developing these activities, the Department has the advice of the Secretary of Labor's Trade Union Advisory Committee on International Affairs, which assures consultation between the United States Government and the top American labor leaders.

Publications of the Department of Labor include the *Directory of Labor Organizations—Africa,* first published in 1958 and then again in revised edition in mid-1962; a biweekly summary of labor developments in Africa and elsewhere; and two monthlies, *Labor Developments Abroad* and *International Labor.* Monographs and summaries of the labor situation in specific African countries are also prepared.

The Department of Commerce

The Department of Commerce promotes U.S. foreign trade and private investment abroad through two bureaus—the Bureau of International Business Operations and the Bureau of International Programs—both under the supervision of the Assistant Secretary of Commerce for International Affairs. The international program provides specific services to business, and helps to formulate and support the foreign economic policies of the United States.

African affairs (excluding Egypt) are the responsibility of an African Division created in September, 1961, within the Bureau of International Programs. This Division has a professional staff of fourteen officers and is organized in three regional sections covering North Africa, Middle Africa, and Southern Africa.

Most Foreign Service posts in Africa have staff officers who cover economic and commercial affairs. Separate attachés for commercial affairs work in several American embassies in Africa, and their number will mount under a Department of Commerce export expansion program. The reports of these officers are reviewed, interpreted, and disseminated to the American business community by the Africa Division and other functional units within the Department of Commerce.

Since 1957, eight trade missions have been sent to Africa, covering various countries in East and West Africa, the Rhodesias, South Africa, and Tunisia. Additional trade missions are planned. The Department has also participated in international trade fairs and exhibitions in Tripoli, Tunis, Casablanca, and Addis Ababa. A Special Trade Exhibit was held in Accra in January, 1962, and others are planned for Lagos and elsewhere in Africa.

Material on Africa appears frequently in Commerce Department publications, including the *Foreign Commerce Weekly* and various country pamphlets in the World Trade Information

Series. The Department has also published useful investment handbooks on Nigeria, Rhodesia-Nyasaland, and South Africa.

The Department of Health, Education, and Welfare

The Office of International Affairs within the Office of the Secretary of Health, Education, and Welfare is under the direction of a Deputy Assistant Secretary and, while it assigns none of its staff exclusively to African affairs, assists in and coordinates the international activities of HEW's five component agencies. One of its major functions is to provide professional backstopping for State, AID, and USIA. For example, experts are supplied to serve on U.S. delegations, international advisory groups, and foreign technical assignments; and technical materials and advice are provided for USIA and other information programs. The Office of International Affairs and the component HEW agencies also participate in the preparation of position papers and related documents for the United Nations and its specialized agencies. During the fiscal year 1961, the Department and its agencies scheduled the itineraries of or gave other assistance to some 6,000 foreign visitors from 91 countries, perhaps 300 of whom came from Africa north and south of the Sahara.

Of the five component agencies of Health, Education, and Welfare, the Office of Education and the Public Health Service are the most closely connected with Africa. The National Institutes of Health of the Public Health Service sponsor grants and fellowships for foreign scientists to work in the medical and biological laboratories of this country and for American scientists to do research or obtain specialized training abroad. Thus far, this program has had little impact on Africa. Out of the 1,185 awards for fiscal year 1961, only 18 went to Africa, and 15 of these went to South Africa alone.

The Office of Education acts as agent for the Department of State in the recruitment of American teachers for the teacher exchange program and in the administration of the training program for foreign visiting teachers. The Office also recruits and services American educators who go abroad under AID technical assistance programs. The Comparative Education Section provides advisory interpretations of foreign student credentials and replies to requests from both government agencies and private individuals for information on educational opportunities abroad. The teaching of 11 African languages was also being sponsored in the academic year 1962–63 under Title VI of the National Defense Education Act.

The Department of Agriculture

In 1961, eight of the fifty-two officers of the Foreign Agricultural Service were stationed in Africa, and each of the eight was responsible not only for the country in which he was stationed but also for a number of surrounding countries. The Africa and Middle East Analysis Branch of the Economic Research Service in 1961 had two agricultural economists for northern Africa and three for southern Africa. Officers in the Foreign Agricultural Service, Commodity Divisions, also covered Africa as part of their wider duties.

Under the Agricultural Trade Development and Assistance Act (Public Law 480) beginning in 1954, the Foreign Agricultural Service has participated in supplying surplus American agricultural products to underdeveloped countries. In fiscal 1961, a total of $173,202,000 of U.S. agricultural exports were sent to Africa under government-financed programs while, in contrast, only $48,030,000 worth of agricultural commodities were exported to Africa in this same period outside of these programs.[1]

The Influence of Congress

Finally, no account of the Africa policy machine would be complete without consideration of the powerful influence of Congress, which is exerted through the control of appropriations and in many other ways. The Secretary of State finds that in addition to the House Foreign Affairs and Senate Foreign Relations Committees, almost every other congressional committee is concerned with some aspect of foreign policy—from the disposal of

[1] For country-by-country breakdown of agricultural exports to Africa under specified government programs, see McKay, *op. cit.*, Table 16, pp. 306–7.

agricultural surpluses to visa and passport policy. In 1962, the support of Congress was vital for American aid to Africa, for American policy in the Congo, and for the Administration's proposal to purchase up to $100 million worth of U.N. bonds to avert a U.N. financial crisis.

As the importance of Africa became more apparent during the 1950's, an increasing number of congressmen devoted attention to it. Each year, two senators or two representatives served on U.S. Delegations to the U.N. General Assembly, where African issues occupied a major part of the agenda. Greater attention began to be given to Africa in congressional hearings and debates.

African and Near Eastern affairs were handled in the same congressional committees until 1959, when both the Senate Foreign Relations Committee and House Foreign Affairs Committee established separate subcommittees for Africa. Between 1955 and 1961, some eighteen congressmen visited Africa. These visits are an excellent means of giving members of Congress a "feel" for the subject of Africa, which can be of real value when they have to form judgments on African issues.

In 1959 and 1960, the Senate Foreign Relations Committee undertook a study of Africa as part of a larger study of United States foreign policy. The statements made to the Committee and the background study prepared for it by the Northwestern University Program of African Studies were widely read and therefore helped to broaden and deepen American interest in and knowledge of Africa.

PROBLEMS OF COORDINATION

The foregoing survey of the overlapping African interests and operations of federal departments and agencies reveals a vast problem of organization and coordination in the Africa policy machine. The committee system of policy-making and policy coordination has been subjected to many caustic criticisms in recent years. In March and April, 1961, President Kennedy abolished fifty-nine such committees. The best-known victim of the President's action was the Operations Coordinating Board

(OCB), in which, since 1953, the heads of major government departments had met periodically to ensure coordination in implementing the recommendations of the National Security Council. The spade work for the OCB was done in "working groups," including one for Africa headed by a senior officer in the Bureau of African Affairs.

Another method of improving policy-making and coordination which is tried from time to time is reorganization of the policy machine. Within the Department of State, there is a continuing disagreement between those who think that all the political, economic, educational, research, and other functions for an area like Africa should be under the authority of the geographical bureau for that area, and those who believe that functional bureaus dealing with worldwide economic, educational, research and other problems should predominate, each having geographical subdivisions. In the proliferation since World War II, the Department has added many functional bureaus to its old geographical bureaus. The geographical bureaus have gone on to employ functional "advisers" in addition to their country desk officers, while the functional bureaus have employed area specialists. In State's Bureau of African Affairs, these functional advisers perform some of the tasks of maintaining liaison and coordination with other bureaus.

List of Contributors

ELLIOT J. BERG is Assistant Professor of Economics and Research Associate at the Center for International Affairs, Harvard University. He is also consultant to the Agency for International Development of the Department of State and was Chairman of the Joint State-AID Task Force on Labor in Africa (1962). He is the author of numerous publications in learned journals.

JAMES S. COLEMAN is Professor of Political Science and Director, African Studies Center, at the University of California, Los Angeles, and President (1962–63) of the African Studies Association. He is author of *Togoland* and *Nigeria: Background to Nationalism*, as well as numerous scholarly articles, and co-editor (with Gabriel Almond) of *The Politics of the Developing Areas*.

ST. CLAIR DRAKE is Professor of Sociology and Director of African Studies, Roosevelt University. He served as visiting Professor at the University of Liberia, 1954, and as Head of the Department of Sociology at the University College of Ghana, 1958–60. In 1961 and 1962, he was a member of the staff training Peace Corps teachers for Ghana. He has published articles in *Présence Africaine, Africa Today,* and *Africa Report*.

RUPERT EMERSON is Professor of Government and Research Associate at the Center for International Affairs, Harvard University. From 1940 to 1946 he served in various government agencies in Washington, including the Department of the Interior, the Foreign Economic Administration, and the Department of State. He has for many years been interested in colonial problems and colonial administration, as well as in the development of nationalism. He has written widely in these fields, particularly with reference to Southeast Asia and Africa. His most recent book is *From Empire to Nation.*

WALTER GOLDSCHMIDT, Professor of Anthropology and Sociology at the University of California, Los Angeles, and Director of the Culture and Ecology in East Africa Project, served as editor of the *American Anthropologist*, 1956–59, and as Director of the Ways of Mankind Radio Project, 1951–53. In addition to studies of American Indians and modern American communities, he did research in East Africa in 1953–54 (under a Fulbright research grant) and again in 1961–63 (under National Science Foundation and U.S. Public Health Service grants). He is the author of *As You Sow, Small Business and the Community, Nomlaki Ethnography, Man's Way,* and *Exploring the Ways of Mankind,* and edited *The Anthropology of Franz Boas.*

ANDREW M. KAMARCK is Lecturer on African Affairs in the School of Advanced International Studies, Johns Hopkins University, and Economic Adviser on Africa at the International Bank for Reconstruction and Development. He has visited most of the African continent, and headed the Bank's economic missions on Rhodesia's Kariba project and Ghana's Volta project. Any opinions expressed are his own and do not necessarily reflect the official views of any institution with which he may be connected.

VERNON McKAY is Professor of African Studies and Director of the Program of African Studies at The School of Advanced International Studies, Johns Hopkins University. He was Deputy Director of the Office of Dependent Area Affairs in the Department of State, and from 1948 to 1956 served on many United States delegations at United Nations meetings dealing with African issues. In 1959 and 1960, he taught at the Universities of Stellenbosch and the Witwatersrand in South Africa. He is the author of *Africa in World Politics* and many articles on African subjects.

Since its establishment by Dwight D. Eisenhower at Columbia University in 1950, The American Assembly has held Assemblies of national leaders and has published books to illuminate issues of United States policy.

The Assembly is a national, nonpartisan educational institution, incorporated in the State of New York. The Trustees of the Assembly approve a topic for presentation in a background book, authoritatively designed and written to aid deliberations at national Assembly sessions at Arden House. These books are also used to support discussion at regional Assembly sessions and to evoke consideration by the general public.

All sessions of the Assembly, whether international, national, or local, issue and publicize independent reports of conclusions and recommendations on the topic at hand. Participants in these sessions constitute a wide range of experience and competence.